The Reason of States

The Reason of States

A Study in International Political Theory

edited by
Michael Donelan

London
GEORGE ALLEN & UNWIN
Boston   Sydney

Burgess
JX
1391
.R4

Printed in Great Britain in 10 on 11 point Plantin by
Willmer Brothers Limited Birkenhead

The Authors

Christopher Brewin *Lecturer in International Relations, The University of Keele*

Peter F. Butler *Lecturer in Politics, The University of Exeter*

Michael Donelan *Senior Lecturer in International Relations, The London School of Economics and Political Science*

Stephen George *Lecturer in Political Theory and Institutions, The University of Sheffield*

Maurice Keens-Soper *Lecturer in Politics, The University of Leicester*

James Mayall *Senior Lecturer in International Relations, The London School of Economics and Political Science*

Cornelia Navari *Lecturer in Political Science, The University of Birmingham*

Barrie Paskins *Defence Lecturer in the Ethical Aspects of War, The University of London, King's College*

Brian Porter *Senior Lecturer in International Politics, The University College of Wales, Aberystwyth*

Peter Savigear *Senior Lecturer in Politics, The University of Leicester*

Philip Windsor *Reader in International Relations, The London School of Economics and Political Science*

Moorhead Wright *Senior Lecturer in International Politics, The University College of Wales, Aberystwyth*

Contents

Preface   *page* 10

Introduction MICHAEL DONELAN   11

1 The Practice of a States-System MAURICE KEENS-SOPER   25

2 Legitimacy in a States-System: Vattel's *Law of Nations*
PETER F. BUTLER   45

3 Patterns of Thought and Practice: Martin Wight's
'International Theory' BRIAN PORTER   64

4 The Political Theorists and International
Theory MICHAEL DONELAN   75

5 The Problem of Meaning in International
Thought MOORHEAD WRIGHT   92

6 Knowledge, the State and the State of Nature CORNELIA
NAVARI   102

7 International Society and International Theory JAMES
MAYALL   122

8 Justice in International Relations CHRISTOPHER BREWIN   142

9 Obligation and the Understanding of International
Relations BARRIE PASKINS   153

10 The Justification of the State PHILIP WINDSOR   171

11 International Relations and Philosophy of History
PETER SAVIGEAR   195

12 Schools of Thought in International Relations STEPHEN
GEORGE   206

Index MOORHEAD WRIGHT   215

Preface

We came together as a group in 1974/6, aware that these are times of reappraisal in the study of international relations, and wishing to restate for ourselves and for others the fundamental issues in the subject. This book is our attempt.

We thank the London School of Economics and Political Science for assistance which helped to make our meetings over the two years possible. We acknowledge with warm gratitude the help in many different ways of many others.

THE AUTHORS

Introduction

MICHAEL DONELAN

The data of the human sciences are the product of thought. The study of international relations is the study of international thought.

Each morning we face a new procession of world events in a vast structure of world organisation. Much that we see is the outcome of luck and chance, recklessness or panic, ignorance or malice. All unfolds through the interaction of many in a way that no one separately intended. Everything done, though, is human; in some way, it is the product of thought.

How like an academic book to picture international relations as 'thought'! Everyone knows that the heart of international relations is war, it is violence, bullet, chemical and electrode. But academics cannot handle the heart, the pain and the suffering. The job of the academic is the thought that inflicts them.

Behind the pain and suffering are ambition and fear for security; group, faction and nation; the customs of nations, the institution of war, intervention and hatred of interveners; and each of these is in some way thought. Because world affairs are bewildering, we sometimes settle for the belief that at least the basic elements are crude and material. We say that in some current conflict the stake is gold, oil, land. We may forget that even these down to earth things presuppose layer upon layer of human activity, which is to say, thought, for their significance. We say easily that a conflict is about 'our' territory. We generalise and say that world politics amount in the end to a struggle for 'power' or for 'economic prosperity'. Perhaps they do. Perhaps generations of theorists have taught us to think so. Either way, all is thought.

The thought that makes the world we live in is basically not the theorist's kind, but thought in response to particular, practical problems. It is our thought as citizens, lawyers, newsmen, company chairmen, heads of governments, day by day. We have our own individual wits and common opinion to guide us. 'It is opinion that rules the world.' The process of world affairs is the movement of opinion.

We make in response to particular, practical problems, bit by bit, the structure within which the process goes on, the boundaries, rules, agreements, companies, organisations. We make 'Britain'; and a division of ourselves into 'Britain', 'France', 'Germany'; and above all, a kind of association among these countries, 'an international system'.

A ruler of a country has the problem of communicating continually with another. He appoints a representative of sorts. Other rulers do the same, only of course differently. It is the diplomatic 'system' growing. After years of war, negotiators meet at Münster and Osnabrück and make, at weary length, cobbled-up, makeshift peace treaties. In the thick of the business, Count Oxenstierna comments like many a statesman before and since, 'With how little wisdom the world is governed'. It is the theorist, looking on, who sees that the Peace of Westphalia of 1648 was the decisive act in an unparalleled European achievement: the formation of a system of sovereign states (Chapter 1).

The first step in studying the world that we make for ourselves in this piecemeal way is the study of history. The reason for saying this is not a perverse preference for the rich muddle of history over rigorous, scientific analysis. It is because of the nature of the data of our science. It is because our thought makes the world, makes the data, and we think historically. The thought that accounts for a conflict, a flow of trade, a foreign policy-making organisation, a state, a system of states or whatever data we turn to, is never fresh thought in a new situation, a rational response to an environment. It is always thought that is formed by remembered experience. If, then, we are to begin to understand our data, we must first of all know the history.

The history that we need for this purpose is not history 'as it really was', but history as it looks to the people concerned in our data. Behind 'a conflict', whether in personal life, company, town, state or world affairs, there are two sets of hopes and fears about the present, springing from two views of the past. Behind more harmonious data, a trade flow, a foreign policy-making organisation, a state or system of states, there is in some measure a common view of the past which makes them what they are. We who form a state, Britain, France or whichever it is, are held together by agreement on what we have been through. No agreement, no state. We who, representing our states, achieve a kind of association with other states, a states-system, can do so only to the extent that we agree on history. Common perception at Münster and Osnabrück of the Thirty Years War as a European war: a European states-system. No agreement in Moscow, Washington, Paris and Delhi on history: no world system.

It follows that in mastering the historical thought behind his data, the scholar of international relations can put aside any scepticism he may have about the science of history and about particular histories. If he reads the histories most admired among the relevant groups at the relevant date, he is reading what he needs, the past as they see it. Let us suppose that he is studying the international system at the present date. He can turn with confidence to the recommended history books. He can read with equanimity their version of past political events and of how past statesmen responded to them. For the thought that constitutes the international system today is the account of the past given in today's history books.

The same is true of any particular part of the structure of the international system, the rules of sovereignty, say, or the idea of non-intervention, or an international organisation. It is true of any part of the process that goes on within this structure, a currency market, say, or a disarmament negotiation. In all cases we can have confidence in the history offered to us by the participants as lying behind the data. Having confidence, we must study it. We shall take the data of international relations, company, state, nation, alliance, conflict, or whatever in the world faces us, too lightly if we treat them simply as rational responses to an environment. Their weight and quality are in large part their history. Perhaps most important of all, the passion in them is revealed in their history. The thought behind conflicts, alliances, organisations, sovereignty, trade arrangements or anything else is not 'rational' thought. It is exalted, furious, embittered, venomous, greedy or coolly determined. To grasp these passions, we have to go into the historical depths. Scholars cannot do without history if they are to understand passion.

Suppose, however, that the scholar wishes to proceed even further than acquiring a full recognition of the quality of the data before him. He wishes to make sense of what he sees. He wishes, perhaps, to find pattern and regularity in, say, the flow of communications between a set of states or even to try to identify the elements of world politics. He wishes to join in the debate about the world's proceedings on his own level, to inquire into the world in a critical spirit, and to say something of interest to his fellow men.

A scholar who sets himself this kind of work cannot be content simply with history as it looks to the actors in the drama. If this is his purpose, he has to believe that there are honest and dishonest histories, that some aim to tell the truth and some aim to tell lies. He has to believe that though we may always disagree and change in our views of the past, this is not because we are imposing our own interested versions, but because our viewpoints differ and alter in time. Within this condition, by reasoning together about the evidence of the past, we attain truth, 'how it really was'.

For if the scholar does not believe this, all his efforts to make sense of the world are nonsense. If there is no truth, no reality, about what has happened in the world, his alleged patterns and regularities of data are nothing but his personal fictions; his alleged elements of world politics are merely the main themes of a play he has written for himself; and his critique of the world's proceedings can be stultified simply by altering at will the history that accounts for them. What he has to say can have no validity for his fellow men. The world he inhabits is a private world.

In the worst case, the scholar escapes from this prison by sundering reason from history, abandoning history as altogether personal, arbitrary, false. His reasoning then ceases to be empirical and becomes rationalist or fideist or voluntarist. In criticising the world's arrangements, he is indifferent to instruction by historical experience. He becomes dangerously interesting to his fellow men. In the best case, the scholar accepts that there is truth, that there is reality, about what has happened in the world. He makes history the first and continual material of his science. History for him is not just an optional subject, something that historians do. It is not just a vital, passionate quality of the thought that makes the data of his science. History is the place he inhabits in his search for pattern, regularity, order, principle. It is the world itself.

I have spoken of 'searching for principle' and of 'making sense of the world'. I will now call this 'theory'. Beyond the study of history is theory. I mean the effort not merely to know the world, but to find coherence.

On that definition, as it stands, everybody is a theorist. For in our ordinary day to day lives, we do not simply know the world in a gaping, passive way; we analyse, we seek coherence and so we act. Some distinctions are needed, then. Everybody is sometimes a theorist. Equally important, indeed crucial for the human sciences compared with the natural sciences, a theorist is like everybody; a biologist is not an enzyme but a theorist is a man. However, in our day to day lives, we face particular, personal or group situations. A theorist does not face his own personal situation or that of another individual, but everybody's. A theorist is by trade, and no doubt by temperament too, an un-self-centred person.

The theorist has some influence on the practical making of the world. In the past he affected how people understood the situations they faced and how they thought they should act. He influenced the way statesmen and lawyers viewed political events and what they thought the rules should be for the future. He stood at the elbow of the historians of his day and helped determine the kind of history they wrote, the view that they and their readers formed of the past. He made people clearer in their minds that they constituted a 'state', that their state had 'sovereignty', that it was part of a 'society of states' and that there was an identifiable 'international system'.

In most cases, perhaps, we have no great need to study a theorist once he is dead. His thought will have been savaged by his successors, the transitory, the erroneous, the evil in the end drained out, the best incorporated in the thought of the theorists of the present day, and we have enough to do reading them. Still, it is always perilous to bury a political theorist; and at least everybody agrees that there are a few great works from the past that deserve a prominent place on our bookshelves.

Why did the theorist influence the practical men of his time, why may it be perilous to bury him, what are these great works of the past? Perhaps some will answer that the theorist was influential because he impressed the practical men as being cleverer at their own business than they were; or because he simply told the people of his day what they wanted to hear. He was the ghost-writer of the rulers or of a whole generation.

Perhaps our answer is that he struck them as in some measure a seer of a deeper aspect of their doings. If we read some forgotten theorist, unwilling to allow only his successors the right to savage him, he may perhaps strike us so. Maybe these works of the past are great because they express in profusion truths that change only slowly in our tradition or not at all. A man today, we might say on this view, would need to be a fool or a genius to talk about the fundamentals of political community without first reading the great political theorists of the past. Does he think that he can reason better against today's assaults of anarchy than they did for him centuries ago?

Take the international sphere. The international system is not simply historical, that is, the thought that constitutes it is not simply the account of the past given in today's history books. The system is also reasonable or unreasonable in the minds of those currently arguing about it. In their advocacy, they might be ill-advised to argue nothing else but their own view of 'the world social-process', accepting no instruction from the theorists of the past.

Let us take a case. Suppose that today we were to set a team of Western scholars to work for some years or to question a Western statesman for some minutes on how to regulate the following kind of world: a chaos of conflicting ideologies; the killing of any man, woman or child by any group that has faith in its cause; inflammatory meddling by one set of people in the conflicts of another far away, armed intervention to overthrow governments, conquests to put down wickedness; right everywhere, power everywhere, neither right nor peace anywhere.

The answer that the scholars or the statesman would give us would be a version of the thoughts of Emmerich de Vattel (Chapter

2). He lived a quiet life two hundred years ago. The statesman (understandably) and the scholars (possibly) have never heard of him. His answer, begun in the Middle Ages, transformed at the Peace of Augsburg, confirmed at the Peace of Westphalia, hacked, shaped and detailed by generations of theorists and at length stated classically by him, was: every man on earth is to make his own life for himself, to co-operate to this end with others, to consent to this end to a state; no state is to interfere with the men of another state, wicked or not; states are to co-operate under freely made treaties; force is to be used only to maintain these arrangements and to be bounded by elaborate rules. Vattel's answer no doubt begs many questions. No doubt there are contemporary theorists who can do better. Perhaps nowadays even a first-year student of international relations sees deeper into world politics than this. Still, at very least, to have read Vattel might save him some trouble as he prepares himself to amaze us. In plain terms, if the first step in the study of international relations is to know history, the second is to know the work of past theorists.

Suppose that we next want to theorise on our own account. The work of our immediate teachers, the scholars of recent years, has rightly the deepest influence on us. It will enslave us if we do not take care. Some of them approached international relations as though it were, not a human science, but a natural science. They treated the data of our world as light things, things without thought, without history, without passion. Commerce, conflicts, foreign ministries, states, whole states-systems were handled like mere phenomena, data without root or earth, units to be culled, counted, compared and correlated like daisies in a summer field.

In their efforts to find coherence in the world, some went from shop to shop to buy readymade patterns to impose upon it: cybernetics, systems theory, economics, decision making from the business schools. Others stayed at home and made their own models and frameworks. Most serious of all, they handled their data uncritically. A biologist does not criticise enzymes, so why, they thought, should a theorist be critical of the data of men? They wanted only to discover how the world actually works, regularities which would allow prediction. Norms and values, they treated simply as part of the data of the world before them, not as elements in their own intelligence with which to assess the data.

Practical men often make a distinction between how the world is and how it ought to be. They would be glad to have the theorist use his intelligence in this area, and reason with his fellow theorists about it and keep up a continuous debate to which practical men could sometimes listen. As it was, these theorists, by being uncritical, by treating good and evil alike as simply data, by mistaking their kind of science, not merely committed an intellectual error; they had nothing to say to the practical men who were making and mismaking the world around them; their work was (in the word of the time) 'irrelevant'.

Even so, these theorists taught us much. They insisted that international relations is a science. They were convinced that there is coherence in the world and that it is our job to try to discover what it is. As to norms and values, they gave us a deep mistrust of the sectarian moralising that had inspired many statesmen and theorists of the generation before them; 'idealism' and 'realism' were swept away. Alas, only that in doing this, they threw out moral reason as well from the science of international relations. They left 'a house swept clean and garnished', defenceless to possession by any creed that might come.

Our other teachers of recent years hesitated to step in. They taught us that the study of international relations begins with history. They insisted that we should know the history of theory, that there is a long tradition of reflection on the arrangements of the world, that much that we might open our mouths to say has been said better (or even more foolishly) long ago. They were historical, philosophical, they were deeply concerned with norms and values; but still they hesitated to theorise.

They presented the realities of the international system; they showed it as a rich, muddled, tragic, funny, haphazard growth, a history of the thought of practical statesmen facing particular problems. They showed us the organisations of the world as constructs of thought. They elaborated three great traditions of international theory, realism, rationalism, revolutionism, three permanently conflictory inclinations of the Western mind in reflecting on the world. But, in each area, they rarely allowed their own theorising to appear. The style was contemplative (Chapter 3).

This hesitation to continue the tradition of international political theory has had serious repercussions in other fields of scholarship. Because political theory has flagged, economics and law are at a loss. For economic theory (save as an abstract logic) always presupposes and depends on political and moral theory. John Locke comes before Adam Smith; and *The Theory of Moral Sentiments* comes before the *Wealth of Nations*. International economic theory, market style, presupposes liberal international political thought. Within a framework given by political theory, economic science can develop vigorously; but only so. In recent years, the economists have been much criticised for remoteness from the real world. They have been urged to become 'political economists'. As though it were the job of economists to work out the framework they need, the political theory of our time!

International law, similarly, grew up over recent centuries within a setting of political theory. Locke came before Vattel also. Later, the historicist theory of the state came before legal positivism. In recent years, some lawyers, thinking politically, have been working out new theories of international law and how it relates to international politics. They would surely welcome co-operation with the political theorists; if we had political theory to offer.

There are strong reasons why our teachers and we ourselves hesitate nowadays to continue the tradition of international theory. The first of these is not high-philosophical, it is pedestrian, but it is powerful. All theorising, above all, all true critical theorising, all reasoning about the world, requires debate with others. Debate can only go on within a group that agrees roughly on the boundaries of what they are debating. What are the boundaries of the science of international relations? We have long been at odds on this. Is our science as wide as a world community of mankind? Or is it restricted to relations between the states into which the world is divided (Chapter 4)?

We at least agree nowadays on all sides that the states are not to be closed and immune from our scrutiny. Some of us want to go into the actual states of the world to see how they make their foreign policies and how their frontiers are blurred and their inhabitants linked by transnational forces. Some of us want to go into the idea of the state to consider the great body of political thought that lies behind sovereignty, nationalism, independence, non-intervention and the rest. In earlier years, a reader of such a book as this might have protested: 'Why, a good half of it is about "the state", about its justification, about its very existence, about the nature of political obligation, about political theorists, about Hobbes and Hegel, about the philosophy of history! What has all this got to do with international relations?' More recently, we have ceased to take the theory or the practice of the state for granted, as something to be assumed before setting out on our work. All of us agree that the study of the state is not prior to the study of international relations but part of it.

Despite this, the question remains at issue among us and paralyses our theorising: is the area of our science still relations between states, as our tradition has been for three hundred years? On this view, the data of the state are to be brought in only to help explain why states relate as they do. Or is the area of our science far wider, one great community of men worldwide, men transnational, men making separate states but still interacting with all other men and morally bound to them?

We can paper over this division of views with a kindly phrase: these are simply 'two different levels of analysis'. We can, alternatively, go further into the relationship between the two, and ask what they are levels of analysis of, and seek some true reconciliation. The practical men who make the world we live in will not wait while we clear our minds on this problem. If we want to say anything, we have as always to hurry. In one academic corner, we talk cheerfully of a world that is quite inevitably divided into separate states and in which these states are the central reality. We offer no argument against the power that will not have it so, that kills abroad for faction whatever the state may say, that is ambitious, grasping a final unity of mankind, to extend its own principles of government over the whole world. In another corner, we talk happily about a world community, a world economy, global interdependence, world politics, the erosion of the state. What political structures do we envisage the while for our security? A world state perhaps? What community, what economy, what interdependence, what politics even, would there be in the world state that power gave us? Let us, if we can, reconcile the opposing corners. If we cannot, let us at least decide which we are in and give the reasons why, which is to say, give our theory.

Beyond the problem of the boundaries of our science, there lie philosophical problems common to all the human sciences. One of these is 'language'. Our data are the product of thought but not at all of silent thought. They are thought articulated in language. The world that faces us is notoriously a flow of talk. Soon we notice that the talk is not all of the same kind. The data of our science are not all of the same kind.

When all the data seem to be about a war, there is in fact one stream of words which expresses the personal pathos of war; another which is social argument about the rights and wrongs of the conflict; and yet another which philosophises about war as an evil of the human condition. When the data are drawn from the harmony of states, there is in a parallel way, first, the language of alliances of states; there is next the social language of international organisations of states; and there is finally the philosophical language of a deeper community of all states.

Often these three kinds of talk are mixed together in a single utterance. In a debate in an international organisation, for example, a representative will speak at one moment of 'my government', the next of 'we, the organisation' and, in his peroration, of 'mankind'. A scholar, as in this book, goes deeper to three 'worlds of meaning' and it is much achieved (Chapter 5). But how, we then ask, do the three languages relate to one another? How does a word glide surreptitiously from one to the other? How is it that one language bursts in upon another, that the personal voice, of Mussolini say, drowns the suave committee-talk of Europe, and the terrible personal pathos of war pictured by American newsmen helps overwhelm the positions of American generals? Above all, in which language, personal, social or philosophical, are we to theorise?

Next among the problems which account for our hesitation to theorise is the formidably named 'epistemological problem' (Chapter 6). Imagine you are on holiday in the Cuillin mountains, happily considering sea, sky and islands. Imagine you are at home, standing on your doorstep, irritably considering how on earth a new gatepost is to be got into an old hole in the flagstone. In either situation, calm depends on confidence that sea, sky and islands are what they are, and that at least a post is a post, a stone a stone, a hole a hole. You have at least that much on your side when you try to paint the picture for others, friends at the hotel bar, the local ironmonger.

In international relations (as in the other human sciences, more or less), we are not so sure. We say that international relations is a science. We speak bravely of our data. When we ask ourselves what our data are, we answer, still quite bravely, island, hole, conflict, trade flow, foreign policy-making organisation, state, system of states. But we are dismally aware that the trouble with our data, the data of the political world, is that they will not keep still. They are always controverted and continuously changing. We are unable to describe them to one another in a manner which is agreed and which lasts. We cannot therefore, we fear, even begin to theorise.

Contrast the natural scientist. He may not be able to understand his world. He may not even be able to explain how he can describe it. No matter. Describe it he can, after arduous inquiry, in a manner which triumphantly convinces his fellows and the rest of us and which enables us to control the world he describes. His description lasts long, until a rare revolution alters the standpoint from which all is viewed.

The natural scientist's world is not our world. Our data are the product of thought. Save in the crassest terms, terms in which there have always been 'conflicts', 'trade flows' and so on since the beginning of human life, our data keep changing over time, over a single decade of our lifetime, leave alone centuries. And not merely are our data the ceaselessly changing product of practical thought; our description of them is the product of our thought. In consequence, even a book that simply attempts to depict current European affairs, to say nothing of a book on the elements of world politics, is instantly challenged or, what is worse, wearily received as just another 'interesting appraisal'. There is never agreement on our data. One way of escaping from this affliction of our science, as in other human sciences, is to pretend that our data are like natural science data and to reduce the human world (as the natural scientist would never reduce his world) to statistics, correlations, abstract logic and model relationships. But this is unfaithful to our data. Most of us avoid infidelity by inertia.

To express the difficulty of the science of international relations in this way is to repeat the well known. The deeper roots of the difficulty need further discussion among us. For a start (so it will be argued in this book) it seems that we think that what we lack is an agreed viewpoint on the world. Scientists need a common mountain, a common doorstep. From such a standpoint, all can agree that the world is to be sliced into data in this way and not in another. The dream or nightmare is to be fixed and parted into the concepts 'sea', 'sky', 'island', 'post', 'stone', 'hole', and not otherwise. A social group agreeing is the source of security of data.

As to some basic things, 'sea' and 'post', the group is perhaps all men. As to others, it is some more particular group. In Europe in recent centuries, the common standpoint for viewing the political world has been 'the state'. From this standpoint, taking it as firm ground beneath our feet, Europeans looked out upon the world happily and irritably. It was seen as divided into islands with a sea between them for the battle of interstate relations. In Europe there were plainly 'states', the battles mitigated by 'a states-system'; elsewhere, there were plainly not states but 'barbarians', 'empires', 'states' perhaps eventually. To this day, a book on current European affairs or on the elements of world politics, and no matter whether it is discussing Britain and France, international business, the nature of human conflict, or anything else, reflects in every line and paragraph the theory of the state or else risks the ultimate condemnation: 'Not an interesting appraisal.'

The trouble is, though, that Europeans have lately become less sure of this standpoint. We do not censure with quite the decisiveness of our grandfathers. Odd stuff, we are inclined to think of some new book, but still, who knows, there may be something in it. For we have discovered that our standpoint for looking at the world is not the firm ground we took it for. The state itself is thought, it is a myth and artifice. We cast about for some other mountain.

We pile the proverbial Pelion on Ossa in an effort to reach a new, higher standpoint. Our European theory of the state is now a slithering heap, so we pile bits and pieces of it into a cairn and call this a world viewpoint. We see from there a vision of a world community, global interdependence, a world economy. Still, is the world with us, we wonder. Could men from Europe, Asia, Africa and the Americas ever agree on what the world is like? We fear that the theorist like any other man is a creature of his own particular culture and can never attain a viewpoint outside it, common to all cultures. Theorists of the five continents, conferring together, do so rootlessly and artificially, except if they lapse from theory into current problems. International theory, perhaps, cannot be worldwide. If it cannot, what in our time is the good of it (Chapter 7)?

So far in this discussion, theorising has been considered in terms of the difficulties of describing the world before us and agreeing on the data. There remains a last, most serious obstacle to theory.

Suppose we agree that theory which merely aims to describe the world is short-sighted. If we agree on this, we shall not be cancelling all that has so far been discussed nor in any way depreciating the work of scholars who concentrate on trying to establish the data of how people, business companies, states, and so on, actually behave. On the contrary, it ought to be acknowledged that such labour is indispensable. Some of us expect to have this at best to our credit and would like it to be honoured.

Still, so far, theory is only just beginning. For to theorise is not just to describe the data of the world, to assemble them in patterns, to observe regularities and to call these norms. That is to make daisy-chains. It is not finding the coherence of the world. A theorist looks critically on the data of the world that he inhabits. Claiming the distinguished title of theorist, he has at least average human intelligence, and this includes a normative faculty. He reasons about the world before him and contrasts for us 'what is' with 'what is done'.

We hold back from a true theorist's work nowadays not just from humility, but from doubt about the standpoint from which the theorist works. We see the world of international relations that we make for ourselves daily. We cannot accept that we have nothing to do but to describe and rationalise it, that scholars of international relations are nothing but the commentators and apologists of the practical men. We desire to reach higher ground. But what could this higher ground be, this standpoint for theory, but some rickety platform of our own personal devising for our own personal moralising?

When sufficiently stirred by the achievements or the atrocities of the world, we pour out praise or condemnation like any other men. Like any other men, we comment daily or quarterly on what is done. In the end, though, we fear that ours, like everybody else's, is an arbitrary standpoint. 'If someone approves, as a goal, the extirpation of the human race from the earth,' says Einstein, 'one cannot refute such a viewpoint on rational grounds.'[1] Accepting this, we think it hardly worth while to expound our underlying critical theory in a formal, structured way. When, as in this book, we treat particular aspects such as 'justice' and 'obligation' in international politics, we feel certain at most of their importance; we do not claim to be certain of what we say (Chapters 8 and 9).

Just as the problem of forming our data centres on the state, so too does this problem of theorising critically. 'State' is central to sovereignty, war, intervention and the rest of the old list, and equally to such rebel ideas as factional violence, economic aid, multinational corporation, transnational organisation and much else that is common coin among us. Correspondingly, the morality of the state has long been the focus of critical theory in international politics. What is the morality of the state, how is a state justified? A state is an arrangement of men to the ends of men. What quality of internal life and external action must a group of men show to call itself a state, separate itself, justify itself? What quality of internal life and external action can the rest of the world in reason condemn? But, above all, what standard can there possibly be for answering such questions? From what standpoint can the critical theorist possibly work (Chapter 10)?

Perhaps much of the insecurity that afflicts us in the science of international relations, both as to the status of our data and as to our standpoint for theorising, springs from our desire for the standpoint of an observer. As in all the human sciences, we in international relations are all in one degree or another powerfully impressed by the example of the natural scientist. We see that the natural scientist is an observer, that is, that he is at a distance from his data, different from them, looking at them as an outsider. We think that to be scientists, we must do the same; that our data must have the same degree of objectivity; that if we are to describe and criticise, we must have the same detached standpoint. We find again and again that none of this is possible. So we are dismayed.

We do not perhaps always keep sufficiently in mind that it is the privilege of the human scientist to be part of the life he studies (Chapters 11 and 12). He is inside his world and, thus, has no radical problem of understanding. Being inside, he is one with his fellow men in making the world, and must expect to have to argue just as they do about what the situation facing them is, what the data are. Being a man, he needs no other standpoint than this from which to criticise the life of men and no other credential than this for reasoning with others about it. He is, as some say who still claim for men the word 'nature', part of nature and can obscurely glimpse its laws. He has, as others would say, the consolation of knowing that he himself is within history and able for that reason to understand and judge.

NOTE FOR THE INTRODUCTION

1 Quoted by Arnold Brecht in *Political Theory* (Princeton, The University Press, 1959), p. 9.

1
The Practice of a States-System

MAURICE KEENS-SOPER

I

That relations between the states of Europe have occurred within a framework of some kind is recognised by all except the most rigorous adherents of 'realism', for whom the clash of political wills is unmediated and governed exclusively by the shifting configurations of power. There is less agreement about and scant interest in the identity of this framework, its bearing upon and relation to the events of diplomatic history and the manner of establishing it and of settling its place in the history of international thought.[1] The purpose of this first chapter is to explore the problems which arise in the pursuit of this identity and to suggest that they lead to a particular view of the relations between theory and practice.

Among the ambiguities which nowadays surround an attempt to establish the framework of European foreign affairs, one at least should be disposed of at the outset. The undertaking is one of imaginative reconstruction in obedience to the evidence rather than of contingent ascription, of examining not whether it makes more sense to us to assume that a framework of some form existed but in what terms, if any, a framework was considered to exist by those directly engaged.

If one keeps in mind that the undertaking is to inquire what framework the evidence obliges us to pronounce and not what constructions it will bear for extraneous purposes, then the answer to one initial question is unambiguous. The states which came to fill the stage of 'Europe' and to exhaust its political space as a prelude to circumscribing the world, were the legatees of a civilisation thoroughly acquainted with the singularity of its own diverse character. That character had come to include, if not to be dominated by, the discrepancies between its cultural and religious unity and its political fragmentation. But so striking was the assertion of princely power by the monarchies of the late Middle Ages and early modern times, and so persuasive has been the force of statehood to a civilisation historiographically dazzled by state and nation, that elements of continuous organisation underpinning extreme diversity have either been denied or regarded as of merely antiquarian interest.[2]

From the point of view of interpreting the relations between the politically separated parts of a once-unified whole this tendency has had several consequences. At its most extreme, it was understood to mean that the multiplicity of states were related only in the ceaseless and bondless strife of an uncivil 'state of nature'. Yet the fact of signal importance, attested to by kings, soldiers, clerics, diplomatic envoys, traders and travellers, philosophers, men of letters and popular entertainers, is that in the very act of asserting and celebrating their emancipation from the rival imperial and papal claims to the government of Latin Christendom, the successor states left untouched the instinctive assumption that they formed parts of a distinctive whole. No Renaissance ruler believed either that his claims to 'sovereign' status as 'emperor within his own kingdom' implied the abrogation of his duties as a prince of Christendom or that the political independence of his realms ruptured the various practices which mediaeval Christendom had adumbrated for the government of its affairs in both peace and war.

Although the last occasion on which a united Latin Christendom is said to have met together (momentarily) was at the Council of Constance (1416),[3] the monarchical states whose standing was enhanced by its failure to resolve the conflicts at issue, were none the less obliged to adapt the pre-existing methods for the papal government of Christendom to the novel conditions of their progressive independence from oecumenical authority. That the implications of political fragmentation did not call in question the continued spiritual and legal unity of Christendom nor curtail the relevance of these considerations to the necessarily piecemeal adaptation to altered circumstances, is nowhere denied by those engaged. The fall of Constantinople (1453) to the Mohammedans, which so glaringly revealed the disunity and the cynical indifference of rulers to the fate of Christendom, was also – for four hundred years – to demonstrate that however close the Turk might bear on their affairs, relations among Christians and Europeans were on a different footing to those that might have to be maintained with outsiders. Mohammedans to the east, and in the next century

Aztecs, Indians and others to the west, might interact with the princely powers of Christendom, enter into their calculations and impinge upon their fortunes, but they were incapable of belonging to the body of the Christian commonwealth. In writing to Mohammed II, the conqueror of Constantinople, the experienced ex-diplomatist Pope Pius II makes quite clear what it was that was threatened. 'We cannot believe,' he wrote in 1458, 'that you are unaware of the resources of the Christian people – how strong is Spain, how warlike is France, how numerous are the people of Germany, how powerful Britain, how bold Poland, how vigorous Hungary, how rich, spirited and skilled in warfare is Italy.'[4]

It has been appropriately remarked that this is not a 'catalogue of Christian peoples, but of *European* Christian peoples'.[5] Not only did the Vicar of Christ hereby identify Christianity with the peoples of a particular area, but also it is clear that the Christendom whose divisions and selfishness he lamented had an 'interior' as well as frontiers threatened by Ottoman conquest. The same pope who had travelled widely within Christendom and who used 'Christendom' and 'Europe' interchangeably also came to coin the adjectival sense of 'Europe'. 'The events which happened among Europeans,' he writes, 'or those who are called Christians.'[6] The notions of Europe and Christendom remained alternative expressions throughout the sixteenth and for much of the seventeenth century. Under humanist influence the *res publica Christiana* became preferred to the mediaeval *Christianitas* or *terra Christiana*, but the point of interest is for how long 'la chose publique de la Chrestiente' retained its hold on men's minds. Perhaps the threatening proximity of the Turk had something to do with the fact that treaties of the sixteenth and seventeenth centuries usually referred to the 'Christian Republic' and 'the Provinces of Christendom'.

The last occasion on which the *res publica Christiana* figured in an official document is said to be the preamble to the Treaty of Utrecht in 1714.[7] If so, this is of perhaps more than incidental interest because the same treaty which sealed the failure of a threatened French hegemony over Europe includes the first explicit treaty reference to the principle of the balance of power as the necessary basis of peace among European powers. There is moreover little doubt that by this time, somewhere between the Nine Years War (1689–97) and the conclusion of the War of the Spanish Succession (1702–13), 'Europe' had come to acquire a political meaning.[8] That meaning is nowhere better expressed than in the deeds and words of the principal architect, William of Orange. He it was whose doggedness in the face of the Sun King's might organised and animated the alliances of European powers whose purpose was to 'defend the liberties of Europe'. To this Dutchman who crossed the

Channel to become King of England as an item in his European agenda, Europe was a single field of diplomatic forces and the liberties he referred to were none other than the independence of its states.[9] The official explanation of the War of the Spanish Succession was 'the great danger which threatened the liberty and safety of all Europe from too close conjunction of the kingdoms of Spain and France'.[10] The remedy for this which would 'establish the peace and tranquillity of Christendom' was declared to be: 'an equal balance of power which is the best and most solid foundation of a mutual friendship and of a concord which will be lasting on all sides.'[11]

II

With such utterances the states-system of Europe had become aware of itself as an association of states. Somewhere between the defeat of the last Turkish attack on central Europe by John Sobieski and the Holy League at the gates of Vienna in 1683 and the victories of Marlborough, the political identity of Europe was defined as a multiplicity of states. It was accomplished in and by war against those, like Louis XIV, who sought to deny its liberties from within, and against those like the alien Turk, who was in but not of Europe. In addition to the sense of Europe as the place where Christians of all kinds lived, the home of peoples responsive to the movements of a single though variegated culture, of subjects of different rulers bound together in material dependencies of commerce, of men who looked back to related traditions of morality, law and government, and forward to the opportunities of the wider worlds beyond Europe, Europeans came to understand foreign affairs as the preoccupations of their rulers with the independence and interests of their states and with the conditions of their coexistence.

Hence what was referred to at the outset of this chapter in purposely anodyne terms as the 'framework' of international relations has to be seen not as an empty shell circumscribing and setting limits to the play of political forces, but as intimately and pervasively related to the substantive issues arising between states. The sense of Europe as a system of states did not emerge suddenly nor was it ever completed or given final shape. The political order which the states of Europe came to comprise and develop was, in its most general formulation, defined by the implications of independence, implications intimated in the practices of men who shared a civilisation and who inherited an entire vocabulary of words and procedures for the conduct of public affairs. As need arose, they adapted past practices to present circumstances, and where, as with 'international law', the past could speak to the present only as echoes, the 'public law of Europe' had to be improvised from the languages of mediaeval canon, feudal and civil war.

It is perhaps with the precepts and practices associated with the enunciation of the balance of power, the elaboration of diplomacy and the formulation of the 'law of nations' that one can most directly grasp the identity of Europe as a political system. Europe came to acquire a novel 'constitution' after its fragmentation into distinct and rival sovereignties whose rulers were moved by mundane considerations of advantage and right rather than by the prescriptions of religious piety. And though we may find the terms and conditions of this association problematical, imprecise, ill-defined, tenuous, fragile, seldom clearly or unambiguously expressed, usually qualified by the imprint of interest and expediency and consequently subject to abuse and adjustment, this leads to the conclusion not that the states-system of Europe was chimerical but that states-systems are the loosest of all political associations and their reality unique. The states-system of Europe remained prescriptive and unchartered throughout its history. Its order was in part implicit in the sense that relations between Europeans, in war as well as in peace, were felt to be of a special kind, and in part more openly proclaimed not by being announced or authorised by any one body of persons meeting at a particular moment, but in the no less instructive reiteration in practice of shared precepts and rules of conduct.

III

Before exploring an illustration of the kind of practice which may be said to establish and embody the states-system, one further comment on the notion of Europe as delimiting a field of diplomatic forces is required. This has to do with the question of Europe's frontiers. Although my principal interest is with the system of Europe as a political association, it is necessary to take precautions against a modern prejudice which declares that where one cannot point with precision (in this instance to unbroken lines of demarcation between political entities) there can exist no actuality to engage one's attention. To the extent that Europe had no fixed or exactly recognised frontiers its existence is deemed suspect.

This line of argument is, however, anachronistic. For men of the seventeenth century, for the rulers and envoys who conducted affairs with all parts of Europe (and of course beyond), no such problem existed. The Turk was physically in Europe but not morally part of its public affairs, subscribing only selectively to its practices of statecraft. The Congress of Carlowitz (1699) was, for example, the first occasion at which the Turks agreed to a treaty in conference. Britain and Holland presided as mediators. The full 'incorporation' of the sultan was long deferred and was formally accomplished only by the Treaty of Paris in 1856. There certainly existed doubt about the position of Muscovy which was not fully resolved until well after the defeat of Sweden at Poltava in 1709 and the determination of Peter the Great to place his capital with ready access to Western Europe. As with the Turk, military might did not alone imply automatic access to the confidence of Europe, and well into the eighteenth century Frenchmen in particular were suspicious of the tsar's civilised, that is European, credentials. Issues of this kind may have attracted uncertainty, but it was not considered a problem casting doubt on the authenticity of Europe among Europeans. We of later times may feel politically ill at ease without maps depicting the exact contours of every item of political space, but to the statesmen and diplomatists of the *ancien régime*, Europe was a mechanism of diplomatic forces in a relatively mapless world. Not only did the eastern frontier of Europe remain vague without damage to the credibility of the states-system – as did the exact whereabouts of Europe's overseas boundaries to west and east – but until the eighteenth century war and peace were made between members of the 'espèce de grande république partagée en plusieurs Etats', as Voltaire called it, without the use of maps as integral parts of treaties.

IV

Summary mention has been made of the origins of the European states-system in the unity of that mediaeval '*societas christiana*, which was the framework of all relationship and all conflict'.[12] Without wishing to qualify the importance of origins to an understanding of the states-system, the issue of origins, as also that of expanding frontiers, may be kept at least conditionally distinct from a consideration of the precepts and practices which constituted Europe's identity. There remains, however, the choice of determining at what point in the development of a prescriptive association – whose capacity to adapt existing and engender fresh methods for its management is among its chief embellishments – to examine its 'constitutional' arrangements. Some at least of them did, however, become progressively manifest as well as more systematically related during the half-century before Europe became a self-consciously political association of states, whose 'liberties' were of general concern to states like France, England, Austria, Prussia and soon Russia (but no longer Spain or Sweden) who were coming to regard themselves as a special class of 'great powers'.

It has been persuasively argued that the significance of the Congress of Westphalia is seriously misjudged when it is taken to mark the 'beginnings' of the states-system rather than its 'coming of age' after some two centuries or so of improvised development.[13] Perhaps more to the point, if one is to illustrate the general argument by reference to one of the characteristic features of the states-system, then choice of period and topic is inescapable. In choosing to dwell on the matter of legal and diplomatic practices in the states-system of post-Westphalian Europe, I do not wish to imply that other considerations are of less relevance. The identity of something is exhausted only when all its features have been named, examined and related to one another. The 'emergence of the great powers'[14] itself calls for special consideration as, of course, does the 'military revolution' in a century that saw only seven complete calendar years without war between European states.[15] Nor would I wish to be taken as denying the importance to the states-system, as to every department of European life, of such considerations as the shift from the theocentric 'meta-system' which stood 'behind' the political system of sixteenth-century Christendom, to the 'meta-system' of 'matter and motion' which in the progress of a century of scientific revolutions gradually suggested different moral bases for human conduct, including the conduct of foreign affairs. Imperceptibly the victory of the 'moderns' over the 'ancients' within the 'republic of letters' came to mean the transition from a world which required justification of conduct in rational terms, which predicated a God-centred universe, to a world which came to construe politics as the arena of power and interest and of men's unhindered and unaided reasoning faculties.[16] By the time the transition had occurred, foreign affairs within Europe had abandoned the spirit of righteousness of the wars of the Reformation and Counter-Reformation for the more flexible vocabulary of calculation, where *raison d'état* occurred as a secularised version of political right, that is, the expediency of state interest raised to the level of principle. Reason of state was also the corollary of sovereignty conceived as the self-authorisation of human associations bound together as states.[17]

V

The 'assembly' of Westphalia whose treaties gave point and definition to the political shape of Europe's foreign affairs served as the major text and referent of diplomatic relations for well over a century. Perhaps it was the closest approximation the states-system had to a textual basis for its 'constitution' between the close of the Thirty Years War and the 'concert of Europe' established at the Congress of Vienna. But the identity we are pursuing is more readily revealed in the 'institutional' animations of the states-system than in the articles of peace in which the outcomes of war were formulated. The states-system of Europe did not of course 'authorise' its 'institutions' in the sense of *establishing* its diplomatic machinery, or *proclaim* a system of law between its states, or *construct* a balance of power. All these were the accomplishments of its members, the outcomes of their conflicts and collaborations and of their selfish and fitful determinations to preserve the system as the necessary underpinning of their own independence. As a political association, the states-system had neither the means, the occasion, nor even perhaps the need to do any of these things. The predicate of the system was universally understood after the Westphalia settlement to be the rejection in right and in power of any political authority to 'give the law', to prescribe conduct or constrain by force the actions of its members. As a result – of the war and not of the settlement taken in isolation—the Empire was transmogrified from the 'universal monarchy' with which the Hapsburgs of the previous century had hoped to pacify all Christendom, heal its spiritual wounds and repel the Turk, into a German kingdom whose greatest princes were thenceforth entitled to make treaties of alliance with powers outside the Empire. It was to make sense of this condition that, in 1675, Pufendorf defined a states-system as 'several states that are so connected as to seem to constitute one body but whose members retain sovereignty'.[18] So far as Christian Europe as a whole was concerned, it had for several centuries lacked the authority and institutional arrangements to govern its parts and had it possessed them, its affairs would belong to the study of constitutional history and not to that of international relations. The uniqueness of the states-system as an association is that although it belongs in the gallery of human political associations, its 'constitution' is composed of 'institutions' like diplomacy, international law and the balance of power, which are not to be found in other quarters. The political space of Europe was subject to government but to government by its independent but connected parts.[19]

The inchoate state of Europe after the Congress of Westphalia can be seen in the apparent paradox that although states had the capacity to devise 'congresses' – itself a new term – for the settlement of their disputes at the conclusion of wars so that it can be said that from then onwards 'the diplomatic history of Europe has stridden from one congress to another',[20] at no time before 1815 did they concert together even for the purposes of rationalising the most elementary rules of their intercourse. As a result congresses, the idea of which may have owed something to the ecclesiastical councils of Christendom and which were one of the most striking additions to diplomacy, frequently spent as much energy in establishing their rules of procedure as on substantive political issues. Precedents were established but the rules of diplomatic conduct were not formally inscribed as part of the 'constitutional' fabric of Europe. Typically, procedural issues easily became the occasion for the continuation of disputes that congresses were called to settle. Diplomacy could be used for the continuation of warfare by other means.

In the case of what we now think of as international law, the task of establishing and formulating, not to mention determining and enforcing its requirements, was generally prodigious. The business of adapting the *jus gentium* of Christendom to the demands of its successor states who had lately engaged in a century of religious warfare from which they had emerged with enhanced powers, was not even contemplated at the Congress of Westphalia. The piecemeal emergence of a *jus inter gentes*, a law between sovereign states, out of the laws of Christendom, was hindered by the habit of Renaissance publicists of downgrading the residues of experience bequeathed from mediaeval experience in preference for the 'authorities' of Greece, Rome and the particularly brutal records of the Old Testament. The force of custom and practice relevant to the relations between members of a states-system was also obstructed by the determination of seventeenth-century natural law thinkers to derive their rules from first principles.[21] What may have been gained in their generalising the 'law of nations' to include the non-European world in a single conception of the 'great society of states' – for example, the implication that the doctrine of state equality applied at least in principle to the non-European world – was paid for within Europe by a gap between the largely unformulated practice of states and the reasonings of publicists.

Much of early international law was concerned with war, the sea and the status of diplomatic envoys. At least for this last, it is possible to detect both the lines of continuity that connected the practices worked out in the states-system with previous experience, and the spirit of adaptation which produced new procedures such as the congresses mentioned earlier. On the one hand, the papal 'international government' of the Middle Ages provided a model of how to organise the 'administrative' affairs of Christendom through the agency of legates and nuncios, while on the other, the insatiable needs of rulers for political intelligence prompted the telling shift from fitful or sporadic to habitual or residential diplomacy. Residence of an envoy at the court to which he was accredited, even though the rulers concerned might have no actual conflicts in need of reconciliation and for the explicit purpose of transmitting regular accounts of the country of his appointment, was an astounding development. At the time there were many who were scandalised by what seemed like the licensed entitlement to pursue systematic espionage, particularly as the new practice of sending ambassadors for 3 years or so at a time incorporated all the traditional immunities and protections which had earlier covered the work of transient envoys. The occasion for the new development, which began in the second half of the fifteenth century with the miniature states-system of Italy as its first theatre, was the pressure of two developments: the independence of states and their close juxtaposition or involuntary coexistence in a restricted political space from which the choice of isolation or indifference had become excluded. As Machiavelli makes quite clear, ceaseless vigilance was the absolute condition of survival within a framework of this kind.

It is sometimes assumed that every need produces its solution. In political life the logic of this style of reasoning leads swiftly to determinism. So far as the 'invention' of the 'honourable spy' who was dispatched abroad 'to lie on behalf' of his country's interests is concerned, the need is evident. But one must also notice the conditions which made it possible as well as necessary to arrive at this fundamental organising element and permit its generalised introduction into the bellicose and unstable affairs of Europe's rulers. These men had no reason to relish the 'eyes and ears' of their rivals in settled and protected positions in their own courts and no obvious reason for undertaking the additional burden of being themselves responsible for protecting the activities of other sovereigns' agents, whose explicit purpose it was to report on their affairs. Part of the explanation is to be found in the precedents afforded by mediaeval experience, though these, as has been suggested, were somewhat indirect and distant. It has perhaps something also to do with the tentative way in which the novelty was first introduced, and in this connection it is perhaps relevant that when the practice of residential diplomacy crossed the Alps from Italy it was among those Western European states who formed the heart of the states-system, that it took on most rapidly. Well into the seventeenth century the kings of Poland were reluctant to allow ambassadors to remain in the country for long periods lest they became engaged in the rival schemes to elect monarchs favourable to the French or the Austrian persuasion. The diplomatists of European rulers were frequently active at Constantinople but the 'unreciprocating will of the unspeakable Turk' had no resident representative at any European court. The reciprocal interest in the flow of information, in facility of negotiation, and in opportunities to 'present' their majesty, which bound the states of Europe together in a continuously activated network of arrangements, was able to find expression in the legal inviolability of envoys and the exterritoriality of embassies because those involved were legatees of a customary order of common understandings.[22] The mechanisms of diplomacy embodied both needs and understandings.

Diplomacy did not, therefore, produce an element of order in the unpredictable 'action and reaction' of foreign affairs where none had hitherto existed, but the means of generating more where some already existed. Even where diplomacy was inverted to become the stalking horse for war, or mobilised to exaggerate rather than mitigate differences of interest, it can be argued that in so far as it facilitated the operations of the system it contributed to the orderly running of its violence. In this sense the elaboration of diplomacy, after it became acknowledged as the staple ingredient of the states-system, provides a profile of the whole, seen through one of its principal institutions.

The shape of the whole is to be seen as the system of states becomes progressively organised as a system of diplomacy. Although the central focus of this story is inevitably the exterritoriality of embassies, there is abundant evidence from other areas which contributes to the picture of an increasingly cogent set of arrangements whose purpose was to focus and articulate the business of the states-system. In the second half of the seventeenth century and under the impress of French example, the diplomatic resources of states were gradually distinguished and organised as separate ministries. Dispatches began to be collected as state property (rather than remaining as the personal property of envoys), housed, arranged and made ready for use as evidence by archivists employed by foreign ministries. Envoys came to be regarded (though slowly) as a separate profession and, with France once again in the forefront, calling for special training in the procedures and arts of negotiating. As Europe by the early decades of the eighteenth century was conceived of as one inter-related field of diplomatic forces, French was more and more accepted as the language of foreign affairs (as widely it became the medium of polite society). The first 'school for ambassadors' founded in 1712 by the French foreign minister Torcy inducted its students into the records of European treaties since the Peace of Westphalia and, less wisely, set them to annotate Grotius. The scheme was lampooned by Addison in *The Spectator*, but a few years later the regius professorships of history were set up at Oxford and Cambridge with the express intention of providing 'a constant supply of persons in every way qualified for the management of such weighty affairs and negotiations' as need might occasion.[23]

The preoccupation with issues of precedence and protocol, particularly during the gatherings of the states-system at peace congresses but also as part of the business of embassy routine, was typical of the social manners of the *ancien régime* and not only of its diplomacy. Moreover the 'compound of formalities, decencies and circumspections' was not always irrelevant to an activity whose *raison d'être* was to be a civilised and civilising force among states frequently inclined to violent remedies. The most matter-of-fact observer of the detail of diplomatic practice in the generation after Westphalia, whose treatise became a reference book for a hundred years, wrote that: 'The ambassador is obliged to conform to the rules that have been agreed upon . . . and cannot fail therein without disconcerting that harmony without which there can be no conversation between public ministers.'[24]

Wicquefort was in no doubt that as a matter of fact there were rules of diplomacy – some of them having the force of legal bonds – and that the voice of 'negotiations' was necessarily conversational. The social life of envoys, gathered and living together in the same capitals while serving the interests of their independent masters, also had its reason. If *raison d'état* was the principle of state policy, then perhaps it is true to say that the civility and corporate sense of the *corps diplomatique* was a visible embodiment of the *raison de système* of Europe.[25] This is evident in the manuals of diplomacy which accompanied, described, reflected and very occasionally reflected upon the art and business of 'negotiations'. At its most informative, this literature is not a digest of fanciful speculations about 'the perfect ambassador' nor merely the most persuasive evidence that international law was a reality in some at least of its parts, but a discussion by practitioners of the manner in which diplomacy was a distinct form of political activity and one unique to the states-system.[26] This is what marks François de Callières's *De la Manière de négocier avec les Souverains* as the finest expression of the diplomacy of the *ancien régime*.[27]

VI

It is one thing to indicate the evidence in support of an argument and another to inquire into the assumptions which must support whatever theoretical burden the argument is designed to sustain. In particular, it is the student of politics, with his professed interest in the nature and workings of human associations, who must be satisfied that the states-system of Europe is sufficiently solid (in the sense of being enough of a 'one' to be more than a mere contingent plurality) to warrant consideration as belonging within the vocabulary of politics at all. For in the absence of all consistency of performance there can be no politics, and were the relations of states taken to be of that sort, there could be no international politics and therefore no systematic study of whatever else one decided to call them. Diplomacy may go on 'in the absence of government', [28] but it presupposes a condition of some order among states even though this may only amount to the existence of a régime of rudimentary rules and elementary understandings. It will not do to argue at one and the same time that the states-system is unique and that it is a political association of a peculiar sort (and therefore subject to political analysis) but so unlike other political associations that it is incapable of systematic exploration. There have been other systems of states besides the European, and there is every reason why a comparison of the members of this species of association might prove illuminating. But even were this to prove unrealisable, it would not prevent the states-system of Europe from lending itself to investigation. It is the character of the relations that existed between the states of Europe and their consequent identification as a kind of political association that determines whether those relations can be systematically studied, not the existence of a species embracing the European, Mughal and Chinese systems.

Political inquiry is not satisfied with the 'investigation of frameworks and procedures as mere pieces of machinery', for the arrangements which men devise for their common association are never solely or predominantly that. And, so long as they are used, they can never become or be reduced to that condition. The reason for this is always present and before our eyes. Political association is the creation of men. It is an example, perhaps a mundane example, of human conduct. And the hallmark of human conduct is that it is purposive or pointed, in the sense of being the activity of intelligent beings. However trivial and transitory, and however unwise the purposes expressed in human conduct may prove to be, the agency of men and the inscription in the world of their demands, is never merely behavioural. The notion of 'political behaviour' is a contradiction; men do not and indeed cannot 'behave' but are condemned to 'acting' politically.

Montaigne observed that men's troubles derive from their congenital inability to remain contentedly within the privacy of their own dwellings. The occasion for politics is the meeting of purposes, and its achievement is the creation of arrangements for the housing together of varied purposes. It is not a matter of 'processes', for a process is what distinguishes the behaviour or identity of the animate or inanimate worlds of things. There are reasons why animal-lovers do not believe in votes for dogs or the representation of lions in the United Nations General Assembly. Both may stand in need of protection but they would not know what to do when called upon to speak in defence of their 'rights'. They are incapable of self-determination or any other kind of determination. Politics is therefore more accurately understood as the activity of intelligent beings who set themselves to achieve purposes and who generate with the aim of achieving purposes, 'institutions' and rules of procedure.[29]

If this is so, then political understanding has not been fully achieved nor the *chef-d'oeuvre* of politics grasped until the thought or purposes at work in political activity have been laid bare and interpreted. So far as international politics is concerned this point may sound uncontroversial if it is understood to refer only to the *substantive* purposes at issue in the conduct of foreign policy. But the point here is that, although undoubtedly foreign policy is the most unequivocal exhibition of substantive political purposes, policy and purpose are not synonymous. Purposes and therein 'thought' are to be detected not merely in the pursuit of the expressly formulated and justified determinations of foreign policy but equally, though differently, in the practices upon which the ability to pursue the substantive ends of policy are themselves dependent. By way of analogy, in constitutionalism, the content of any legislation is unimportant; it is the procedures that matter. And diplomacy is to foreign policy what constitutionalism is to legislation.

In the absence of established diplomatic and legal procedures, it would be strictly impossible to conduct foreign policy. Without agreement among states about how relations are to be conducted, there could be no meeting of understandings in terms of which conflicts of policy could be mediated. The contingent meeting of unrelated wills might produce a fitful clash of recognitions, but of itself it could not be the occasion for political dealings because these presuppose a basis of consistency. Even war, the most risky and violent of substantive purposive political acts, is unintelligible divorced from a framework of legal and prudential understandings whose purpose is to regularise its conduct. To those caught up in war, the laws 'governing' its conduct may be real enough to make the difference between life and death. In their absence, war would lose its identity as a 'continuation of policy by other means' and become inseparable from gratuitous blood-letting.

Viewed in this manner, the stock of diplomatic practices discussed earlier is more than one of the prerequisites of foreign policy. To regard it as of no more significance than a set of instrumentalities is to confuse the categorical distinction between rules of procedure and policy and to wrongly suppose that only the latter is capable of revealing the agency of purpose. The identity of the states-system is that it is a system of rules of procedure and hardly at all a political association for the achievement of common substantive purposes. The history of the European states-system reveals how these rules of procedure were adumbrated as 'institutions'. Abraham de Wicquefort understood the character of these rules and perhaps came closest to giving them formal expression in the years after the Peace of Westphalia:

'The necessity of Embassies makes the security of Ambassadors by the universal consent of all the nations of the Earth; and it is this general consent that constitutes what is called the Law of Nations. It holds a medium between the Law of Nature and the Civil Law, and is by so much the more considerable than the last, that it can neither be changed nor altered, but by the same unanimous approbation of all peoples. There is no sovereign that can assume the authority to explain the laws which compose this right. Neither is there any judge that can extend his jurisdiction over those persons whom this law protects, because he would thereby disturb a commerce, the freedom whereof is founded on indispensable necessity, and he would deprive mankind of the means of maintaining society, which could not subsist without this principle, which is more than mathematical.'[30]

With its flavour of universalism, rationalism and contract, this is unmistakably a voice of the seventeenth century. But its conception of a system of law between sovereigns who must sustain that law because they will not suffer a judge above them, and who cannot do without the institution of diplomacy for the regularisation of their inter-related affairs, is also the reasoning of a European intimately familiar with the historical identity of Europe's states-system.

The 'mechanism' of diplomacy is perhaps most expressive of the determination of states, or rather of generations of their human agents, to equip themselves with means appropriate for the conduct of their substantive affairs. In the creation and adaptation of this body of practices, in the tentative, circumstantial and provisional character of their formulation, through unrelieved attention to the dictates of foreign affairs by nameless and numberless hands, one glimpses the involvement of thought.

VII

The bearing of my argument on the business of theorising relations between states may be briefly and tentatively stated. Much attention has been directed towards trying to theorise the substantive relations of states. What stands in the way of this is their independence – the uniqueness and particularity of separate states. Attempts to say something general and systematic about their 'goals' have produced an untiring circumlocution of banalities.[31] Less attention has been paid to areas where what is typical is what states share and not what they do not have in common. This may be due to a belief that the study of foreign policy and of other 'international processes' is the most important topic in the study of international relations. One may, however, question this kind of assumption. Perhaps a less ephemeral centre is to be found in the study of the determination of the 'rules of the game' in states-systems and of the political conflict the adumbration of these rules has occasioned.

In so far as one seeks to go beyond this to the requirement of situating the 'institutions' of diplomacy, international law and the balance of power as the constitutive parts of the states-system, and so of raising the whole to the level of 'idea' or system of thought, the implications of the foregoing are clear. The pursuit of a theoretical understanding of human conduct[32] is to be engaged in, not by establishing models of the 'things' to be theorised, by contriving an unnecessary divorce between 'theory' and 'practice', and so licensing an inconclusive and wanton dilemma about 'isomorphism'. The task is misunderstood as a need to create models which 'allow one to think systematically' and is better regarded as a commitment to the exploration, in as ordered a manner as the evidence permits, of the thought already embodied and at work in practice.

NOTES FOR CHAPTER 1

1   I discount those whose interest is restricted to exploiting the past in search of data relevant to their models of the international system. This is a fanciful abuse of the past, though earnestly disguised as scientific endeavour.

2   There are signs that the focus of attention is changing from nationally inclined histories to a greater awareness of the European setting. An example is the *Fontana History of Europe* under the general editorship of J. H. Plumb.

3   Martin Wight, *Systems of States*, ed. H. Bull (Leicester, The University Press, 1977): 'It is the last Ecumenical Council of undivided Latin Christendom, whose failure to effect reform of the Church makes revolution inevitable. It attempts to reform the international system of Christendom, which is the papally centralized Church. Its failure leads directly to the breakdown of the system and rebellion within the Church' (p. 132).

4   Quoted in Denys Hay, *Europe* (Edinburgh, The University Press, 1957), p. 83.

5   ibid., p. 84 (emphasis added).

6   ibid., p. 87.
7   Garrett Mattingly, *Renaissance Diplomacy* (London, Cape, 1955), p. 285.
8   See D. H. Schmidt, 'The Establishment of "Europe" as a Political Expression', *Historical Journal*, vol. IX, 1966.
9   See Stephen B. Baxter, *William III* (London, Longman, 1966), esp. ch. 26. 'Il faut considérer que tous les Etats dont l'Europe est composée' wrote François de Callières in his treatise *De la manière de négocier avec les Souverains* (1716), 'ont entr'eux des liaisons et des commerces nécessaires qui font qu'on peut les regarder comme des membres d'une même République, et qu'il ne peut presque point arriver de changement considérable en quelques uns de ses membres qui ne soit capables de troubler le repos de tous les autres' (p. 12).
10 Anglo-Spanish Treaty of Utrecht, 13 July 1713, in *The Consolidated Treaty Series*, ed., Clive Parry (Dobbs Ferry, Oceana, 1969), vol. 28, p. 325.
11 ibid.
12 Martin Wight, op. cit., p. 26.
13 ibid., ch. 5. This is not to deny that the Peace of Westphalia has, as a matter of opinion, established itself in this way; e.g. Clive Parry writes in the preface to his monumental *Consolidated Treaty Series* which begins in 1648, that 'it is proposed to make a beginning with the year 1648, classically regarded as the date of the foundation of the modern system of States'. Grotius's reputation as the 'father of international law' seems in a similar way to owe more to zealous late nineteenth century opinion in search of a prophet of internationalism than to his just deserts in the history of international law. In his own day he was famous for his writings on Christianity rather than for the *De Jure Belli ac Pacis*. These modern judgments are perhaps not surprising since there is no history of the European states-system, no agreement about how it might be tackled, and no comprehensive history of international law. One can, however, detect phases of internal differentiation and development in the elaboration of the states-system that are distinct from – though associated with – both the extent of the system and its principles of membership. They may be detected as proceeding from the 'Oecumenical' *order* of mediaeval Christendom; through a phase marked by the fragmentation of that order into independent states and by the pursuit, at first instinctive but later contrived, of a *balance of power*; through a phase indicated by the pursuit of a *concert of power* among the 'great powers'; on to a half-phase of *codification*; until one reaches in this century the breakdown and universalising of the system in the phase of *international organisation*. The point of significance in these movements of political expression within the states-system is that they did not succeed one another by replacing or destroying the phase before. Each phase overlay and inherited part at least of its predecessor, so that not merely did the balance of power emerge within the remnants of an order which defined its 'field of political forces' but the phase of balance was in turn incorporated into and, so to speak, underpinned the phases of concert, codification and organisation. On this reading, changes within the states-system from (at least) the seventeenth century have been so many adaptations of the balance of power which is thereby considered as the principle of plurality among a manifold of independent states. The Concert of Europe did not go beyond, though it did something to, the balance of power. It made explicit the presiding role of the great powers, giving them an official status. Similarly, the generation of international organisations has embedded the balance of power – and the concert of power – within these arrangements.
14 See John B. Wolf, *Toward a European Balance of Power 1620–1715* (Chicago, The University Press, 1970).
15 See Michael Roberts, 'The Military Revolution 1550–1660', an Inaugural Lecture delivered before Queen's University, Belfast, 1956.

16   For the way in which the notion of 'interest' enters the vocabulary of international relations we have as yet no study. One place to begin is with the Huguenot warrior, the Duc de Rohan, who finished by working for Richelieu to whom he dedicated his *De l'Interest des Princes* of 1638. 'The Princes command the People,' his preface begins, 'and the Interest commands the Princes. The knowledge of this Interest is as much more raised above that of Princes' actions, as they themselves are above the People. The Prince may deceive himself, his Counsell, but the Interest alone can never faile. According as it is well or ill understood, it maketh States to live or die' (English trans., 1643(?)).

A generation later Samuel Pufendorf developed some further distinctions: 'Interest may be divided into an Imaginary and Real Interest. By the first I understand, when a Prince judges the welfare of his state to consist in such things as cannot be performed without disquieting and being injurious to a great many other states, and which these are obliged to oppose with all their power; as for example, the monarchy of Europe, or the universal monopoly, this being the fuel with which the whole world may be put to flame. The real interest may be subdivided into a perpetual and temporary. The former depends chiefly on the situation and constitution of the country, and the natural inclinations of the people; the latter, on the condition, strength and weakness of the neighbouring nations; for as those vary, the Interest must also vary.' (*An Introduction to the History of the Principal Kingdoms and States of Europe* (English trans., London, 1702), Preface, p. v).

17   Small wonder, therefore, that the pope castigated the settlement of Westphalia and by the bull *Zelo domus Dei* declared it null and void. The decline of the Papacy from its position as the 'international government' of Christendom to that of a minor Italian state, via its position as mediator, guarantor and observer, is the reverse image of the emergence of the secular states-system.

18   Quoted in Martin Wight, op. cit., p. 20.

19   By the second half of the seventeenth century the 'political space' of Europe was taken to include sea as well as land. The Mediterranean was won back from the Turk as a 'European lake', while the pirates of the Barbary coasts of north Africa were increasingly pressed by the navies of European states.

20   'The use of congresses was a new method of diplomacy, for the working of which, etiquette, amongst other things, had to be altered and adapted. Only one kind of earlier gathering, the ecclesiastical councils of the late Middle Ages, bears a resemblance and that by no means a near resemblance, to these congresses. Their organisation is one of the great land-marks of the century' G. N. Clark, *The Seventeenth Century*, 2nd ed. (Oxford, The Clarendon Press, 1947), p. 134. He lists the following: Westphalia (1648), Pyrenees (1659), Oliva (1660), Aix-la-Chapelle (1668), Nijmegen (1676–9), Frankfort (1681), Rijswick (1697).

21   See Arthur Nussbaum, *A Concise History of the Law of Nations*, rev. ed. (London, Macmillan, 1954), esp. ch. V.

22   See E. R. Adair, *The Exterritoriality of Ambassadors in the Sixteenth and Seventeenth Centuries* (London, Longman, 1929).

23   Quoted in my 'The French Political Academy, 1712: the School for Ambassadors', *European Studies Review*, vol. 2, no. 4, 1972.

24   Abraham de Wicquefort, *The Embassador and his Functions* (Digby's trans., London, 1716), ch. XXI, p. 191. Wicquefort is interesting for a number of reasons. A Dutchman who served several masters including Richelieu and de Witt, he moved in the half-world of diplomatic agents and spies typical of the times. Apart from a voracious historical knowledge of the period before 1648, his book is full of examples taken from the negotiations of Münster and Osnabrück which he may have attended in person. His treatise conveys both the necessity of diplomacy and its range. It also reveals, through a command of the 'administrative' detail of ambassadorial life, the most concrete sense of the

states-system as an association complete with a set of indigenous and recognised practices and rules of conduct. The growing importance of French practice as a model for the rest of Europe is marked. The fact that he wrote in French and not in Latin is indicative of the changing times. The book was first published in 1681 and went into five editions before its appearance in an English translation in 1716.

25 Antoine Pecquet was an official with long experience of foreign affairs in the early eighteenth century. He described the *corps diplomatique* in the following terms:
'Le corps des ministres étrangers dans un pais, forme une espèce de société indépendante dont les membres vivent entre eux proportionnément pour l'intimité à la manière dont leurs souverains sont ensemble; mais toujours avec politesse et honnêteté, même quand les maîtres sont en guerre; conduits par des intérêts différents et souvent opposés, ils ont cependant tous un objet commun qui consiste a connaître le pais où ils sont, et à faire réussir les vues qui leur sont confiées. Il sont liés en même-temps par une communauté de privilèges, dont l'infraction au prejudice de l'un devient le cause de tous, parce que chaque souverain est lésé dans ses pareils, quand même ils ne vivront pas bien ensemble'. (*Discours sur l'Art de Négocier* (1737), p. 134.)

26 Mattingly, op. cit., ch. V. The word 'diplomacy' and its correlates 'diplomat' and 'diplomatist' are nowhere used in the manuals. Callières, for example, refers to 'les négociations' and to 'un bon' or 'un habile négociateur'. According to the OED, the 'original' meaning of *diplomatic* was 'Of or pertaining to official or original documents, charters, or manuscripts'. In 1681, Jean Mabillon published *De re diplomatica* and he is acknowledged as the founder of 'diplomatic(s)' which the OED, quoting Webster, defines as '"The Science of diplomas, or of ancient writings, literary and public documents, letters, decrees, charters, codicils, etc., which has for its object to decipher old writings, to ascertain their authenticity, their date, signatures, etc."'. There is a second stage when *diplomatic* is defined as 'of the nature of official papers connected with international relations'. 'The transition,' one reads in the OED, 'appears to have originated in the titles of the *Codex Juris Gentium Diplomaticus* of Leibniz (1695) and the *Corps universel diplomatique du Droit des Gens* of Dumont. In these titles *diplomaticus, diplomatique,* had its original meaning as applying to a body or collection of *original official documents*. But as the subject-matter of these particular collections was *international* relations, "corps diplomatique" appears to have been treated as equivalent to "corps du droit des gens" and *diplomatique* taken as "having to do with international relations".'
    In the third sense of *diplomatic,* the connection with documents has disappeared. The definition reads:
'Of, pertaining to, or concerned with the management of international relations; of or belonging to diplomacy. *Diplomatic body,* the body of ambassadors, envoys and officials attached to the foreign legations at any seat of government; *diplomatic service,* that branch of the public service which is concerned with foreign legations.'
In a comment, the OED says 'This sense became established in English at the time of the French Revolution, and its French origin comes out emphatically in the writings of Burke on French affairs'.

27 On Callières, see my 'Francois de Callières and Diplomatic Theory', *Historical Journal*, vol. XVI, 3, 1973, pp. 485–508.

28 The expression is C. A. W. Manning's.

29 I have left the word 'institution' in quotes throughout because I am aware of two things. The burden of some of my argument depends on the appropriateness of describing diplomacy, international law and especially the balance of power as institutions. Unless one is clear about what an institution is

and what are the conditions which qualify a practice to be named as such, this may beg some important questions. The literature of international relations is vague to the point of permissiveness on this issue and in this respect our subject is a reflection of the social sciences at large. F. F. Ridley has drawn attention to this vagueness in a valuable recent article, 'Political Institutions: the Script not the Play', *Political Studies*, vol. XXIII, nos 2–3, 1975, pp. 243–58. He demonstrates the entire lack of unified usage, but unfortunately his solution cuts away too much. He comes close to identifying an institution as something that is established with conscious deliberation and for explicitly stated purposes; institutions are very nearly organisations. It should be clear that the meaning adopted here is much more anthropological, i.e. a set of practices may become institutionalised without any moment of establishment and achieve a considerable degree of differentiation without acquiring charters, rule-books or organisational paraphernalia. But how much embodiment of a precept is required in practice before one recognises its title as an institution? I have found the discussion in S. F. Nadel, *The Foundations of Social Anthropology* (London, Cohen & West, 1951) helpful. He defines institution as 'a standardised mode of social behaviour or, since social behaviour means co-activity, a standardised mode of co-activity' (p. 108). His discussion is directed towards three aspects: the degree and nature of the standardisation visible in the coactivity; the group of individuals or the 'personnel' who are its carriers; and the purposive orientation, the aim-contents, of the activity (p. 111).

30 Wicquefort, op. cit., ch. XXVII, p. 246.

31 Charles Reynolds has indicated the shortcomings of this style of exploration in his *Theory and Explanation in International Politics* (London, Martin Robertson, 1973).

32 For a recent discussion of this see, Michael Oakeshott, *On Human Conduct* (Oxford, The Clarendon Press, 1975).

2
Legitimacy in a States-System:
Vattel's *Law of Nations*

PETER F. BUTLER

Classic texts, whose authors therein seek to elaborate their ideas of the general moral and practical principles underlying the interaction of states, are not much studied these days. In this chapter, I expound the main ideas of Vattel's *The Law of Nations* and suggest that an acquaintance with those ideas can contribute to a fuller understanding of both the period in which that work was written and the present international situation. I suggest that the significance of the work has two main aspects. First, the popularity of the work in its time reflected and contributed to the maintenance of a set of ideas about the nature of right relationships between sovereigns and subjects and among sovereigns, which in turn sustained a society of states in Europe. Second, Vattel's ideas have a contemporary significance in as much as the ordered conduct of present-day international relations requires, as a prerequisite, continued adherence to those ideas by states.[1]

The Argument of The Law of Nations
Emmerich de Vattel, sometime diplomat and sometime Privy Councillor in the cabinet of Augustus III of Saxony,[2] published *Le Droit des Gens, ou Principes de la Loi Naturelle, appliqués à la Conduite et aux Affaires des Nations et des Souverains* in 1758.[3] He hoped 'to establish on a solid foundation the obligations and rights of nations' (Prelims, 3) and thereby to provide rulers 'with weapons for the purpose of defending the cause of right, and compelling the unjust to observe at least some measures, and to keep within the bounds of decency' (IV, IX, 127).

According to Vattel, previous writers on the law of nations, while they had correctly realised that natural law was applicable to the inter-relations of both men and nations, had failed to realise that natural law in its pure form—a set of rules applicable in a state of nature and deduced from the natural requirement that individual men preserve and perfect themselves—cannot be immediately applied to nations (Preface, ix). Vattel, therefore, agreed with Wolff, who had argued that 'the principles of the law of nature are one thing, but the application of them to nations another, and this produces a certain diversity in that which is inferred, in so far as the nature of a nation is not the same as human nature'.[4]

Vattel argued that when the law of nature was applied to nations in a manner that was appropriate to that subject matter, it had to be divided into two components: first, the necessary law of nations, consisting of inferences from the natural law which 'nations are *absolutely* bound to observe' (Prelims, 7) and which 'is always obligatory on the *conscience*' (Prelims, 28); and, second, the voluntary law of nations, 'whose maxims are devoted to the safety and advantage of the universal society of mankind', and which must be consulted by a nation 'when there is a question of examining what she may demand of other states' (Prelims, 28).

Three main ideas formed the foundation for Vattel's elaboration of the content of the necessary law of nations: the nature of a nation; the 'society established by nature between all mankind' (Prelims, 10) and 'the great society established by nature *between all nations*' (Prelims, 12).

With regard to the nature of a nation, Vattel argued that 'a nation or a state is . . . a body politic, or a society of men united together for the purpose of promoting their mutual safety and advantage by their combined strength' (I, I, 1). It is formed as a remedy to the unsatisfactory and dangerous situation that exists in pre-political society—the natural society of the state of nature—wherein 'the depravity of the majority' (Preface, xiv) prevents men from fulfilling their natural obligations to act in such a way that that society is not endangered. The response to that situation is for men to subject themselves 'to the authority of the entire body, in every thing that relates to the common welfare' (I, I, 2) and to entrust the exercise of that authority either completely, or in a manner restricted by fundamental laws, to a sovereign, which may be the body of the people themselves, a number of them, or one individual (I, I, 3).

This special nature of a nation—its contractual basis and its naturally ordained necessity as a response to a situation where the dictates of natural law in its pure form were being flouted—was seen, by Vattel, to be the main determinant of the primary obligation of a nation and, hence, of the rights which derived from that obligation. The agreement among men which leads to the establishment of a nation 'can no otherwise be fulfilled than by maintaining the political association. The entire nation is then obliged to maintain that association; and as their preservation depends on its continuance, it thence follows that every nation is obliged to perform the duty of self-preservation' (I, II, 16). It may be inferred from this obligation that a nation has a right to that which is necessary for its self-preservation. In addition, as a moral being, it has an obligation to perfect itself, 'to procure for the citizens whatever they stand in need of for the necessities, the conveniences, the accommodation of life, and, in general, whatever constitutes happiness' (I, II, 15) and the necessary law of nations in consequence bestows on nations the right to conduct themselves in a manner which furthers their attainment of these objectives.

The importance of these primary rights and related obligations was uppermost in Vattel's mind when he dealt with the question of 'whether the aggrandisement of a neighbouring power can authorize a war against him'. The problem is a difficult one, for,

'On the one hand, a state that increases her power by all the arts of good government, does no more than what is commendable … on the other hand, it is but too well known, from sad and uniform experience, that predominating powers seldom fail to molest their neighbours, to oppress them, and even totally subjugate them, whenever an opportunity occurs, and they can do it with impunity.' (III, III, 42)

Vattel's answer was that where a 'reasonable presumption' of intended aggression was present, preventive war was justifiable. For example.

'If two independent nations think fit to unite … who is authorized to oppose them? I answer, they have a right to form such a union, provided the views by which they are actuated be not prejudicial to other states. Now, if each of the two nations in question be, separately and without assistance, able to govern and support herself, and to defend herself from insult and oppression [i.e. to meet her primary natural obligation to preserve and perfect herself], it may be reasonably presumed that the object of their coalition is to domineer over their neighbours. And, on occasions where it is impossible or too dangerous to wait for an absolute certainty, we may justly act on a reasonable presumption.' (III, III, 44)

The primary obligation of a nation to preserve and perfect itself also informed Vattel's treatment of the question of whether the fundamental precept of natural law, that 'he who does an injury is bound to repair the damage', is applicable to the relations between nations. Vattel argued that this precept required modification in the necessary law of nations because of the different, corporate nature of the subjects of that law, nations. For, in the case of a sovereign who leads his nation into an unjust war – fought purely for territorial gain, for example – it will often be impossible for recompense to be made without affronting those principles of natural law which recommend a particular relationship between the sovereign and his subjects within the state:

'The prince's private property will not be sufficient to answer the demands. Shall he give away that of his subjects? – It does not belong to him. Shall he sacrifice the national lands, a part of the state? – But the state is not his patrimony: he cannot dispose of it at will. And although the nation be, to a certain degree, responsible for the acts of her ruler, – yet (exclusive of the injustice of punishing her directly for faults of which she is not guilty) if she is responsible for her sovereign's acts, that responsibility only regards other nations, who look to her for redress: but the sovereign cannot throw upon her the punishment due to his unjust deeds, nor despoil her in order to make reparation for them. And, were it even in his power, would this wash away his guilt, and leave him a clear conscience? It is a strange kind of justice which prompts a man to make reparation for his own misdeeds at the expense of a third person: this is no more than changing the object of his injustice.' (III, XI, 186)

Nor can the soldiery be justly put upon to make good the damage caused in an unjust war, since, in causing such damage, they acted under the orders of the sovereign, and 'what would be the consequence, if, at every step of the sovereign, the subjects were at liberty to weigh the justice of his reasons, and refuse to march to a war which might to them appear unjust?' (III, XI, 187).

Thus, for Vattel, natural law's requirement that recompense be made for injuries done, could not be fulfilled in the relations between states because of the very recommendations of natural law. For natural law, in consequence of the nature of the relationship it recommends between sovereign and subject for the purpose of preserving and perfecting the nation, prevents the sovereign from making amends for his misdeeds at the expense of his subjects, and those 'alterations which the civil law makes in the rules of the law of nature, with a view to render them more suitable to the state of political society' (III, XII, 189) – alterations approved of by natural law – prevent the use of the military to make amends, since they cannot be blameworthy. For it is essential to the functioning of the state that the military in particular, and subjects in general, do not question the motives of the sovereign, except on infrequent and momentous occasions. 'It often happens that prudence will not permit a sovereign to disclose all his reasons. It is the duty of subjects to suppose them just and wise, until clear and absolute evidence tells them the contrary' (III, XI, 187). Thus, the attempt to apply natural law in its 'pure' form to relations between states, in the matter of recompense for injury, leads to inconsistency, and some alteration is required if this is to be avoided. The alteration is that, in general, according to the necessary law of nations, recompense cannot be had for injuries done under these circumstances; the nature of nations prevents it.

The natural requirement that nations preserve and perfect themselves also determined Vattel's views on the application of the necessary law of nations to treaties.

Initially, Vattel gives the impression that he regards 'the faith of treaties' as the foundation of international stability. He asserted that 'treaties are sacred between nations', that 'the faith of treaties is sacred', and that 'he who violates his treaties violates the law of nations' (II, XV, 219–21). He argued that

'An injury cannot ... render a treaty invalid. He who enters into engagements ought carefully to weigh everything before he concludes them.... If we might recede from a treaty because we found ourselves injured by it, there would be no stability in the contracts of nations. ... Sovereigns are subject to no superior judge. How shall they be able to prove the injury to each other's satisfaction? Who shall determine the degree of it sufficient to invalidate a treaty? The peace and happiness of nations manifestly require that their treaties should not depend on so vague and dangerous a plea of invalidity.' (II, XII, 158)

Yet, for all this, Vattel clung to the view that 'treaties which are pernicious to the state' are invalid:

'Though a simple injury, or some disadvantage in a treaty, be not sufficient to invalidate it, the case is not the same with those inconveniences that would lead to the ruin of the nation. Since, in the formation of every treaty, the contracting parties must be vested with sufficient powers for the purpose, a treaty pernicious to the state is null, and not at all obligatory, as no conductor of a nation has the power to enter into engagements to do such things as are capable of destroying the state, for whose safety the government is intrusted to him.' (II, XII, 160)

Similarly, in connection with peace treaties, although 'the treaty of peace binds the nation and successors', although 'it is to be faithfully observed', and although 'the plea of fear or force does not dispense with the observance' (IV, IV, 35–7):

'To take up arms for a fresh cause is no breach of the treaty of peace: for though a nation has promised to live in peace, she has not therefore promised to submit to injuries and wrongs of every kind, rather than procure justice by force of arms. The rupture proceeds from him who, by his obstinate injustice, renders this method necessary.' (IV, IV, 40)

The two remaining main ideas which informed Vattel's elaboration of the content of the necessary law of nations were, as I have mentioned, those of 'the society established by nature between all mankind', and 'the great society established by nature *between all nations*'. Signs of the impact of these on Vattel's thought should already have been detected; for example, in his view that 'the peace and happiness of nations . . . require that their treaties should not depend on [any] vague and dangerous . . . plea of invalidity'.

With regard to 'the society established by nature between all mankind', Vattel held that the limited endowment by nature of men with 'the same strength and natural weapons of defence with which she has furnished other animals' was 'convincing proof of her intention that they should . . . mutually aid and assist each other' (Prelims, 10). This obligation, arising from nature, could not be cast off by men 'by any convention, by any private association'.

This view influenced Vattel's remarks on 'the great society established by nature *between all nations*', for

'since the object of the natural society established between all mankind is – that they should lend each other mutual assistance, in order to attain perfection themselves, and to render their condition as perfect as possible . . . nations [too], considered as so many free persons living together in a state of nature, are bound to cultivate human society with each other, [and] the object of the great society established by nature *between all nations* is also the interchange of *mutual assistance* for their own improvement and that of their condition.' (Prelims, 12)

However, the obligations which accrued to a state as a result of its membership of this 'great society' were, according to Vattel, to be fulfilled only when doing so did not threaten the individual nation's ability to preserve and perfect itself. Unlike an individual human being, who, we may suppose, may sacrifice himself for others (though he is not obliged to do so), the state is obliged not to make such a sacrifice, for to do so would be to contradict the naturally ordained contractual basis of the state.

Ever mindful of this limitation, Vattel sought, in general and in detail, to articulate those rules of the necessary law of nations to which the obligations of states to the 'great societies' of men and states bound them.

In general, 'one state owes to another state whatever it owes to itself, so far as that other stands in real need of its assistance, and the former can grant it without neglecting the duties it owes to itself. *Such is the eternal and immutable law of nature*' (II, I, 3). Indeed, to refrain from assisting when assistance is due and can safely be given is, according to the necessary law of nations, to commit an injury.

More particularly, the natural 'society established by nature between all mankind' was also the foundation of Vattel's assertion of each nation's obligation to engage in commerce, for 'if trade and barter take place, every nation, on the certainty of procuring what it wants, will employ its land and its industry in the most advantageous manner, and mankind in general prove gainers by it' (II, II, 21). A still more detailed elaboration of a provision of the necessary law of nations arising from men's obligations to the 'great societies' may be found in Vattel's treatment of lakes.

What happens, for example, when a lake which is part of a state, but whose far shore is part of the boundary of that state, increases in extent on that far shore? Vattel answered that it depended on the nature of the increase. If the increase is 'insensible . . . real, constant and complete', then 'the whole of the lake thus increased still belongs to the same state as before', but

'if this increase be not insensible, – if the lake, overflowing its banks, inundates a large tract of land, this new portion of the lake, this tract thus covered with water still belongs to its former owner. Upon what principles can we found the acquisition of it in behalf of the owner of the lake? The space is very easily identifiable, though it has changed its nature: and it is too considerable to admit a presumption that the owner had no intention to preserve it to himself, notwithstanding the changes that might happen to it.' (I, XXII, 275)

Seasonal flooding does not give rise to seasonal changes of ownership, for 'were it otherwise, a town overflowed by a lake would become subject to a different government during the inundation, and return to its former sovereign as soon as the waters were dried up' (I, XXII, 275). This plainly inconvenient arrangement would be quite inconsistent with nature's dictates that the societies of men and nations be so organised as to contribute most effectively to human preservation and perfection. Such, then, are some aspects of the necessary law of nations regarding the increase in extent of lakes. These problems may arise but rarely, and the natural law in its pure form is not clear in such matters. Instead, the natural law directs states to adhere to more specific rules covering such instances, and Vattel attempted, using environmental signs and presumptions about the intentions of states, to formulate such rules.

Thus far, I have attempted to convey an impression of Vattel's treatment of what he called the necessary law of nations, and to show how the content of that law arose, for Vattel, from his acceptance of certain ideas about the nature of nations, and the natural societies of mankind and of all nations. I wish now to turn to the second major component of Vattel's thought on the law of nations: the voluntary law of nations. For Vattel argued that the particular situation of states gave rise to a need not only for the transformation of pure natural law into the necessary law of nations, but also for that law to be supplemented by the voluntary law of nations, which dealt with the demands that a state could rightly make of another state.

Vattel's account of the content of the voluntary law of nations was rooted in his view that, morally, nations are equal, that 'a dwarf is as much a man as a giant; a small republic is no less a sovereign state than the most powerful kingdom', and that 'nations composed of men, and considered as so many free persons living together in the state of nature, are naturally equal, and inherit from nature the same obligations and rights' (Prelims, 18).

But the equality of nations gives rise to problems when breaches of the necessary law of nations occur. Within a nation, breaches of the civil law – the natural law modified to take account of the condition of civil society – may be punished by the sovereign authority, for the members of civil society have perceived the necessity to consent to this for their mutual well-being. But nature has made no such recommendation in the case of nations, for

'it is easy to perceive that the civic association is very far from being equally necessary between nations, as it was between individuals. We cannot, therefore, say, that nature equally recommends it, much less that she has prescribed it. Individuals are so constituted, and are capable of doing so little by themselves, that they can scarcely subsist without the aid and the laws of civil society. But, as soon as a considerable number of them have united under the same government, they become able to supply most of their wants; and the assistance of other political societies is not so necessary to them as that of individuals is to an individual.' (Preface, xiv)

Therefore, nations remain moral equals, and as such have no right to pass judgment on the intrinsic justice of each other's acts. Their obligations, stemming from their membership of 'the great society of nations' are, therefore, imperfect; that is, nations have a perfect right to request that a nation comply with its obligations under the necessary law of nations, but that nation has a right to decide for itself whether or not the situation in which it finds itself is one that permits it to fulfil those obligations without violating its primary obligation to its own preservation and perfection.

Vattel made this point most plainly in his treatment 'of the common duties of a nation toward others; or, of the offices of humanity between nations'. Although, by the law of nature, nations are 'bound to cultivate human society with each other', the fact that the nation has a duty to itself means that 'common duties . . . consist, generally, in doing everything in our power for the preservation and happiness of others, as far as such conduct is reconcileable with our duties towards ourselves' (II, I, 2). But

'since nations ought to perform these duties or offices of humanity towards each other, according as one stands in need, and the other can reasonably comply with them, – every nation being free, independent, and sole arbitress of her own actions, it belongs to each to consider whether her situation warrants her in asking or granting any thing on this head. Thus, 1. Every nation has a perfect right to ask of another that assistance and those kind offices which she conceives herself to stand in need of. . . . [But], 2. These offices being due only in necessity, and by a nation which can comply with them without being wanting to itself; the nation that is applied to has, on the other hand, a right of judging whether the case really demands them, and whether circumstances will allow her to grant them consistently with that regard which she ought to pay to her own safety and interests.' (II, I, 8–9)

In other words, a nation that is refused assistance by another has to accept that refusal, whether or not it is convinced by the reasons offered in justification of it. There is no authority to judge between states in the matter, or on any matter concerning an alleged breach of the necessary law of nations which the breacher defends on the grounds that to have obeyed the law would have been to endanger his state. This was something which, according to Vattel, nations simply had to accept. Indeed, 'it is . . . necessary, on many occasions, that nations should suffer certain things to be done, though in their own nature unjust and condemnable; because they cannot oppose them by open force, without violating the liberty of some particular state, and destroying the foundations of their natural society' (Prelims, 21).

However, although he argued that actions that may be at variance with the dictates of conscience must often be tolerated, Vattel did not want to conclude that there was no law of nations at all in such matters. For

'the law of nature, whose object it is to promote the welfare of human society, and to protect the liberties of all nations, – that law, I say, recommends the observance of the voluntary law of nations, for the common advantage of states, in the same manner as it approves of the alterations which the civil law makes in the rules of the law of nature with a view to render them more suitable to the state of political society, and more easy and certain in their application.' (III, XII, 189)

The voluntary law of nations, Vattel held, proceeded from the 'presumed consent' of nations (Prelims, 27). It was the law to which individual nations, conscious of their obligation, binding in conscience, to obey the necessary law, yet also of the impossibility of enforcing it, were to be presumed to have consented for the sake of the natural societies of men and of nations.

Vattel was, perhaps, most clear about the way in which necessity required the application of the voluntary, rather than the necessary law of nations, in his treatment 'of the voluntary law of nations, as it regards the effects of regular warfare, independently of the justice of the cause'.

Vattel held, as had Grotius and most other writers on the law of nations, that natural law directs that 'he alone whom justice and necessity have armed, has a right to make war' (III, XII, 188). Yet he also saw that there was no way in which this dictate could be made to prevail among equal, sovereign states in a state of nature without infringing the rights of nations to be judges, however partial, of the dictates of their own consciences. Moreover, in a conflict with

'each party asserting that they have justice on their own side, [each] will arrogate to themselves all the rights of war, and maintain that their enemy has none, that his hostilities are so many acts of robbery, so many infractions of the law of nations, in the punishment of which all states should unite. The decision of the controversy, and of the justice of the cause, is so far from being forwarded by it, that the quarrel will become more bloody, more calamitous in its effects, and also more difficult to terminate. Nor is this all: the neutral nations themselves will be drawn into the dispute, and involved in the quarrel.' (III, XII, 188)

Vattel argued, therefore, that any attempt to impose the necessary law of nations on states would, in fact, be counterproductive to the aims of the great society of nations, for it would lengthen and expand wars. Natural necessity therefore recommended that a different set of laws – the voluntary law of nations – apply in war.

The first rule of the voluntary law with respect to war was 'that regular war, as to its effects, is to be accounted just on both sides' (III, XII, 190). Such a rule would serve the interests of the natural societies of men and nations by diminishing the ferocity, and limiting the scope of war. The second rule was that 'whatever is permitted to the one in virtue of the state of war, is also permitted to the other' (III, XII, 191). As well as logically following from the first, this rule made for peace by ensuring that a state, which believed that it had justice on its side, would, nevertheless, restrict the amount of violence it perpetrated, because it would know that the other side, regarding its own cause as just, would feel no qualms about meeting like violence with like, and would not be subject to pressures and hostility from non-belligerent states on account of any injustice in such response. This latter point was connected with Vattel's espousal of the third rule, which was 'that this voluntary law of nations, which is admitted only through necessity, and with a view to avoid greater evils, does not, to him who takes up arms in an unjust cause, give any real right that is capable of justifying his conduct and acquitting his conscience, but merely entitles him to the benefit of the external effect of the law, and to impunity among mankind' (III, XIII, 192). Exemption from punishment would make it more likely that states would call a halt to a war, whereas the fear of punishment would lead to a prolongation of war until the state which believed that other states viewed its cause as unjust had obtained a position from which it could defend itself against attempts to punish it.

Further examples of provisions of the voluntary law are to be found in Vattel's treatment of a state that wages war without first attempting to obtain redress peacefully, and in his remarks on the subject of acquisition by war. He argued that although by the necessary law of nations it was obligatory to attempt first a peaceful solution of disputes where there was some chance of this being successful, the existence of situations where a recourse to peaceful attempts could be dangerous to the state seeking redress and the impropriety of one state judging another meant that 'nations are bound to consider as lawful the conduct of that power who suddenly takes up arms in a doubtful cause, and attempts to force his enemy to come to terms, without having previously tried pacific measures' (II, XVIII, 335).

With regard to acquisition, although, by the necessary law of nations, only the wager of a just war has a right to title over territory and property captured (for how can just title accrue from unjust action?), the voluntary law of nations, Vattel held, dictated that simple conquest, without reference to the justice of the matter, was sufficient to provide just title. This rule of the voluntary law of nations was evidently intended to diminish the number of disputes in the great society of nations (III, XIII, 195–6).

The Significance of The Law of Nations

While the presentation of an outline of some of the main arguments of a classic text such as Vattel's *Law of Nations* may seem merely an interesting intellectual exercise, concern with the work need not in fact end there. In this section, I shall comment on the significance of the work. The significance of *The Law of Nations* has two main aspects, which I will call the contextual and the general, and in each of these aspects that significance is, in a sense, moral. I will deal with the aspects in turn.

One of the main distinguishing features of a society is its members' attachment to a set of ideas about morality. Indeed, one might argue that such an attachment is both a necessary and a sufficient condition for the existence of a society. It is an attachment that includes both a universal acceptance of an empirical environment – an agreement on the identities of the contents of that environment – and also an agreement in significances or moral priorities. The agreement is, in other words, an agreement about what, empirically, there is, and about the ways in which what there is can be located in a moral hierarchy in such a way as to indicate the relative importance of the various kinds of things that there are.

Vattel's contextual significance consists in his having encapsulated in his views, and helped sustain by his influence, those agreements about identities and moral priorities that characterised eighteenth-century Europe. *Prima facie* evidence for this can be found in the popularity of Vattel's work. One commentator, distinguished in his time, held that the stage in the development of the law of nations from 1770 to 1914 'may safely be called after [Vattel]'.[5] Charles G. Fenwick, the translator of the Carnegie Classics edition of *The Law of Nations*, wrote (1913) that 'a century ago not even the name of Grotius himself was more potent in its influence on questions relating to international law than that of Vattel'.[6] And Robert von Mohl wrote that Vattel's work attained the status of 'a kind of oracle with diplomats, and especially with consuls'.[7] The number of editions and translations of the work is also evidence for its popularity, with 20 new or reissued editions between 1758 and 1863, 29 printings of English-language translations (19 of them American) between 1759 and 1863, 6 Spanish translations between 1820 and 1836, and 1 German and 1 Italian translation in 1760 and 1805 respectively.[8]

It seems to me possible to expand on a recent explanation of the work's popularity, which puts this down to its readability, resulting from Vattel's choice of French rather than Latin; its relevance to contemporary affairs, 'especially state sovereignty'; and the systematic presentation of its ideas 'whereby Vattel's system was given coherence as well as grace and relevance', and which appealed to eighteenth-century taste.[9]

The contextual significance of the work can, I suggest, be highlighted by pointing to the symbiotic relationship that existed between, on the one hand, the Vattelian system of ideas and the use that could be made of it, and, on the other, the moral climate, the political and administrative structure, and the interests of members of the political élites of eighteenth-century Europe. Vattel, I suggest, recognised the major components of political life that were identified in eighteenth-century Europe: the sovereign, the individual, the transnational moral order, and property. He also dealt with these components in a way that settled their relative moral significance. Acceptance of the general thrust of his arguments contributed to the maintenance of the balance of power system.

During the period of the emergence and consolidation of nation states in the seventeenth and eighteenth centuries, there appear to have been contradictory pressures on the minds of men who thought about politics, which stemmed from the existence of doubt and dispute about the relative moral worth of the components of political life. The requirement for the state to predominate over its subjects was widely acknowledged and informed political practice, but at the same time, the hindrances to individual freedom, to the ability of groups subordinate to the state to pursue their interests, and to the desire to conform to a higher moral order than that provided by mere *raison d'état* (if that was a *moral* order), were recognised. In the seventeenth century, evidence of these contradictory pressures is to be found in the popularity of and hostility to the contents and author of *Leviathan*, and in the circumstances of the composition of, and views expressed in, Locke's *Second Treatise*. And in the eighteenth century, Rousseau warned men of the threat of the state to their self-realisation: 'so long as government and law provide for the security and well-being of men in their common life, the arts, literature, and the sciences, less despotic though perhaps more powerful, fling garlands of flowers over the chains which weigh them down.'[10] And elsewhere, Rousseau also resignedly accepted the irresolvability of the tension between the claims of a universal moral order and the fact of the existence of states: 'beyond doubt, a lasting peace is, under present circumstances, a project ridiculous enough. But give us back Henry IV and Sully, and it will become once more a reasonable proposal.'[11] Rousseau was here alluding ironically to Sully's plan for peace in Europe. Sully's master, Henry IV, would convince the nations of Europe that it would be in their interests to unite against the House of Austria, and the campaign would be conducted so that Henry would emerge as paramount in the end, securing 'peace' by his extended power.[12] In Rousseau, then, the tension between the practical requirements for political order and the moral claims of the individual and the broader society of the human race are plain to see.

It is not difficult to suggest reasons why such tensions were felt during this period. The rise of sovereign states, as identifiable components of the public realm, and the establishment of their control over fairly definite areas had supplanted the institutional functions, though not the sentiments and institutional forms, that had characterised an earlier, more inclusive order that Rome had generated and Christianity sustained. Indeed, these tensions continued to manifest themselves in the nineteenth century. It was no accident that the author of 'Diplomacy' in the 9th edition of the *Encyclopaedia Britannica* assessed past attitudes to his subject thus:

'There has, indeed, ever been a reluctance in the English nature to acknowledge the art of transacting international business as a pursuit worthy of a British statesman, or as one entitling its adepts to honourable fame. It is popularly looked on as the art of carrying into the business of nations a morality condemned in the intercourse of men with each other.'[13]

He then justified the practice of diplomacy, especially British, by pointing to the contribution it made to the maintenance and extension of a broader political and moral order, thus permitting the development of British institutions and practices over a widening area. The justification of the state, in other words, lay in its contribution to the world.

The period which we are considering, however, was not only a witness of tensions between political requirements and the demands of abstract morality. Individual, selfish interests, especially in property, were being increasingly impinged on as sovereigns increased the range of their concerns. In the writings of the time, attempts were made to reconcile the pursuit of such interests with submission to political control by showing that the latter was a prerequisite of the former. And attempts were also made to show that certain forms of political submission threatened proprietorial interests and that individual proprietorial interests threatened the establishment of a just political order.[14]

Now no doubt Vattel's popularity was, in part, a product of the relative brevity and elegance of his work. Some also probably read the work simply because others did. The specific issues with which the work dealt may have been of particular relevance at the time. But, in addition to all this, an acceptance of Vattel's main arguments would have permitted the resolution of the tensions that I have described as they manifested themselves in two related areas: among the politically conscious subjects of a sovereign, and in the relations between such subjects and their sovereign. Among subjects, tension may have arisen during the contemplation of what, in international relations, their state should do. Ideas of what was morally good for the subject as an individual, of what was in his proprietorial interest, of what was morally good for mankind as a whole, may have suggested differing courses of action each of which may have also been disconsonant with the interests of the state. And these potentially contradictory pressures may also have been the source of tensions that arose between a sovereign and his politically influential subjects; George II's concern for Hanover, for example, was regarded as the product of a proprietorial interest at variance with the interests of Britain.

First, let me consider tensions that might have arisen among subjects, and produced by the disconsonant pressures of duty to oneself and the moral claims of broader human society. Hypothetical situations can be imagined in which such disconsonant pressures exist – where, for the individual to seek self-fulfilment, the claims of the broader society of the human race must, it seems, be ignored. And the different courses of action suggested by these pressures may both conflict with the survival and advancement of the state. Vattel reconciled these tensions by arguing that natural law established the necessity of the state for individual well-being; by arguing that a set of rules – the necessary and voluntary law of nations – was deducible for the collectivity of states and applicable to them in a manner that did not affront their sovereignty and equality and which, moreover, contributed to the health of the broader society of men by facilitating 'the maintenance of order and liberty' in the 'kind of republic' that was Europe *as a whole* (III, III, 47). The moral life of the individual was shown to be subsumable within the interests of the state, and the pursuit of those interests – in conformity with the primary obligation of the state to have regard for its own survival and perfection – contributed to the maintenance of a wider order by preventing the predominance of any one state.

Second, let me consider those tensions that might have arisen because of the contradictory pressures of, on the one hand, subjects' individual proprietorial interests and, on the other hand, the reconciled requirements of duty to oneself, one's state, and the broader society of all men. Vattel's arguments made it quite plain that a self-interest that contradicts the moral requirement that the state survive and perfect itself is merely an apparent self-interest; for the consequences of behaviour disconsonant with the interest of the state is the possibility of the destruction of the state, and hence of the very context within which real self-interest may be pursued.

Third, Vattel's views on the sovereign provided the means for reconciling tensions that might otherwise have characterised the relationship between the sovereign and his interested subjects. For Vattel, natural law directed that the sole responsibility for response making in international relations be located in the sovereign. The fact that 'prudence will not permit a sovereign to disclose all his reasons' permitted the acceptance by subjects of action by the sovereign that did not conform to their ideas of what was right. Here, the Vattelian framework was particularly important in providing a means whereby conflicts between sovereigns and the growing foreign services of the eighteenth century could be reconciled. Furthermore, Vattel's argument that subjects could not be held to account for the actions of their sovereign furthered their readiness to tolerate otherwise dubious behaviour by the sovereign. Vattel's arguments, therefore, provided a rationale for accepting the direction of a sovereign even though it might appear inconsistent with ideas of what the reconciled pressures of duty to oneself, to the society of all men, proprietorial interests and *raison d'état* suggested.

A significant consequence of Vattel's reconciliation of the competing demands to which political actors were subject was the ability of those actors to regard their own and other states as unitary actors. This contributed to the maintenance of the system of European states by enabling international actors to exist in and respond to a world in which there was a limited number of entities, all of a kind, which was consequently less complex and more susceptible to balance of power method than the present. While such a world survived – sustained by the general acceptance of the Vattelian framework and made less horrendous by the nagging thought that the nations of Europe did indeed form a great society – there seemed little reason to depart from that framework.

I come now finally to the general significance of the arguments of *The Law of Nations*. I wish, briefly, to do what is these days regarded as somewhat unfashionable, and to suggest the utility of its ideas in the contemporary international situation.

Fundamentally, the contemporary international situation is not much different from that of eighteenth-century Europe. The concept of the state remains prime in the international area of the public realm, as evidenced by the assiduousness with which the status of statehood is sought by groups – Palestinians, Zimbabweans, Azanians, Scottish Nationalists, and the rest – who do not enjoy it. Furthermore, and *pace* the environmentalists, the apocalypse, if it occurs, is still more likely to result from the confrontation of states than from any other context; and problems arising in other contexts are likely to be transformed into and dealt with as state problems. The idea of the state, in other words, retains its paramountcy.

I wish to suggest that, in general, the acceptance of a Vattelian framework is more likely than others to render life within an environment of states amenable, if not perfectly satisfactory. The fact is that stability – the preservation of a relatively untroubled context within which progress is possible – is more likely to be a feature of an environment of equals where those equals are formally committed to respect for one another's equality, and where there is formal adherence to a common set of ideas about the rules of conduct of those equals in their inter-relationships. In such an environment, there will of course arise occasions where one or another of the equals will feel constrained to breach the rules of conduct. Yet the very fact of general adherence to those rules will make such breaches infrequent and, usually, limited; and the breacher will sense the necessity of offering a justification for the breach which is at least *prima facie* convincing. Furthermore, those equals will feel constrained not to behave in a way which could be used to justify a breach by another. Also, ordered and predictable relations between the components of a state, and between states, are more likely if they accept the Vattelian framework as an alternative to the random determination of behaviour by an unreconciled variety of pressures of duties and interests. Vattel's ideas on equality, on a state's right to be the sole judge of the dictates of its conscience, on sovereignty, and on the existence and ground of the necessary and voluntary law of nations have a relevance for contemporary circumstances, stemming from their general appropriateness for any collectivity of equals among whom unification is not likely.

Finally, with reference to the contemporary international situation, we might reflect on Vattel's view that 'the civic association is very far from being equally necessary between nations, as it was between individuals . . . [who] can scarcely subsist without the aid and the laws of civil society' (Preface, xiv). We might well ask whether there have not been changes in the international situation which preclude an easy acceptance of that view. Certainly, the potential scope – geographical and technological – of war has increased to the extent that war between some states is likely to become war among all, in spite of the superpowers' skill in containing such conflicts. It may also be suggested that, nowadays, the prime responsibility of states to themselves precludes them from supplying those ecological goods on which, in the long term, the survival of the planet depends. We may, in other words, ask whether there is not now a moral obligation to create an institutionalised *civitas maxima*. But if this is so, it does not mean that the significance of Vattel is merely antiquarian. For the *civitas maxima* will only emerge out of negotiations between states who, in the course of those dealings, have respect for their equality, are willing to admit the force of cosmopolitical moral claims, are circumspect about ignoring those claims, are regarded by their subjects as the legitimate representatives of their real interests, and who conduct themselves with the solemnity that these characteristics require.

NOTES FOR CHAPTER 2

1   I am grateful to the other authors of this volume for their comments on various drafts of this chapter and especially to Maurice Keens-Soper for his detailed observations. I am also grateful to members of the staff–postgraduate seminar of the Department of Politics, University of Exeter, to which I read an early version, and to A. H. Birch and M. M. Goldsmith for specific comments.

2   M. Avenal, 'Vattel', *Nouvelle Biographie Générale* (Paris, Fermin Didot, 1860).

3   I have used Vattel, *The Law of Nations or Principles of the Law of Nature applied to the Conduct and Affairs of Nations and Sovereigns*, ed., Joseph Chitty (London, Sweet & Maxwell, 1834). Quotations from *The Law of Nations* in this chapter are referenced in the text, where (except for references to the Preface and Preliminaries) the numbers of the book, chapter and section are given, in that order.

4   Christian Wolff, *Jus Gentium Methodo Scientifica Pertractatum*, vol. II, trans., Joseph H. Drake (New York, Oceana, 1964), a reprint of the Carnegie Classics edition, 'Prolegomena', s. 3.

5   C. Van Vollenhoven, *Three Stages in the Evolution of the Law of Nations* (The Hague, Nijhoff, 1919), p. 32.

6   Charles G. Fenwick, 'The Authority of Vattel', *American Political Science Review*, vol. 7, 1913.

7   Quoted in Arthur Nussbaum, *A Concise History of the Law of Nations*, rev. ed. (New York, Macmillan, 1954), p. 161.

8   'The Law of Nations, Bibliography of the Different Editions,' in E. de Vattel, *The Law of Nations*, vol. 3 (Washington, Carnegie Institution of Washington, 1916), pp. lvi–lix.

9   F. S. Ruddy, 'The Acceptance of Vattel', in C. H. Alexandrowicz, ed., *Grotian Society Papers 1972* (The Hague, Nijhoff, 1972). Ruddy's paper has subsequently appeared as Chapter IX of his book *International Law in the Enlightenment, The Background of Emmerich de Vattel's Le Droit des Gens* (Dobbs Ferry, Oceana, 1974). I regret that this book was not available to me while I was writing this chapter. In addition to attempting to explain Vattel's acceptance and expounding in some detail the arguments of the text, Ruddy also traces the development of international legal theory from the Romans to the eighteenth century and elucidates the main strands of thought during the eighteenth century.

10 J.-J. Rousseau, *A Discourse on the Moral Effects of the Arts and Sciences*, in *The Social Contract and Discourses* (London, Dent, 1968), p. 120.

11 J.-J. Rousseau, *Judgement on Saint-Pierre's Project for Perpetual Peace*, in M. G. Forsyth, H. M. A. Keens-Soper and P. Savigear, eds, *The Theory of International Relations* (London, George Allen & Unwin, 1970), p. 166.

12 Maximilien de Béthune, Duc de Sully, *Memoirs* (London, 1761), vol. III, bk. XXX.

13 (Edinburgh, Black, 1877), vol. VII, p. 251.

14 See, for example, J.-J. Rousseau, *A Discourse on the Origin of Inequality*, in *The Social Contract and Discourses*, op. cit.

3
Patterns of Thought and Practice: Martin Wight's 'International Theory'

BRIAN PORTER

Past thinking about international relations needs to be put into order as present thinking needs to be put into perspective. Yet few scholars have attempted to meet this need. The realist-idealist or realist-utopian analysis was a product of the late 1930s, chiefly owing to the writings of E. H. Carr and most notably treated in *The Twenty Years' Crisis* (1939). A later and more elaborate attempt to clarify patterns of thought and practice in international relations was made by Martin Wight, and so influential (whether at first or at second hand) has his work been in university teaching in Britain, and so challengingly does it merit consideration as the basis for an advance of theory, that we should turn next in this book to an exposition and a discussion of it.

I

Martin Wight (1913–72), an Oxford-trained historian, was Reader in International Relations at the London School of Economics and Political Science from 1949 until appointed Professor of History at the University of Sussex in 1961. Although his published writings on international relations were few, they showed him to be a scholar of rare erudition and one who brought to the study of the subject a profound mastery of Western thought, classical and mediaeval no less than modern.

In 1946 Wight wrote for the Royal Institute of International Affairs a brilliant and influential essay entitled *Power Politics* which explored the role of power in the post-mediaeval states-system, and he also contributed chapters on the balance of power to *Diplomatic*

Investigations (1966) and *The Bases of International Order* (1973).[1] But apart from his papers 'Why is there no International Theory?' and 'Western Values in International Relations', likewise to be found in *Diplomatic Investigations*, and 'International Legitimacy' which appeared in the journal *International Relations* (May 1972), his main contribution to the theoretical study of the subject was made in the series of lectures he delivered at the London School of Economics and Political Science in the 1950s, and to which he gave the title 'International Theory'.[2]

In these lectures Wight delineated three main traditions of thought and practice, to which he initially gave the names Realism, Rationalism, Revolutionism – adding for certain purposes a fourth, which he designated Inverted Revolutionism.

How did Wight define these terms? There was no simple definition offered but an understanding of them emerged as they were used as approaches to certain leading issues in political thought: the nature of international society, human nature, the nature of history, the role of power and of diplomacy, the nature and conduct of war, the theory of national interest, theories of international law and ethics and relations with 'barbarians'.

Wight largely drew his traditions from the works of classic Western thinkers, and it is interesting to note that in the later versions of these lectures he had come to prefer, as descriptive of his three main categories or 'paradigms' as he called them, the terms Machiavellian, Grotian and Kantian.[3] But he did not confine himself to the classic writers, seeing these three or four categories of thought exemplified in all sorts of ways, and not least in political practice and in writings which had a strictly political function. Thus, in the bibliography which accompanied the lectures, Hitler rubs shoulders with Hobbes, and Nasser with Kant.

The primary exponents of realism were, of course, Machiavelli and Hobbes although Wight also drew upon writers as varied as Bacon, Hegel, Treitschke, Spengler, Hitler, Freud, E. H. Carr, and Hans Morgenthau, among others, to illustrate aspects of the realist tradition. The characteristics of this tradition in its most thoroughgoing form were a pessimistic view of human nature; a preoccupation with power for its own sake; the likening of international society to the jungle – in effect the denial of any such society; a belief in the primacy of foreign policy – the aims of which should be freedom of action, self-sufficiency and self-reliance; an opportunistic approach to international law; a belief in the immanence and inevitability of war and a penchant for ruthlessness in its conduct; the exploitation of 'barbarians' (that is, those of an alien culture); and, in the realm of ethics, justification by necessity and justification by success.

(

For rationalism, on the other hand, the chief exemplars were Grotius, Locke, Montesquieu, Rousseau (in regard to the *Project for Perpetual Peace*), Bentham and Burke, with its modern expression to be found in writers of the League of Nations period, perhaps the most notable of whom was Zimmern. Rationalists, Wight held, acknowledged a duality in man; thus they were neither unduly pessimistic nor optimistic about human nature. This recognition of a basic tension in man was to be found in the mainstream of Stoicism, Christianity, and Western mediaeval thought generally. Rationalists differed from realists too in their view of the state of nature. For them it was not a savage state of competitive survival, but, as Locke held, a milieu of goodwill and mutual assistance. For Locke, international society was a true society which lacked a judiciary and a sovereign, but which depended for its ordering upon custom.

Political power for rationalists was a problem: it had to be justified by some source beyond itself, as the pursuit of virtue or justice. The prime role of politics being to ensure the good life, foreign policy took second place to domestic policy. In foreign policy the end of the political art was 'harmony', and in order the better to achieve this it was important to minimise the number of vital interests. Self-interest should, as far as possible, accommodate itself to the interests of others. Thus, the rationalist approach to international law was one of adhering honourably to its pacts and commitments. With regard to war, the rationalist saw it not as a continuation but as a breakdown of policy. It could therefore only be resorted to in a just cause, and had to be limited as far as possible and terminated as quickly and fought as humanely as practicable. Much of this was rooted in Thomas Aquinas's theory of the just war and in the liberal view of war which arose in the nineteenth century but had been rendered obsolete by the changing nature of war. The rationalist solution to the problem of 'barbarians' was one of trusteeship. And the ethical standard to be adopted in a necessarily imperfect world was that of choosing the lesser evil.

The third category of Wight's analysis was revolutionism. The roots of this tradition he saw in mediaeval theory, ultimately derived from the idea of Rome. Central to the tradition was belief in the world state, divinely ordained. The idea was enshrined in Virgil and channelled into political theory through Dante. It had immense influence upon Latin, Byzantine and Russian political thought – indeed, upon all who have claimed to inherit the Roman mantle.

But a universalist imperialism was but one aspect of revolutionism. It also postulated the community of mankind. And if this, which although immanent, was not at present realised, the fact must be attributed to the machinations of a heretical minority that it was imperative to convert or liquidate. Hence the necessity for ideological homogeneity. Kant himself, in his essay *Perpetual Peace*, stressed the importance of this in a world federation of states. A requirement for international peace, he held, was that all governments should have republican constitutions. Wight saw this idea as emerging in a number of historical instances: in the Reformation and Counter-Reformation, in the ideological conformity desired by the autocrats of the Holy Alliance (who described themselves as 'fellow countrymen'), in Mazzini's view that the peace of the world depended upon the prevalence of nation states, and in President Wilson's desire that the League should consist exclusively of democracies. The communist view that international conflict is simply an expression of class conflict and would disappear with the triumph of the revolution was but the latest example of the Kantian idea.

Wight saw cosmopolitanism as the most revolutionary of revolutionist doctrines. It ignored the state altogether, holding that the only true international society is one of individuals. This idea had a great influence upon American attitudes, leading to a yearning for relations between peoples rather than governments (and explaining, perhaps, the extraordinary degree of hospitality accorded by Americans to foreign visitors).

In revolutionist eyes, all men were good and human nature was perfectible. (Perhaps there is rather more than cynicism in the subjecting of Soviet dissidents to psychiatric treatment.) Power was justified by the furtherance of the doctrine, and war by its role as the catalyst of the millennium. The 1914–18 slogan of 'the war to end war' was an aspect of liberal revolutionism. Indeed, to the revolutionist, wars in which he was not engaged were invariably 'unjust'; those in which he was engaged partook of the character of holy wars.

In discoursing about holy wars, Wight made a rare excursion into non-Western thought, seeing their probable origin in the early history of Islam. The destiny of *dar al-harb* ('the abode of war' – the rest of mankind) was absorption into *dar al-Islam* ('the abode of Islam') by means of *jihad*. The crusade was the Western equivalent, a penitential war, through which, as with *jihad*, those participating received spiritual privileges.

Wight saw three principles in revolutionist war doctrine: the division of the world into two parts dependent upon acceptance or rejection of the faith; acceptance of a state of war between them; and submission to the victor's doctrines as a war aim ensured by ruthless conduct of the war, and leading in extreme cases to extermination. Whereas, he held, the realist love of power produced violence or even massacres, revolutionist ideals called for the alternatives of assimilation or extermination. This derived from the claim of Judaeo-Christianity, its Islamic religious heresy, and its Marxist-Leninist secular heresy, to possess positive final knowledge.

This tremendous claim naturally governed the theory of revolutionist ethics. One could see it in the communist belief that the violation of word or treaty is not an arbitrary act but justified by a higher principle. One could see it too in the doctrine '*Cum haereticis fides non servanda*', leading to the burning of John Huss by the Council of Constance after promise of safe conduct and Imre Nagy's execution after a similar promise. Unlike those who distinguish between the ethics of private and public life (love and justice respectively for the rationalists, morality and amorality for the realists), the true revolutionist made no such distinction. As with primitive Christianity, however, revolutionism asserted an interim ethic, and what is permissible or even desirable before the revolution (for example, industrial strike action) would be completely unethical after it.

Wight's fourth category he termed 'inverted revolutionism' by which he meant uncompromising pacifism. It occupied a much smaller place than the others in his lectures, but is of a more personal interest because he himself adopted this stance during the 1930s and held to it throughout the 1939–45 war. This utter repudiation of power (other than the power of love) he termed revolutionist because of its missionary character and its claim to universal validity. He saw it as deriving chiefly from Hindu thought and primitive Christianity. Whereas mainstream Christianity came to adopt a rationalist position, the earlier tradition trickled through the Middle Ages (with the Franciscans, for example) and re-emerged at the Reformation. Some Anabaptists and Baptists upheld it but its chief adherents were the Quakers. In our own time it has found champions in such diverse figures as Tolstoy and Gandhi.

Inverted revolutionism stemmed from a pessimistic and not an optimistic view of human nature and in this differed from revolutionism proper; the pacifist had no illusions about the character of his persecutors and acknowledged that his stand required the willingness to die. He died, however, in the hope that a revolutionary transformation of man and society might ultimately result from his action. There was no double standard: the Sermon on the Mount remained as valid in public as in private life. There was no choosing the lesser evil, for there could be no compromise with evil.

II

The foregoing, I trust, will give something of the flavour of 'International Theory' even though I have had to give only the barest sketch of it and sacrifice much of the more detailed analysis and profusion of illustration which characterised these lectures. Nor could one hope to convey the wit and pungency with which they were delivered. They were the work of a Christian pessimist who had no belief in progress, and who thus saw the happenings of distant times as being as pertinent to his purpose as those of the present or of the recent past. Indeed Wight once observed that the writer who most effectively and fruitfully discussed the relations of states was Thucydides, and much of his own last work lay in the realm of the interstate politics of the ancient world.

It must next be asked, however, what precisely was Wight doing in these lectures? And how far do they help us towards an understanding of international political realities? A minor matter but one which needs to be explained is the question of the title. How, if he wrote a celebrated paper called 'Why is there no International Theory?', could he have compiled a whole series of lectures under a heading the validity of which he apparently denied? In fact, there is no contradiction. A man expecting El Dorado might exclaim on the banks of a gravelly stream 'Why is there no gold?', only to be told that there is, but that it must be panned for. International theory, by which Wight meant 'a tradition of speculation about the society of states, or the family of nations, or the international community',[4] he saw as lying embedded in the writings of international lawyers and historians, or as something to be distilled from the speeches, dispatches and memoirs of statesmen and diplomatists. As for philosophers, these, it is true, did on occasion turn their attention to the international world, but never more than incidentally to their main concerns. Wight is almost contemptuous of such international theory, describing it as 'scattered', 'unsystematic', 'mostly inaccessible', 'repellent and intractable', and, in a much quoted phrase, 'marked, not only by paucity but also by intellectual and moral poverty'.[5]

Is, then, this poor, wilting stuff the main content of his lectures? Surely not. For, as we have seen, the lectures were concerned with human and state behaviour on the grandest scale, and in all their fascinating variety. The pieces of a jigsaw puzzle may be paltry things when loose but assembled in a proper way they may form a picture that none had suspected was there. And for his grand design Wight by no means restricted himself to the commentaries of others, since his real subject was the impulses and ideas that move all men, not merely a select few, even if those few have been the only ones to articulate them in an intellectually respectable way.

The objections to such a method of proceeding may, however, be cogent. If Wight constructed a grand design, fitted so much of human thought and behaviour into his threefold structure, may he not have falsified reality, seen pictures in the fire or in the clouds, imposed a bogus order upon the intractable complexities of history, been the artist whose art improves upon nature? And then is not the structure a little too neat, recalling that symmetry beloved of the Latin mind – or in this case the mind steeped in Latin culture? Indeed, as Wordsworth compared his greatest poem to the groundplan of a Gothic church, so 'international theory' is suggestive of a Palladian villa complete with hall and two wings, with 'inverted revolutionism' as a smaller structure set a little apart, like the stables – or perhaps the folly.

The danger of such an arrangement is that the categories may be more Procrustean, and their subject matter more Protean, than may at first appear. Wight himself suggested that pacifists, if and when they entered the fray, usually took up a realist position, as did 'hard revolutionists' under stress, and his examples all too clearly show that men and situations cannot always be easily docketed. Bismarck, for instance, although a realist in his contemptuous dismissal of the notion of 'Europe', was nevertheless completely rationalist in his sparing and precise use of war.

Moreover, how are these three modes of thought and behaviour to be explained? Is each derived from a particular historical experience? Or form of economic production? Or cultural tradition? And how universal are they? Wight was steeped in Western history and philosophy, but can the attitudes and policies to be found in non-Western civilisations be similarly categorised? In the world of the Bedouin, for example, life was very much 'a war of everyman against everyman', with fratricide being not infrequently the means of succession to a sheikhly throne. Realism could scarcely be taken farther. But for travelling in the desert a different code prevailed: guests were sacrosanct, and if strangers were encountered the sharing of food and water was an obligation that was absolute. And then in the Wightean scheme there seems no mention of honour. Yet much that passes for realism, particularly if it ultimately derives from a warrior way of life, must surely be tempered by this.

Again, there is a sense in which we may seriously question Wight's use of the word 'tradition'. It may be that in the chain of thinkers from Machiavelli to Morgenthau each was consciously influenced by the work of his predecessors, but a much more potent influence is likely to have been the circumstances of the time in which each wrote. And in any case, Wight is not merely concerned with the thinkers, but also with the practitioners, and here the influence of 'the tradition' will be remote or non-existent. 'The tradition' then is a device, as the arranging of stars in constellations is a device, for the convenience of the observer; it has scarcely any such meaning as when we speak of the tradition of militarism in Germany or of violence in Ireland. 'Permanent propensities of the political mind' might be a better, though more cumbersome, way of putting it.

In posing such objections and qualifications we should recall that Wight himself made no especial claims for his theory. The three 'traditions' were to be taken only as paradigms: a convenient way of arranging not only a multitude of ideas but also international politics 'in action' throughout the long history of Western civilisation. And he was always experimenting with new ways of assembling this material.[6]

Were the categories, then, no more than a pedagogical device, the culminating teaching aid of one who, by all accounts, had begun his career as a schoolmaster of genius? The concern and supreme aptitude that Wight had for stimulating youthful minds should not be overlooked, but to claim that this, though important, was all that he was doing, would be to claim too little.

III

Whether as definable types of behaviour, or as 'traditions' of theorising which have either reflected or advocated such behaviour, one may see the Wightean categories not simply as co-existing, but in a state of dynamic relationship one to another. And from the clash of the categories, from their mutual criticism, their modification and transmutation, important insights can be gained into both what is going on in the world, and what is going wrong in the world.

Indeed, do not the categories largely owe their existence to the perception that each gives of each? If all human behaviour were realist, would realism have any meaning? Would Machiavelli be famous if he were not thought in some way to be shocking, by advocating conduct which even in the ruthless world of Renaissance politics was considered abnormal, and because abnormal, successful?

But this leads to a paradox. If realism succeeds by virtue of its superior cunning, ruthlessness, and absence of moral inhibition, how comes it that it has not everywhere conquered? An answer in Wight's terms would be that a good deal of realism reflects the behaviour and the philosophy of the underdog, or at least the aspirant; that 'establishment' behaviour, in contrast, tends to be rationalist because it can afford to be, because success having been achieved, there is less need to struggle for advantage than to conserve it, and because the ethos of accommodation and compromise is better calculated to underpin a *status quo* which serves well the interests of the affluent and contented.

Not all established power, of course, is of this character. Unassailable power, such as was possessed by Rome, or even by the British Raj in its heyday, tends to be associated with markedly realist attitudes and conduct. And if Victorian England pursued policies that were weighted towards realism in the East, and towards rationalism in Europe, the explanation is clear. Such rationalism flourished within a 'disguised' realism. A Great Britain could produce a Gladstone, and a United States a Woodrow Wilson, only because the ultimate realism of sea-power, and therefore unchallengeable security, allowed them to do so. In the much harder, rougher, political environment of continental Europe, such would never have been the case. If the French today have little scruple in selling arms to all and sundry, we might see such un-British realism as a consequence of their more tumultuous history.

Looked at as the philosophy of the deprived, the vulnerable or the buffeted, even realism can argue a moral case, and it was the moral dimension that was of particular interest to Wight. Indeed it was the debate among the categories, and the moral tensions that this gave rise to within both international and human society, and even within the same individual, that especially engaged his attention, and which for him was of the essence of international politics.

But the clash of the categories is not only to be seen on the intellectual or moral plane. A field of inquiry opens up of an even more fundamental nature. Wight warned against confusing being realist with being realistic. In a world of competing philosophies, wherein lies their viability? Under what circumstances does each arise and flourish? And when they are in conflict, what is the likely outcome of that conflict?

This was a line which, as far as I am aware, Wight did not fully explore, but a possible answer to the last question seems to lie in a transmutation of the categories. When, for example, rationalism and realism come into conflict, what tends to happen? At first the former will attempt to treat the latter as being of its own kind. It will seek to accommodate, to harmonise, much as the Chamberlain government sought to accommodate the demands of Hitler. But then, when it finds that such a policy is being taken advantage of, not only will it have itself to resort to realism in order to survive, it will be likely, if it has the strength, to become *ultra-realist* in order to preserve the rationalist milieu. One senses that the strategic bombing of Germany, the devastation, say, of Dresden, for which there was no military necessity, was undertaken, whether consciously or subconsciously, in the pursuit of such an object.[7] The line of thought might be expressed as follows: 'You, the German people, who gave your support to leaders who dared to subvert the rationalist scheme of things, must be made to realise the enormity of what you have done.' The phenomenon might be explained as preserving – or perhaps transforming – the milieu by shock. When Walter Nash, the Prime Minister of New Zealand, lightheartedly informed Khrushchev that he had a family connection with Russia – his grandfather had fought in the Crimean War – the Soviet leader turned on him with unexpected ferocity for appearing to condone so heinous a crime. Revolutionists, of course, are particularly prone to this type of behaviour in an attempt to effect an almost geological shift in prevailing attitudes.

Perhaps, however, revolutionism is itself the most subject to change as it is brought face to face with unyielding reality. The heavy realist lesson taught the Bolsheviks by the Treaty of Brest–Litovsk is a case in point. And if, in contrast, a revolutionist movement is too successful it comes up against a situation which may force it into something like rationalism. For unless power spreads with the spread of the ideology, the result is likely to be the burgeoning of heresy and a threat all the more deadly because it poses a rival claim to orthodoxy. A communist China is a greater danger to the Soviet Union than the old China ever was, and would not a communist United States be a greater danger still?

Wight's categories, I suggest, enable us to envisage political situations with more facility and with deeper insight than we might otherwise do. And because they link theory with history, because they transcend the distinction between international and all other forms of politics, and because they comprehend competing world-views and are intimately related to values, they represent the sort of theory of which the times we are entering would appear to stand peculiarly in need. And if the policies or the statesmen or the situations we face do not fit readily into Wight's categories? Then we might discover some interesting things about them. We might also have further to refine or subdivide the categories. For Wight's 'International Theory' was never just a response to the problem of ordering past thought; it was perpetually a challenge.

NOTES FOR CHAPTER 3

1   H. Butterfield and M. Wight, eds, *Diplomatic Investigations* (London, George

Allen & Unwin, 1966); Alan James, ed., *The Bases of International Order: Essays in Honour of C. A. W. Manning* (London, OUP, 1973).

2   Further papers by Wight, written for meetings of the British Committee on the Theory of International Politics and referred to in the notes to Chapters 1 and 7 of this book, were published while the book was in press: Martin Wight, *Systems of States*, ed. H. Bull (Leicester, The University Press, 1977). The lectures are unpublished and until Professor Bull's exposition of them in the second Martin Wight Memorial Lecture delivered at the LSE in January 1976, remained generally unknown except among Wight's colleagues and former students. See H. Bull, 'Martin Wight and the Theory of International Relations', *British Journal of International Studies*, vol. 2, no. 2, July 1976.

3   Hedley Bull also prefers these terms to the 'three Rs', holding the latter to be not comparable to one another in their usual meanings. In philosophical terminology, the counterpart of realism is idealism; of rationalism, empiricism; and of revolutionism, conservatism. But I have retained the 'three Rs' here not only because in the Wightean sense they are now familiar, but because the three archetypes, although probably the best or most suggestive available, are themselves not altogether satisfactory. Machiavelli, as Wight himself pointed out, is not strictly 'Machiavellian', and there is far more to Kant than revolutionism.

4   Butterfield and Wight, op. cit., p. 18.

5   ibid., p. 20.

6   H. Bull, op. cit., p. 106.

7   See Sir C. Webster and N. Frankland, *The Strategic Air Offensive against Germany 1939–1945* (London, HMSO, 1961), vol. III, pp. 109, 113–16, and particularly the exchange of letters on p. 115. The policy of unconditional surrender may be viewed in the same light.

4
The Political Theorists and International Theory

MICHAEL DONELAN

Among all the fields of learning, international relations has two unique features, one bad, one good, by chance or providence balancing each other. On the one hand, it is the saddest of subjects. On the other, the title of its greatest work is a pub-sign, Kant's *Zum Ewigen Frieden*.

Suppose that, like cricketers in winter, we were to survey the centuries of political theory and pick up a team of immortals for an evening's discussion at The Perpetual Peace. Who would they be? The selectors' list anyway is this: Aristotle, Augustine, Machiavelli, Hobbes, Locke, Montesquieu, Smith, A., Rousseau, Kant, Hegel, Marx. The 'Twelfth Man', from among the moderns, is left for argument. The question which Kant, captain, chairman, clubbable at last, puts to the company is this: why have they so little to say about international relations?

It is not through lack of concern as men, they protest. Aristotle mutters about time spent on Alexander. But as theorists they say nothing because there is nothing to say. It transpires that they think this on the basis of three assumptions.

With the most basic of these assumptions, the listener can hardly quarrel. It is that in setting out to study politics, the starting-point must be men. Obvious as this is, we who do 'international relations' once spent much energy implicitly quarrelling with it and made much trouble for ourselves in consequence. If the inhabitants of the earth in front of us were states as (to take our familiar analogies) the inhabitants of the solar system are planets or of the snooker table, snooker balls, then states would be the proper starting-point of the study of politics. It would then be possible, indeed mandatory, to develop an 'interstate theory' with balance of power concepts and the like. This is what 'political theory' would be. But, in fact, not even the most fervent believer in the state as an Organism or as a Collective Personality really believes that states are the basic entities of the earth. It was the deracination of the subject 'international relations' from the subject 'politics' and the carving out of its area as 'relations between states' (from motives which we respect) that led us into our difficulties. Nowadays, among all schools of international theorists, there is a revulsion. We all accept in our various ways that the starting-point of theory is not states but something more basic: men.

The next assumption heard from the company around the table is more questionable. It is that these men, who are the theorist's starting-point, are creatures who live in association with others under government, members (to be brief) of a state. Some of the company envisage a more basic condition of man of some sort, a paradise in which it was not so, a withering away of the state, a Senecan Golden Age. But this is only a casting of light outwards from the true focus of illumination: man in the state. The concern around the table is to understand the nature of the state and the terms of man's membership.

What we may question about this assumption is not what it says but what it conceals. It says that man is a creature who lives in a state. Yes, no doubt. Anarchists have challenged this, but, on the whole, we are against them. Still it glides over an important question: is this state in which man lives one or many?

We gather from the conversation, after a while, an answer to this question. Numerous passing remarks and a few extended passages that the company quote from their works (Rousseau and Kant read whole essays to great applause) show us how the land lies. They assume (it is their third assumption) that man lives in many states. In their various ways, they indeed raise the international question; but even in Rousseau and Kant there is no wavering in the assumption that man lives and always will live in a separate state. This is their starting-point with man and here, not in some wider human community, are the roots of his being. Though they begin with man, they do not begin with mankind and inquire into the reason and unreason of the separate states into which he is divided. They simply take man's membership of a separate state as the primordial fact.

In this third assumption, we may see the reason why the political theorists have nothing to say about international relations. They do not discuss the assumption in their writings; they give no reason in their writings for their silence about international relations; still, we can easily guess the reason. If the roots of man's being lie in the separate state, if what is right and good for him are centred there, what can there be for the theorist to say about international relations? The area of international relations is just a wasteland between states. The most that can be said about it, the most that can be shot out into this space, is the implications of the theory of the state. As Hobbes pictures the state bristling at the edges with guns, so all theorists must see it bristling with ideas against the outsiders, Leviathan porcupine, powerful and good. The shooting between states, the extrapolation of the implications of statehood are, as we may be sure, for our company of political theorists, a very important affair. The international arena is heroic, tragic. But it is an arena for soldiers, politicians, businessmen and other able practical men, and as to thinkers (we seem to hear them say) the 'Second Eleven'. There are the Spaniards and that interminable Grotius, and (after all those terrible mercenaries) the good Swiss, Vattel, who extrapolated Locke with a lot of Leibniz, and the Red Cross. We should drink to this succession of men who reduced our miseries. But they are different men with practical skills and pragmatical reason. There is no job for the theorist in the international arena. There is no *res publica* there.

Anyone who does international theory, any student of international relations, anyone interested in international affairs, anyone at all, might well be disturbed by this line of talk. He might be willing to continue for a while the fiction of an evening's discussion among the political theorists at The Perpetual Peace. A fiction of some sort is, after all, the best we can do; the political theorists did not handle the matter explicitly in their writings.

Let us imagine, then, that Kant, as chairman and as friend of international relations, presses the company to defend their assumption of a world of separate states, source of their lack of interest in international relations.

Their first defence is to beat a courteous retreat. They did indeed assume that the state about which they were writing was one of a plurality of states; but they meant no harm by this, still less to insult anyone. They were not seriously concerned with the point at all. Their concern, their life's work, was the problem of man, in association with others, under government. To this problem, the issue of one state or many states is neither here nor there. It is merely a matter of contingent historical fact whether the problem is worked out in practice in one state or many. The basic issues are the same.

No doubt, on a superficial view, it seems crucial to reasoning about the nature of the state to decide whether it must expect to go to war (because there are many states) or whether it need not (because there is only one). Undeniably, the character of all the states that have ever actually existed has been profoundly influenced by the threat and experience and, above all, the changing methods of warfare. But all this belongs to history and is not the kind of matter with which political theory can grapple. It has no bearing on the reasonableness of the *polis*, its constitution, the contract of society, obedience to government, liberty and tyranny, the state as manifestation of Divine Will or of the relations of production and all such issues. Political theory (say the company, warming to the argument) is untouched by war or peace and, for that matter, the other horsemen of the international apocalypse either, Disease, Famine, Beasts. It knows nothing of this issue 'the One State or the Many'.

We may imagine the political theorists pleased at first with this defence of themselves. It is courteous to outsiders and yet it insists on the proper dignity of their subject. The place of quiet reasoning about politics is not to be flooded out by the inrush of history. We are not to be knocked senseless in thinking about the state by wars and rumours of wars and all the other evils which distort reason when it comes to practice. The timeless truths of government are not to be swept aside by some tyrant with a plea of encircling enemies or some expert armed with alarming statistics about the plight of 'planet Earth'.

This much is agreed. Soon, however, discontent spreads around the table, started by Augustine. Any political theorist who dismisses the issue of the One or the Many States and the consequent issue of Peace or War simply on these grounds is in danger. Such a theorist insists on the place of reason in human affairs, he marks it out, he is determined to defend it; but he gives to us, his supporters, no explanation of the enemy. He cannot say why the onslaughts of Unreason and War keep on coming, wave after wave. We must fight for him blind; and the worst of it is that we know that the enemy is not some inexplicable Beast from the Beyond but belongs to our world, is indeed indistinguishable from ourselves. The place of reason is an abstract place (as yet) and so in principle encompasses all reality. But the theorist accounts only for a part, perhaps the most noble part, not the terrifying whole of man's experience of himself and his fellow men.

Thus challenged, the political theorists stop being courteous and, from now on, with all continued respect for all concerned, start to hit out. They no longer express disinterest in the question of the One or the Many States; they answer it. They no longer dismiss as harmless their assumption that the primordial arrangement of the world is a plurality of separate states; they insist upon it. They reject the alternative notion of a primordial moral community of mankind from which the separate states are derivative. And they expect that this second line of defence of their position will end matters swiftly. Deferring to seniority, 'Speak out, Aristotle', they say.

Aristotle appears to shake his head. Why so? For surely we owe to the Greeks the very name of the human phenomenon we are studying, 'politics', with its built-in assumption that politics begins and ends with the *polis*, the separate state. We owe to Aristotle himself the statement, and one of the greatest elaborations of it, that 'Man is by nature a political animal', meaning precisely that he is a member of a *polis* and not of something else. But still, uncertainties arise. For the thrust of the famous statement, we recall, is a denial of the sufficiency of family and village and an assertion that 'the good' is to be achieved in the *polis*. It has no decisive bearing on our question, which is whether the good is One or Many as between men in separate polities, and whether, if it is One, it does not entail some kind of ethical community of them all. We can find fire-power on this question in both directions in Aristotle's writings. We cannot, it seems, find a definite defence of the assumption that man's only community is the separate state.

We hear next, then, from those of our company of political theorists more or less influenced by the Judaeo-Christian tradition. What they say differs on many important points from one to the other and there is lively argument; but what seems to emerge on the whole is the following well-known answer to the question before us.

There was indeed an original moral community of mankind, a paradise, wherein man lived in a condition of natural integrity, fulfilling the absolute natural law of his being. There was originally no state at all, leave alone many states (or only, one of the company adds, for the administration of things). But the men with whom we actually have to deal are not like this. Scripture and everyday observation alike inform us that they are 'fallen', degenerate, self-seeking. These men need to associate with others for the satisfaction of their desires, but only up to a number which is sufficient and which can be regulated by a single government. The roots, not indeed of man, but of actual, fallen man are thus in the separate state, first in the sense of sad, selfish isolation, then as the separate political association. Between these associations, these separate states, the fallen condition continues unmitigated, degenerate, self-seeking, unreasonable and warlike. The separate states of the world are islands in a sea of evil.

The deep ambiguity in this account of the human condition is as well known as the account itself. It is part of a great issue far wider than political theory, which has run through the whole of European intellectual life over the centuries up to the present, the issue of Decline and Progress, Flesh and Spirit, Nature and Grace, Reason and Faith, Matter and Mind, Necessity and Freedom. We shall not need to go far into this tremendous labyrinth and, for the present, the very shortest of steps will suffice down to the first parting of the ways. We are concerned simply with this: what is supposed to be the extent of the moral blindness which struck man at his first disobedience? In prosaic terms, is actual man of the account before us supposed to have moral reason or is he not?

The most prominent feature of the account is that in one respect man's reason is in very good health. He sees very well what he must do in a wicked world. He sees the means to ends. He sees, at the broadest, that he needs to associate with others under government. He has, in short, Prudence. Over the centuries, by and large, few have quarrelled with this much; the apparent quarrels have been artificial. There is no fundamental question that man has the innate capacity to use his reason as the slave of his passions. Man is, without doubt, an excellent pragmatical fellow.

The parting of the ways comes a little further on. Are the passions of man to any extent reasonable or are they utterly degenerate and selfish? Is Prudence, accordingly, one of the great virtues or is it mere cleverness? Let us put the issue more broadly. Is man supposed to have a conscience that he is a being under orders and that there is a Right in means and a Good in ends, and some capacity for discernment with some will to fulfilment? Or is the moral sensitivity of man a radically new creation of Grace (among those aware of Redemption)? Is it (for the majority of mankind) merely a pragmatical, clever ability to see the need for association with others, subject to government?

The ambiguity in our political theorists about this question is deep. To report what they say on it at length, let alone the apparent conclusion, would prolong matters unendurably. The general opinion seems to be that Augustine darkened his description of our human moral paralysis to extremes in outrage with Pelagius. He suffered, centuries before, the long, later exasperation of the world with the moral obtuseness of the English. (Those who say that Pelagius was of Irish extraction are scoundrels.) Machiavelli turns out to be too Roman to be properly questioned on these mysteries. Hobbes seems to be another case of English moral idiocy. He says that our alleged moral reason is really nothing but pragmatical reason for our self-preservation; he says that we must show to others justice, gratitude, modesty, equity and mercy for our self-preservation; but where, all wonder, do these sentiments that we must take care not to affront, come from? Locke says that men have moral reason if they will but consult it; he then goes on to picture their society as a mere pragmatical device for protecting themselves against lapses and for settling uncertainties; the findings of their moral reason may thus be thought rather limited and negative; but, nevertheless, possess it they do.

This is what Locke, the reasoner of civil government, says. What Locke, the reasoner of human understanding, the theorist of reason, says may be inconsistent with it. Rationalist conflicts with empiricist, explain the epistemologists. We shall have to venture a step or two into that part of the great labyrinth a little later. Meanwhile, we end our report of this part of the discussion at The Perpetual Peace, and we have to do so on a note of fearful violence. We hear the decisive critic of men who think that society is merely a pragmatical convenience. We hear Rousseau denouncing them to the guillotine and slaughtering pragmatism with a fable.

No association of men, he says, no association whatever, can possibly begin, or endure, on the basis of mere pragmatical self-interest. I do not care whether you are talking about a company of merchants; or about a state; or about a group or a whole world of states. It makes no difference. Those who study the world of states continually hear statesmen and (this drives them to despair) many of their own number arguing that co-operation between states is a pragmatical imperative, grounding international co-operation on obvious national self-interest. The least stupid of them are uneasy. They add adjectives from a dimension that they do not understand. 'Enlightened' self-interest, they say in my century. 'Long-term' self-interest, they will say after the good Hegel. But I tell them all this, I whisper it in a fable that the élite of my century understands: among the self-interested, the stag-hunt does not hold together when someone starts a hare.

Let us now recapitulate the question before us, and, having done so, notice the implication of our answer. Do we have moral reason in some measure; or is it really only Grace or our own self-interested, pragmatical need of society? If the latter is our answer, then our whole discussion here is at an end. For the Sons of Grace can have no community with the Sons of Wrath once the bond of common moral reason is denied; and self-interested, pragmatical men can only associate with others up to the number which is sufficient for their needs and which can be regulated by a single government. We are thus basically, radically, creatures of separate states. The defence of the assumption of a world divided primordially into separate states stands.

If, on the other hand, we credit ourselves with a measure of moral reason, then there is a primordial moral community of the whole of mankind from which our separate states are derivative. For our moral reason cannot assume prior to its own working a distinction between one man and another, one group of men and another group; all men are the constituency of its gaze and all at first are indifferently claimants upon us. Selective benevolence to our fellows may be how we behave and may very well be reasonable; but it has to be grounded and the extent of it reasoned through; it cannot be simply assumed.

If we take the view that there is a primordial moral community of mankind, the work of the political theorist begins in subordination to moral philosophy which seeks to establish the scope of the moral community, a man's claims on other men. The political theorist's own proper province opens with a finding of the grounds on which men may then give priority to some of their fellows over others, of the terms on which they are required and entitled to segregate themselves from others in separate states, and of the obligations to all mankind which may be renounced and those which continue. The political theorist gives us, in other words, the terms on which we can reconcile our sense of the unity of mankind with our obligations to our separate states. His work speaks to us in critical tones in that it confronts one aspect of actual men, moral reason, with another, how we are presently behaving in the affairs of the world.

Before pursuing this any further, we should heed a brutal warning against any such effort. It comes in the shape of a third and last style of defence of the assumption of the separate state. Even the most hard-of-hearing listener cannot credibly report that the company of political theorists have now exhausted their defences. The theorists of the eighteenth and nineteenth centuries, our nearest and most powerful masters, have so far hardly spoken. They have a formidable defence of the assumption of a world of separate states, which is (first in brief) this. To do political theory is not, as all so far said suggests, to engage in rationalist speculation about an abstract being called man; it is to theorise something confronting us; and that something can only be the separate state. For that alone is given to us by History.

In setting out to discuss the previous defence of the assumption of the separate state, we recalled the wider background, the centuries-old controversy of Decline and Progress, Flesh and Spirit, Nature and Grace, Faith and Reason, Matter and Mind, Necessity and Freedom, discernible in every area of European thought. The present defence belongs to the modern chapter of this wider story. Since the heart of it is that man is above all historical, it may most appropriately be deployed in the historical terms of how it originated and developed. We must listen to our theorists speaking one after the other.

We need, before we do so, a preliminary from the wider story. We have seen that for Augustine and, more than a thousand years later, still for Machiavelli or Hobbes or Locke, the fundamental problem of morals and so of political theory was whether man was entirely corrupt or not, whether he had some measure of genuine moral reason or whether he had none. Whichever side they came down on, all four had one trait in common, as did all the others, philosophers, theologians, preachers, humanists, over the centuries who reasoned or ranted upon the issue. For all of them, the controversy was about the soul and intellect of individuals. Individuals were the first and last entities of human life, before Church, before State. If there was moral reason in the world anywhere, it was in individuals; and individuals used it in debate with one another to make their society.

When we listen to Montesquieu, all this has begun to change. The ancient problem of the moral corruption of man casts little shadow; man is, by and large, certainly good. But also, the focus of interest is no longer the moral reason of individuals and the use of it to make and criticise society; reason is beginning to be under a cloud. Montesquieu sets out to give us, not a theory of government, but a theory of why different peoples have the kind of government they do. Only once does he check on this course which will lead in the end to resigned relativism about the political institutions of the various peoples of the world. He gives at one wonderful moment his own reasoning, an analysis of liberty, a declaration of the constitution that liberty requires.

The cloud upon reason has been thickening for a hundred years. In the days of Descartes, the philosophers had excogitated a new, tremendous dichotomy of European thought. They had sundered Mind from Nature and enthroned the mind of man as 'master and possessor of Nature'. They may have assisted, in consequence, the glories of natural science. They certainly faced in consequence the problem of how it was that one kind of stuff knew another kind of stuff, how Mind knew Nature, man the world; and they could not solve it. Answer had followed answer from the philosophers, the theorists of reason, the epistemologists, in dreadful combat. The naïve empiricists of Bacon's day who believed in a given world of fact, 'out there', simply to be observed by man's mind, had perished for their shallowness at the hands of the rationalists. The world, the rationalists had declared, was not known simply by looking at 'the facts'; knowledge depended upon ideas innate in the mind and was developed by reasoning into certainty of what the world must be like. Now this rational world was, in its turn, under attack. England sent forth a new, terrible breed of empiricists. (Not Scotland; the Humes only claimed to be Scottish.) Nothing was certain but experience; all other knowledge, all other alleged certainty, was a fabrication of men's minds. Under their fearful blows, Reason, save only the most pragmatical, was dying.

With this in mind, we hear next among the political theorists from Rousseau. In place of the old, aristocratic, despotic Reason of individual men, Rousseau proclaims a new principle: popular social will. The great paradox of modern European history, detectable in Montesquieu, is now made brilliantly clear in what Rousseau has to say. Man's goodness is more radiant than ever before over the centuries; man's reason is degraded to a depth not achieved by any of the religious zealots of the past. The Fall of man is a lie, we hear him say; men in themselves are good. The Fall of man is true, we hear him say, in my new version: men, basically good and free, fall through interaction with each other. Here, in society, not in men themselves, lies the problem of men. You have heard it said of old, as in one man all men died, so in one man all shall rise again. Here is my echo of that religion, my transformation, my better gospel: as in society lies the corruption of men, so in society lies their salvation. Morality for men lies in social morality; virtue for men lies not in individual reason, but in social reason; freedom for men, their basic property, lies in equal conformity with that sublime, ineffable, rationally incomprehensible, passionate principle of the good society: the General Will.

Troubled by the sceptics of Reason and impressed by Rousseau and his moral will, Kant makes one last superlative effort to reform and save the old tradition, to delimit afresh the old dichotomies of European thought, the Kingdom of Nature and the Kingdom of Ends. But Reason, rationalist reason, cannot be saved. What is left is Will and only one other perspective on man and the world: History, national History. The historical perspective was not discovered by the men of the eighteenth century; it was as old as the Judaeo-Christian tradition; it was left in solitary power, vastly enhanced, by the collapse of Reason.

So, in the end, we hear from Hegel. He draws all together. The great dichotomies are reconciled in the movement of the Spirit within the World in the dialectic of History. The world is indeed a fabrication of our own ideas, as the sceptics had said, but the source of these is the Eternal Idea. What makes a good society and a good citizen is not just the General Will but the Divine Will which is the State. In the understanding and acceptance of this, men are free.

There is no need to prolong this summary of what our political theorists from the eighteenth and nineteenth centuries have to say. It will seem already too long. Most of the main ideas that dominate us today are now before us: Society, State, Nation, History, Will, Equality, Freedom. We lack, it is true, Marx's contribution of Class but this can be accommodated in the further going. We lack Freud's reassertion of the fallen nature of man, but this is, in principle, no novelty. The summary has been prolonged only so that the highest resources of the political theorists for the third defence of the assumption of the separate state may not seem to be neglected.

In making that defence, we lesser immortals pick and choose the resources that suit us. A standard contemporary version is easy to construct, however. With some attempted echo of the good-humoured vehemence to be heard at The Perpetual Peace, it may be put like this.

Thanks to the efforts of the philosophers of the seventeenth and eighteenth centuries, we cannot nowadays, without crass obscurantism, picture ourselves as beings with access to an 'objective reality'. We know that we have no secure grounds for thinking that there is such a reality at all or, if it exists, that we could have secure knowledge of it. It follows that we cannot appeal to a reality called 'Natural Law', 'Reason' or the like for the foundation and continual correction of our moral life, our laws, our constitution, or any of our other institutions and practices.

All that we can truly know is that we and everything we see about us are the product of an evolution over many millennia, an evolution which proceeds (on the lowest view) by the accumulation of one pragmatical insight after another or (on the loftiest) according to an inner dynamic. And in what setting has our evolution proceeded? It has always been the setting in all recorded history of a particular animal species, a particular culture, a particular nation, a particular class, regulated by a particular manifestation of the state.

It follows that all our reason is cultural, national, class reason, the *Staatsräson* of the separate state or kind of state that we have inherited. Any attempt to turn upon the separate states in which we live and to question them in the name of some alleged reason beyond their history is absurd.

The general epistemic weakness in the whole earlier discussion of the separate state (whether for the defence or for the attack) is enough to kill it, the weakness, that is, of conjuring up such unhistorical fantasies as an original moral community, a Fall, a state of nature, a contract of society, a contract of government. And the weakness of that style of discussion comes to a precise point in this: it cannot accommodate the most obvious fact of our political experience, that our lives are led, not just in a separate state, but in a particular separate state.

That style of theorising tells us (for the defence) that actual, fallen, selfish men associate only up to a sufficient number for the satisfaction of their ends. It tells us (for the attack) that the surviving moral sense of these men requires them to justify themselves in separating from their fellow men. But it does not give us at any point, and could not give us in fidelity to its own abstract, unhistorical style, any principle on which these supposed men, all equally selfish or all equally morally sensitive, could possibly choose one set of their fellows rather than another to associate with in a separate state.

This is the final exposure of the earlier style of political theory as playing with a figment, an abstract man, a fantasy of rationalist reason, a man who does not inhabit this earth. The first thing that we can truly know is particular men, associated with others in a particular state, products in every respect of the history of that state or kind of state. Political theory cannot pretend to criticise them and their states from an external standpoint because there is none. Political theory must take the separate state as it is, the one, given, substantial thing on which it can get a grip, and theorise it, look on at it, look into it, try to understand what is this 'going-on', here, now. Political theory, like all theory in human affairs, follows practice. The owl of Minerva flies at dusk. Cookery books come after cooking. If a man has not the wit to write a cookery book, let him at least keep out of mischief. Let him just do the history of the political thought of some chosen separate state.

Against this towering modern defence of the assumption of a world of separate states, what could an opposing modern find to say? Let us see what he might say, and again with an echo of the good humour at The Perpetual Peace. The basic trouble with the defence is (first in brief) this. All appearances notwithstanding, it is founded not on humility, but on pride. It demands for the human mind the status of the gods, and, denied this, it would rather reign in Hell (or anyway, the kitchen) than serve in Heaven.

It is true that we cannot adopt, without crass obscurantism, the theory of reason which satisfied men in the sixteenth century. We accept the criticisms of Locke, Berkeley, Hume and Kant. Suppose, however, that after a period of consternation, we accept from Hegel a new theory. The old dichotomy of Mind and Nature, which like all the others in European history, had threatened to become an impossible Manichaean dualism, is broken down. Mind is restored to the world. Now there is no longer a problem of knowledge. Mind makes what it knows and knows what it makes. But suppose next that we read some nineteenth-century criticisms of Hegel. The Hegelian picture no longer satisfies us. New consternation. And so on to today.

What is of final interest in this story of incessant upheaval is that it is throughout a process of reasoning, of knowing and criticising. Reason is being used to achieve ever new understanding of reason. We change our minds from time to time over the centuries about the nature of reason, about how we know and how we criticise; but that we know and that we criticise is confirmed to us in the very procedure itself. If the ordinary man (for example, a political theorist) is uncertain whether men can validly know and criticise, he has the highest possible human authority for the fact that they can: the epistemologist cheerfully at work in his trade, carving up his fellows. Even the epistemologist cannot undercut that. To demand some further absolute validation of reason, of our capacity to know and to criticise, is a demand to be, not human, but a Creator. To question reason with reason, to say that we do not know whether we can know, to criticise criticism, is self-contradictory and absurd. It is an illness, the dreaded *morbus epistemologicus* in its final, hopeless stage, hypertrophy of the epistemic gland.

Let it be accepted, then, that we have a basic, unchallengeable capacity to reason, to know and to evaluate. Next, some phantom from the nineteenth century frightens us with this question: can this capacity ever be our own, is it not always saturated with the ideas of our culture, our society, our class, our time? There can be no doubt on this. Tradition is a constant friend in our minds, prejudice a constant enemy. We look all the time with the eyes of the last moralist, economist, artist, epistemologist who has impressed us. We think by reaction to the views of the men who came before us.

Yet it is impossible that our cognitive, critical capacity should itself be artificial, made for us and given to us by our culture, society, class or tradition. For that would entail (which is absurd) that we are all nothing but the ventriloquist's dummies of one another, all sitting on one another's knees and speaking with the voices of one another. We are not condemned to a perpetual shaking of the same old kaleidoscope of predetermined ideas into new patterns. The brilliant bits of glass come from somewhere. Did Rousseau and Marx round on the society of their day with nothing else but the ideas of the society of their day? Did Marx turn on the epistemology of Hegel with nothing but the ideas of Hegel? If our modern political theorists really believe that it was so, then we owe them an apology; they are not, after all, too proud; they are too humble. They underestimate their power over us. They underestimate the small, vital element that they bring from themselves to their writings. They overlook, that is, the reason of Rousseau, of Hegel, of Marx, of the 'Twelfth Man', of themselves, which knows, criticises and so changes us.

Our modern political theorists underestimate the grandeur of that very aspect of man's experience which is their pride, man's history. Like some old Baconian empiric, they take society, state, a plurality of separate states in the world as brute facts, 'out there', given, an objective reality simply to be observed by the receptive mind. They add nothing to the sixteenth-century view but to stress that these facts have a history. Yet if we look into this history, what do we see? We find men, century after century, from the beginning of recorded time, from the highest to the lowest, from the historian and epistemologist right down to the cellar-man of The Perpetual Peace, each knowing a world and his life and work in it, physical nature, institutions, customs, methods, and questioning it and thinking some things right in it and some things wrong, and if enough others agree, changing it.

Why should this long history of knowing and criticising be made to stop when a man comes to the question of a world of separate states? Who can in reason say so? A man, for example, notices that an Englishman behaves in certain respects very differently to a fellow Englishman than he does to an Indian. If the fellow Englishman starves to death, there is an uproar; if the Indian starves to death, there is a smaller uproar. The man seeks an explanation of this and very soon, he is asking why we are 'Englishmen' and 'Indians', why we have separate states at all. Perhaps in the end, he satisfies himself on this, perhaps he does not. But he cannot be told that he must not ask the question.

More than this, our inquiring man is entitled to press this question on the political theorists. He is entitled to say that, in reason, the political theorists should be willing to be concerned with this question. They may not simply assume a world of separate states. If they assume it, they must defend their assumption with reasons. And it now seems, at the end of the day, that they cannot.

Stay a moment. At this last minute, the gallant defenders are coming again in a final, desperate charge, a cavalry charge, with a heavy cannon in support. They attack the inquiring man thus: if you, you pestering fellow, if we, the professional men of political theory on your behalf, were to use our reason and engage in this international line of inquiry, we should soon be saying that some aspects of the behaviour of actual states are reasonable and some are unreasonable. Is it not so? The earnest inquirer assents. Then where should we get our (here comes the cannon-ball) 'norms' from?

Alas, the brave horse; alas, the proud rider. All is still misconception for them. The charge stumbles and perishes in the dark. For the last time against this last rally: critical reason, the ability of an individual to say 'this is right and that is wrong', cannot be asked where it comes from, cannot be criticised, cannot be told to validate itself before it is permitted to criticise. It is basic; no one can go deeper; it is free. No epistemologist, no political theorist and finally (for this is the dark end of the proud demand for a grounding for values) no tyrant is entitled to say 'You may not criticise my will. You have no ground on which to stand'.

Though critical reason cannot be questioned in advance of its activity, it can and must be questioned in its findings. All our reasoning, knowing or criticising, faces the test of other reasoners. Criticism expects and desires criticism. The worst problems are those of courage and honesty and patience with the freedom of perpetual inconclusiveness, matters on which reason needs faith. As to lesser problems, in all our reasoning, we are often simply parading the standard ideas of our culture, society and time, unreasonably, uncritically, indefensibly. We are often tempted to 'rationalism in politics', to great schemes for our society, for all humanity, for the world of states, ideas glittering in the sky but with no discoverable anchor in the earth. We are vulnerable as captious and arbitrary, one approval contradicting another, one disapproval incoherent with another.

The pursuit of order in our reasoning, of the integrity of our reason, leads in the end to the science of Being. We know from our experience of reasoning with others that we are disordered, disintegrated, or (it is a roll of distant thunder) degenerate, fallen. The reordering of ourselves in respect of reason culminates in metaphysics. About this, an ignoramus has nothing to say, except for the old, emboldening comment. There can be no notion that metaphysical understanding gives a transcendent standpoint (that, say, of a Creator) and that only those who attain it are licensed to reason. For metaphysical understanding is itself attained by knowing and criticising and can thus never be used to endorse or prevent the use of these capacities by others. Knowing and criticising are basic, natural, they are man's freedom of the very first creation, and nothing, not even Grace itself, takes that away.

The pursuit of order in our reasoning has implications of a simpler sort. It means that there is something to be said for the style of political theory which we were discussing before the debate with the Historical School. A characteristic of that style is that the reasoner presents a whole case, an ordered, coherent account of the human political condition, not one set of thoughts today and another tomorrow. There is perhaps, in the end, no difference on fundamentals between that old style and the style which springs from what we have lately been saying. On the international issue, the old style brings before us a human species, declares a common moral sense, posits a moral community of mankind, argues the reason and unreason of separate states, and puts before us the obligations to men in other states that fall away and those that persist. The new style notices that we treat one man differently from another. It seeks an explanation. It receives a set of answers. It asks for further explanations. And so on. The only difference between the two styles of reasoning may be that the old is more rigorous, more ordered than the new.

We may perhaps go farther. The new, we might say, is the method that produces the old. It is the critical questioning that leads in the end to a coherent theory, to the presentation of a whole case, an ordered account of human politics. The mighty objection of the Historical School to the old style of political theory was that it is rationalist, that it treats men as mere abstract man, proved by its inability to provide any principle whereby men can be supposed to choose particular associates. Locke seems to give us in passing an answer to this. Perhaps it is too sentimental. He says that the principle is friendship.[1]

It is now time to bring this whole discussion to a close and to attempt some conclusions. First, a brisk recapitulation: the question put at the beginning to the company of great political theorists was why they had so little to say about international relations. Their answer appeared to be that they assumed a world divided into separate states. Thenceforth, the discussion turned on whether this assumption could be defended or whether it could not. Three defences were advanced and criticised.

Who won, who lost? It would not be seemly to trumpet an answer here. The fiction we have used throughout has been that all has been a report by a hard-of-hearing listener at an evening passed in a pub by the great political theorists. Probably that listener has missed much, perhaps something decisive. He has revealed his inclinations plainly enough in the going. He had best now submit the question to others.

Why does an answer to the question under discussion matter, why does it matter whether we must assume a world divided into separate states or not? It matters, first, because if the starting-point of the study of international relations is a world of separate states, a political theorist is right not to be interested in the subject. There is nothing for him to say. International relations is concerned with a mere space between states, a desert of crude power, mitigated at best by a network of pragmatical customs and by pragmatical, unstable co-operation. This is a place for great intelligence and the highest qualities of character but only on the part of practical statesmen and their attornies and historians and commentators. There is no international theory to be done.

If, on the other hand, we must not start with this assumption of separate states, there is all the international theory in the world to be done. For there is now a primordial community of mankind; separate states are but an arrangement of it. The international sphere is no longer a mere space between states; it is this community. 'International' no longer means between nations but shared by the nations.

Political theory now opens as international theory. It begins as reasoning about the arrangements of this community of mankind, about the necessity of separate states, about the quality that justifies a particular state, and about the rights and obligations towards others that states and other international entities have and do not have. Political theory must next perhaps divide into specialisms of the state, interstate relations, transnational entities, and whatever else is decided. But each specialism is no longer a starting-point; thought in each is determined by consideration of the whole.

Some practical implications of abandoning the assumption of primordial separate states can perhaps also be dimly discerned. When, as practical men, we consider world affairs, we see not only constantly changing problems but perhaps also something unchanging. We perhaps see in ourselves a tension between awareness of ourselves as part of mankind and awareness of ourselves as members of our own separate states. We grasp that safety and justice require allegiance to the wider community and to the narrower, but we cannot reconcile them. We are perplexed as to the claims of each. We are thus impeded in the handling of our problems. Perhaps a change in the basic framework within which we think, the assumption of the separate state, would give us some help. It might help us to work out anew from the beginning what obligations we have to men of other states and what obligations we do not have.

To intervene in the affairs of another state is unsafe and unjust; to leave it to its tyranny and poverty is unsafe and unjust. The state must not use in warfare the hideous resources of modern technology; the state must do anything at all necessary to its survival. The products of animal and plant life many millions of years before men appeared on the earth are 'our' oil, aren't they? Or are they? Perhaps political theory could be of some help to us as practical men on all this. After all, practical men are dominated by theory.

Let us imagine, for example, that the last word in the discussion around the table at The Perpetual Peace goes to one of the company who has not yet spoken. He has been preoccupied and silent throughout the evening, because he knows that he will be expected by the others at the end to apportion the bill accurately or pay it all himself. Now, at last (having had to pay it all himself), we seem to hear him saying this. He never intended that economics should become a mere pragmatical logic of choice rather than a branch of moral philosophy. He would like to think again about the fact that economics begins with the individual (micro), goes on to the separate state (macro) and ends with international economics (optional). Perhaps the reverse order would be more reasonable?

NOTE FOR CHAPTER 4

The writer of this chapter acknowledges with thanks the especial help that he had from the works of Collingwood, Lonergan and Oakeshott, and from the discussions with the other authors of this book.

1   John Locke, *Second Treatise of Government*, s. 107.

5

The Problem of Meaning in International Thought

MOORHEAD WRIGHT

In setting out to think and theorise afresh about international relations, an initial problem arises common to all thought about human affairs. We see the phenomena of the world before us. They have meaning for us, but how do they have meaning? What kind of meaning is it?

Any satisfactory approach to this problem must begin by distinguishing between verbal meaning as the denotation of words, and material or 'real' meaning as the nature of things which we wish to understand. The problem of meaning resides in the relationship of the two. We cannot formulate and express real meaning without the use of words or other symbols, so that language in large part structures our thinking about the nature of things. Yet the objects of thought are strongly resistant to our efforts to pin them down in language, as the chapter entitled 'Word against Object' in George Steiner's *After Babel* emphasises.[1]

It is in this interdependence and antagonism of the two types of meaning that problems arise. One solution has been offered by Morris R. Cohen, who argues that 'verbal meaning is derivative and presupposes some recognition of a common world'. He elaborates this in the following terms: 'if we fix our attention on the actual process by which words acquire meaning, or, more generally, on the way objects become signs or symbols, we find that such objects are originally parts of larger situations or complexes, and their meaning is their pointing to or representing something beyond themselves'.[2] Erich Kahler puts it this way: 'When we say that something has a meaning we want to indicate that it forms part of something larger, or superior to itself, that it is a link, or function within a comprehensive whole, that it points to something beyond.'[3]

Assuming that real meaning is related to context, I shall explore three important 'comprehensive wholes' within which the phenomena of international relations acquire meaning. Although conceptually autonomous, these three contexts overlap in the real world. I shall refer to them as 'worlds' or 'domains' or 'realms' in order to exploit the spatial metaphor which these terms suggest.[4] The three worlds are the *Lebenswelt* (literally 'life-world', but usually translated as the world of everyday life), the public domain, and the ultimate realm.

I shall assume that a world is constituted by its form, following Aristotle's lead: 'And why is this individual thing, or this body having this form, a man? Therefore what we seek is the cause, i.e. the form, by reason of which the matter is some definite thing; and this is the substance of the thing.'[5] In R. P. Blackmur's words, 'Form is the limiting principle by which a thing is itself'.[6] In comparing the three worlds, I shall explore three aspects of form: wholeness or synoptic quality; a consistent internal structure; and a history or development over time. The role of language in each domain will also be indicated, and in a concluding section I shall briefly show how each of the three domains provides a context for elucidating the meaning of war – a characteristic problem in international thought.

The first domain, then, is the world of everyday life, a central notion of phenomenology. This is 'the world in which I live' or 'the concrete reality of the individual's lived experience'.[7] Its wholeness is determined spatially by 'horizons' and temporally by birth and death. A consistent internal structure is achieved by putting the 'self' firmly in the centre and making everything in the world of everyday life radiate out from and return to this centre. The temporal dimension of this world is essentially biographical – the story of a person's life from birth to death. The essence of the world of everyday life is what the phenomenologist calls the 'natural attitude' within which 'the world and our experience in the world are taken directly'.[8] The human body is seen as an instrument for the discovery and articulation of experience, and the situation of the self is described in terms of a complex of attitudes, projects and interpretations which form the ground for the emergence of any problem.[9] In this world everything is related to the self and takes on meaning only in so far as it affects the self. All criteria, values, norms and goals 'are both conceived and realized in *Lebenswelt* terms'.[10]

The social aspect of the world of everyday life is based on the principle of intersubjectivity, or the 'reciprocity of perspectives' between interacting selves.[11] The social counterpart to the physical world of objects and events is the face-to-face relationship in which people experience each other directly as unique individuals. It is the concrete social encounter in everyday life which provides the archetype for all extended forms of social relations.

Language and communication are vital constituents of the world of everyday life. Kurt Riezler makes the point in somewhat overly dramatic terms:

'Every language is the whole of a world, a space in which our souls live and move. Each word breathes the air of the whole.... A language is not an aggregate of words and rules. It is a potential world, an infinity of past and future worlds, merely a frame within which we speak and can create our world, actualizing ourselves and our language.'[12]

Speech or discourse is seen here as the medium in which the self is realised or made actual.

In turning from the world of everyday life to the public domain, we shift from a world which is 'self'-constituted to one which is constituted by the interaction of competing entities, whether individuals or groups. The wholeness of the public domain is best conveyed by the term 'arena'. In its literal sense, the term denotes the central part of an amphitheatre in which combats took place; in its figurative sense, it denotes any sphere of public or energetic action. In the latter sense it is both open and circumscribed; that is, the public domain is potentially bounded even though it may not actually be so at any one moment.

The main point is that the boundaries of a public domain are determined by the activity which takes place in it. For example, the shape and extent of the spaces marked out for tennis, cricket and football are determined by the nature of the activities which they enclose. Furthermore, these spaces are demarcated in common by those who take part in the activity, or their representatives, even though their purposes are mutually exclusive. The delineation of the arena is thus itself a public enactment, the result of which is embodied in a convention or 'constitution', whether formal or informal. This obviates the necessity of enacting a new arena each time the activity in question is to take place.

Whereas the framework of everyday life is naturally given or taken for granted, the public domain is only conventionally given or taken for granted. In the latter case, the framework was once problematic and may become so again. Those who participate in the public domain may attempt to change the framework or 'ground rules' to their own advantage. When this happens the nature of the framework itself becomes a stake in competitive activity. The prevalence of this tendency in international politics hardly needs underlining. Hannah Arendt argues that 'Limitations and boundaries exist within the realm of human affairs, but they never offer a framework that can reliably withstand the onslaught with which each new generation must insert itself'.[13] The public arena is constantly being made and remade, defined and redefined.

The interaction of opposing forces determines the internal structure of the public domain. Any order which is attained will be provisional and negotiated because it is based on an unstable constellation of pressures and a conditional reconciliation of conflicting interests, or alternatively on a tolerance of a certain level of disagreement. H. U. E. Thoden van Velzen has described an arena as a setting for antagonistic interaction which aims at achieving a publicly recognised decision.[14]

In its temporal aspect, the public domain transcends the limits of birth and death which mark the world of everyday life; it has a history rather than a biography. Public arenas are constituted, evolve, decline, merge, disappear. The similarity of some of these phases to the natural cycles of birth and death, growth and decay, has encouraged in the past the attribution of organic unity to public domains such as the state. The dangers of this analogy are by now so well known that it has become less common. In more neutral terms, the outstanding feature of the public arena is the interplay of actuality and potentiality, that is, the 'being' is also the 'becoming'. An alliance treaty, for example, is both an actuality in that it defines an existing juridical relationship between the signatories, and also a potentiality in that it envisages future military co-operation in the event of war.

The role of language and communication is a central one in the public domain. The complex system of shared relevances which structures the world of everyday life is translated into the interests and principles which form the basis of the claims and counterclaims of political activity. These interests and principles are articulated and represented by spokesmen, and their effectiveness in action largely depends on the rhetoric of identification and division, which Kenneth Burke has thoroughly explored.[15]

In the ultimate realm, the conflicting viewpoints of the public domain are reconciled and ordered according to ideals and principles which by their nature resist the complete appropriation by one side or other in the arena of public life. The 'space' which these ideals and principles occupy is bounded by the definite relationships which they have with each other and by the limits established by the 'most ultimate' of their number.

The internal structure of this domain is governed by the principle of hierarchy, usually involving an ascending, developmental sequence. For example, Iris Murdoch writes of 'The Sovereignty of Good over other Concepts', while Max Scheler postulated 'master ideals'.[16] In addition to the Good (first advocated by Plato), other candidates for the dominant ideal include Peace (Kant), History (Hegel), and Love (Christian theologians). This is pre-eminently the domain of what T. E. Hulme called the 'capital letterists' who attempt to find 'a framework outside the flux, a solid bank for the river, a pier rather than a raft'.[17]

In the temporal dimension, this realm by its nature tends to be relatively unchanging: it is usually seen to be eternal or outside time. Yet the history of thought does point to shifts in the dominant ideals which men have espoused, both within a civilisation and from one civilisation to another. The main point is that there is a certain economy of ideals. As J. N. Findlay puts it, the Kingdom of Ends cannot 'permit unmeasured growth towards infinity in any direction'.[18]

The language of the ultimate realm is characterised by metaphysical concepts, which tend to be the fruit of pure speculation or some form of transcendental experience. John Macquarrie has aptly described this type of concept:

'By a metaphysical concept, I mean one the boundaries of which cannot be precisely determined, not because we lack information but because the concept itself turns out to have such depth and inexhaustibility that the more we explore it, the more we see that something further remains to be explored. The more we grasp it, the more we become aware that it extends beyond our grasp.'[19]

As in the other domains, speech or discourse is of vital importance for those whose conduct is inspired by the ultimate realm: there is an imperative to 'voice' one's ideals, to give them expression, to urge others to attend to them.

It is not possible here to illustrate fully these three domains with the subject matter of international thought, but some idea of their relevance for the problem of meaning may be gained by placing within each of them in turn the question: what is the meaning of war?

To illustrate the *Lebenswelt*, I draw upon Stephen Crane's short story, 'An Episode of War'.[20] In a respite from the fighting and apparently safe behind a breast-work, a lieutenant divided equally each man's share of coffee into brown squares with his sword. Suddenly he cried out as a stray bullet from the fighting in a nearby wood ripped through his upper arm. Gently placing the lieutenant's sword in its scabbard, the orderly-sergeant

'did not allow even his finger to brush the body of the lieutenant. A wound gives strange dignity to him who bears it. Well men shy from this new and terrible majesty. It is as if the wounded man's hand is upon the curtain which hangs before the revelations of all existence – the meaning of ants, potentates, wars, cities, sunshine, snow, a feather dropped from a bird's wing; and the power of it sheds radiance upon a bloody form, and makes the other men understand sometimes that they are little.'

In search of medical aid, the lieutenant made his way from the line of battle back to the field hospital. As he left he 'was enabled to see many things which as a participant in the fight were unknown to him'. The battle sights appeared in such vivid detail and colours that they seemed to the lieutenant 'precisely like a historical painting'. He met some other officers on the way, one of whom clumsily bandaged his arm with a handkerchief while scolding him: 'The lieutenant hung his head, feeling, in this presence, that he did not know how to be correctly wounded.' A busy surgeon he met saw his bandaged arm and treated him with the same contempt, as if he were on a 'very low social plane'. But when the surgeon examined the wound, he took the lieutenant towards the field hospital, an old school-house. Both, jokingly, tried to deny the reality of what must be done, but the lieutenant struggled with the doctor, his glance fixed on the door of the old school-house, 'as sinister to him as the portals of death'.

The final paragraph of the story follows immediately:

'And this is the story of how the lieutenant lost his arm. When he reached home, his sisters, his mother, his wife, sobbed for a long time at the sight of the flat sleeve. "Oh, well," he said, standing shamefaced amid these tears, "I don't suppose it matters so much as all that."'

The lieutenant and his self-conception dominate this story. If we recall the phenomenologist's emphasis on the *embodiment* of the self, it is evident that the meaning of war in this story is found in the lieutenant's wound and the amputation of his arm. Crane emphasises the contrast between the general evaluation of battle wounds which give their recipients 'this new and terrible majesty' and the particular evaluation of the wound which the lieutenant received in such an inglorious situation as cutting up coffee with his sword. The lieutenant's own humiliation and shame are reinforced by the reactions of the others he meets, even though the latter could not have actually known the circumstances in which the wound was acquired. There is also the ironic contrast between the grandeur and emotion which he perceives in the battles he witnesses after being wounded, and his own dejected and futile journey to the field hospital. In *Lebenswelt* terms there is also, of course, the all-pervading atmosphere of death, of which 'the wound' is a symbolic foreshadowing.

Compare the self-orientated world of the lieutenant in Crane's story with an essay on war by the military historian, Michael Howard.[21] He is in accord with Crane that war is about suffering, but he is concerned with the relationships between the separate communities or peoples who are at war. The object of war, writes Howard, is 'to inflict on one's adversary such suffering, or to threaten him with the prospect of such suffering, that he abandons his political objective, whatever that may be. Conversely, war demands the capacity to endure suffering until the adversary abandons all hope of breaking your will'. In modern warfare, Howard stresses, this competition in endurance involves civilian populations as well as formal combatants; for both, the willingness to endure and to inflict suffering and death is crucial. It is in calculating these relative dispositions that each adversary population defines itself and the other. War is above all the arena where such public evaluations are put to the critical test.

Howard illustrates his argument with a wealth of historical examples, among which is the American Civil War:

'If the willingness of the Confederates to endure suffering had not been exceeded by the willingness and capability of the North to inflict it, the Southern States might today be a nation as independent and distinct as Mexico. The United States would never have developed as the power that it is, and the history of the world would have been very different.'

Here the meaning of war is to be found in its historical consequences, especially the integration and disintegration of various public arenas. Civil wars are the most obvious cases for this interpretation of war, but it is also true of international wars. The latter have the same capacity for establishing and overturning relationships in the international public domain. The evolution of the international system, for example, can be largely described in terms of the general wars and ensuing peace settlements which have occurred periodically, for example, the Wars of Religion (Westphalia), the War of the Spanish Succession (Utrecht), the Napoleonic Wars (Vienna), the First World War (Versailles) and the Second World War.

In exploring the relations between war and law, Norberto Bobbio considers the function of war in the creation of a new international order as analogous to that of revolution in the creation of a new internal order between a state and its citizens:

'Puisque nous sommes dans le domaine du problème de la légitimité, remarquons que ce qui change dans le passage de la théorie de la guerre-sanction à la guerre-révolution, c'est le critère de légitimation: la guerre est toujours considérée en fonction d'un droit à faire valoir, mais il ne s'agit plus de *rétablir* un droit passé, mais de *préétablir* un droit futur, non pas de *restaurer* un ordre ancien, mais d'*instaurer* un ordre nouveau.'[22]

War and law can be seen to have such an intimate relationship only in the public domain, which provides a framework for registering the outcomes of wars. In the broadest sense this framework is history. As Alexis Philonenko observes, 'Le propre de la guerre *est d'être une action violente s'inscrivant dans une histoire*'.[23] In the sense which concerns us, the framework is the states-system or international society, the subject of other chapters in this book.

Finally, compare Howard's analysis with that of Kant in his *Idea for a Universal History with a Cosmopolitan Purpose*.[24] Like Howard, Kant is concerned with the role of war in history, but his notion of history is a teleological one. He admits the strangeness of the enterprise: 'It is admittedly a strange and at first sight absurd proposition to write a *history* according to an idea of how world events must develop if they are to conform to certain rational ends; it would seem that only a *novel* could result from such premises.' Kant would agree with Howard that, retrospectively, wars are seen to have served local and parochial ends, but Kant goes on to argue that wars and all they entail prepare the ground for their own transcendence:

'Wars, tense and unremitting military preparations, and the resulting distress which every state must eventually feel within itself, even in the midst of peace – these are the means by which nature drives nations to make initially imperfect attempts . . . [to form] a federation of peoples in which every state, even the smallest, could expect to derive its security and rights . . . from a united power and the law-governed decisions of a united will.'

Kant concedes that the idea may appear 'wild and fanciful', but maintains that 'it is nonetheless the inevitable outcome of the distress in which men involve one another'. Howard, in contrast, must assume the continued willingness of people to endure and inflict suffering and death within the context of the public domain.

For Kant the striving to realise the ideal of peace enters as a new factor in history – a factor which must in time breed its own consequences. Just as religious wars in his day had become anachronistic, Kant looked ahead to the time when the irrationality of war would also become generally apparent; and peace, which would be no mere truce between powers, no temporary secession of hostilities, but a civilised life, would become so rooted that appeal to violence would be inconceivable.

The meaning of war for Kant thus lies in its potentiality for eventual self-transcendence, a process which can only be envisaged in the Kingdom of Ends. This is most clearly illustrated by the conclusion to his *Metaphysical Elements of Right*.[25] He declares that

'moral-political reason within us pronounces the following irresistible veto: *There shall be no war* . . . For war is not the way in which anyone should pursue his rights. The moral law within us makes it a duty to act as if perpetual peace could really come about.'

Kant appeals to metaphysics more than to experience as the guide to the best way of achieving this end: it should be derived '*a priori* by reason from the absolute ideal of a rightful association of men under public laws'. He concludes: 'If we try instead to give it reality by means of gradual reforms carried out in accordance with definite principles, we shall see that it is the only means of continually approaching the supreme political good – perpetual peace.'

Crane, Howard and Kant all place suffering and distress at the centre of their conception of war, but each locates this suffering within a different context or level of existence. The lieutenant in Crane's story endures both physical suffering in the loss of his arm and mental suffering in the shame and humiliation which he experiences in his social encounters with his fellow soldiers and his family. In Howard's essay, the collective suffering of peoples acquires meaning in the context of specific political outcomes, principally the creation, maintenance and alteration of the independent entities which comprise the international system. In Kant's philosophical history, war becomes meaningful in the context of a plan of nature which aims at a perfect civil union of mankind, in other words perpetual peace. In the understanding of these three basic contexts and of their intermingling in thought and conduct may lie the future development of international theory.

NOTES FOR CHAPTER 5

1   George Steiner, *After Babel: Aspects of Language and Translation* (London and New York, OUP, 1975), ch. 3.

2 Morris R. Cohen, *A Preface to Logic* (New York, Meridian Books, 1956), pp. 58–9.

3 Erich Kahler, *The Meaning of History* (New York, George Braziller, 1964), p. 18.

4 T. E. Hulme has suggested that, since space is 'essential to clearness', we can profitably put 'all ideas (purely mental states) into terms of space', *Speculations* (London, Routledge & Kegan Paul, 1924), pp. 239–40

5 Aristotle, *Metaphysics*, bk. VII, ch. 17, 1041b, 5–9.

6 Quoted by Erich Kahler, 'Artistic Form and the Human Condition', *University* (a Princeton, quarterly), December 1967, p. 10.

7 Maurice Natanson, *Literature, Philosophy and the Social Sciences* (The Hague, Martinus Nijhoff, 1962), p. 39.

8 Natanson, *Phenomenology, Role and Reason* (Springfield, Ill., Charles C. Thomas, 1974), p. 6, paraphrasing Husserl.

9 Natanson, *Literature, Philosophy and the Social Sciences*, op. cit., p. 39.

10 ibid.

11 Alfred Schutz, 'Symbol, Reality and Society', in Lyman Bryson *et al.*, eds, *Symbols and Society* (New York, Harper & Row, 1955), pp. 163ff.

12 Quoted in Natanson, *Literature, Philosophy and the Social Sciences*, op. cit., p. 131.

13 Hannah Arendt, *The Human Condition* (Chicago and London, The University of Chicago Press, 1958), pp. 190–1.

14 Quoted by Victor Turner, *Dramas, Fields, and Metaphors: Symbolic Action in Human Society* (Ithaca, NY., and London, Cornell University Press, 1974), p. 133.

15 Kenneth Burke, *A Rhetoric of Motives* (New York, George Braziller, 1955).

16 Iris Murdoch, *The Sovereignty of Good* (London, Routledge & Kegan Paul, 1970); J. R. Staude, *Max Scheler: An Intellectual Biography* (New York, The Free Press; London, Collier-Macmillan, 1967).

17 Hulme, op. cit., p. 222.

18 J. N. Findlay, 'The Structure of the Kingdom of Ends', *Proceedings of the British Academy*, vol. XLIII, p. 113.

19 John Macquarrie, *The Concept of Peace* (London, SCM Press, 1973), p. 63.

20 Stephen Crane, *The Red Badge of Courage and Selected Prose and Poetry*, 3rd ed. (New York and London, Holt, Rinehart & Winston, 1968), pp. 625–9. The setting of this story is not specified, but it is probably the American Civil War.

21 Michael Howard, 'War', *The Listener*, 8 August 1968, pp. 169–70.

22 Norberto Bobbio, 'Esquisse d'une théorie sur les rapports entre guerre et droit', in *La Guerre et ses théories; Annales de philosophie politique 9* (Paris, Presses Universitaires de France, 1970), p. 11 (italics in original).

23 Alexis Philonenko, 'Guerre et langage', *Etudes polémologiques 14*, October 1974, p. 36 (italics in original).

24 *Kant's Political Writings*, ed. Hans Reiss, trans. H. B. Nisbet (Cambridge, The University Press, 1970), pp. 41–53 (italics in original).

25 ibid., pp. 174–5 (italics in original).

6

Knowledge, the State and the State of Nature

CORNELIA NAVARI

It behoves one to begin at the beginning, but what is the beginning? Our subject is curiously unblessed with one. 'There have always been international relations' says one school; 'the Chinese had them and so did the Babylonians.' Even the school that posits beginnings seems to relegate these to pre-history: the state was preceded by a state of nature but at such a remote point in time that the beginnings of the state are virtually irretrievable.

The difficulty arises from assuming a precession. In fact, the state and the state of nature are twin concepts which entered the world together towards the end of the seventeenth century and which denoted a particular kind of state and a particular kind of nature, each discrete and delimited. The denotation of the one gave rise to the denotation of the other, and both were sub-clauses to a history which preceded them and of which they marked the end and a round of new beginnings. It was a break so radical that everything which had preceded them did fade into pre-history.

The Problem of Knowledge
The break concerned doubts about nature as a validator of knowledge. (In this sense, nature did come first.) These doubts arose from the competing views of nature's structure which dominated the seventeenth century. They were confirmed by the victory of the view that nature was a kind of machine or field of forces. The appearance of a mechanistically-ordered nature not only cancelled out nature as a validator; it raised doubts about the possibility of any external validation and whether true knowledge could be determined at all.

By nature, seventeenth-century men did not mean a realm of

trees and flowers. They meant creation, or reality, or order. In the seventeenth century, nature was a field of reality to which man stood in relationship as a sensor or perceiver. The exploration of nature was designed to uncover that reality, to reveal its structure and, by the act of discovering it, prove that man was capable of sensing it, prove indeed that it *could* be sensed. For unless it could, man would not be considered capable of knowledge of 'highest things'.

This, at some levels, very modern notion of the connection between sense, knowledge and a field containing ordered and sensible 'matter', was an elaboration of Thomistic epistemology, of Thomas Aquinas's concern to bridge the gap between knowledge by reason and knowledge by dogma. To close that gap, Aquinas elevated 'sense' into an independent property, no longer merely informed by good or evil, and set it into a relationship with reason as an independent operator in the world. For, unless reason were connected with something independent, something which operated in the world and gave it separate access to Truth, the battle between reason and dogma would be insurmountable. Hence, the origins of empiricism.

As this search went on, however, something very strange began to occur. The supposed single order of nature began to dissolve. What emerged was quite another nature, one never dreamt of and yet there, a nature of multiple structures, of random processes, of numerous small mechanisms, ticking away to various mysterious orders of their own.

The problem of this nature is the problem of what might be called taxonomies. Did its structure begin with small essences moving into greater, or did it begin at the top in great and move downward? Was there a single process in it, or many processes; and single or many, where did one break into them to establish their beginnings – their prime movements? One could, it appeared, begin anywhere and move back to the beginning again in this strange world.

Even more strange, the various elements which comprised this world themselves appeared amenable to varieties of differentiation into different systems altogether, in each of which they changed their rank. That is to say, whosoever looked at this world could structure it in any number of different ways, relating winds to currents, or currents to tides without doing an injustice to its perceived causal structures.

This world was not only its own problem, it became *ipso facto* man's problem as well, a problem which may be defined as the significance of meanings already arrived at. What this world indicated was that sense or experience could be amenable to a *variety* of orderings; on what basis therefore had experience been ordered before this astonishing fact had been discovered? The world, now called the world of 'man', had not after all stood still until the discovery of this other world, the world of 'nature'. It was full of meanings and differentiations, of what purported to be 'knowledge'. Where had they come from? What was their status? How were they to be validated?

It was Hobbes who posed these questions, and in doing so he was deliberately breaking with his age. Indeed, he called its main impetus nonsense. Of course, the epistemologists of his time *might* discover formulae in the stars or other more internal essences which, bending down, might bless order from afar. But meanwhile, did not their disagreements themselves tell them anything? To Hobbes they were as primitive as alchemists, ignoring the main discovery which was their *non-discoveries*, that meaning had no observable, felt base outside of itself. Nor could continued regression be the solution. The more one regressed, the more curious would become the world of meaning, for the more the regression, the more remote to the senses it would be and the more men would differ.

The nature of Hobbes's radicalism has been as much misunderstood as maligned. In fact, Hobbes was a sociologist of knowledge before he was a power-politician. He began from the not very extreme supposition that since his age had gone on a deliberate search for the prime mover, it ought to have found one if there were one to be experienced. Since no prime mover could be experienced or felt, the problem of knowledge was evidently a different problem ·from what the epistemologists of his age were assuming. It was not a problem of discovering what mover, what hidden and external spring, had given rise to the present and palpable order, but how in the absence of any such perceptible spring, order, meanings and knowledge had arisen *at all*.

The absence of the 'hidden spring' Hobbes expressed by the metaphor of the state of nature. This was the condition of men when they wandered 'outside' to locate their external sources and were bound to locate nothing but the random and variable causes of nature itself. The 'nature' of the state of nature is a new, alienated nature. The separate, independent status of agreements, meaning, knowledge, he expressed by the notion of 'compact'. Both concepts – nature and compact – are in their essence epistemological concepts which express the curiosity of what purported to be knowledge once it was seen that there was no 'natural' correspondence between what happened 'here' and what happened 'out there'. They emerged together in that the discovery of the one, the variable order of creation, had resulted *ipso facto* in the discovery of the other, the separate and perplexing status of knowledge.

Of course, by denuding knowledge and meanings of their external sources, Hobbes had already answered, or rather established the field for an answer to, the question of derivation. Without God or nature, the only other possible source was man and his collectivities. It could only be from there, given a non-sensible God and random nature, that knowledge and meanings could possibly have derived.

But the discovery that knowledge is 'social', that it arises in some manner out of the affairs of man, immense as such a discovery is, does not in itself solve the problem of *true* or *non-mythological* knowledge. And for all his reputed nominalism, for all his 'men call things what they will', Hobbes did not believe it did. Nominalism in Hobbes is a crude, early method of naming knowledge an artefact.

Indeed, it is the essence of the problem. For what is the Hobbesian mythology about but that any perceived mechanism or causal interaction can simply give rise to a random bit of myth, and a myriad of 'compacts' would ensue, recapitulating the state of nature itself. This, indeed, is the very problem which Hobbes saw in his own time of the civil wars. Compact in Hobbes does not justify or validate itself.

What Hobbes inherited as a single problem he passed to his successors as two. One is the problem of derivation; the second is the problem of how, given 'the absent source', such meanings as have emerged are to be validated, are to be judged as true and not merely random correspondences of the unprincipled causality of nature itself. If nature represents both absent source and absent validator, 'compact' expresses the need for some kind of new, unnatural validator which can rid the compact of its false or mythological derivations; that is, if the problem of knowledge is to be solved at all.

Hobbes's own solution is a very famous one, although its specifically epistemological function has seldom been noted. This is Leviathan, the great beast which in political terms imposes peace among the warring compacts, but which in Hobbes only does so through a specific knowledge-producing function. It stands in the history of knowledge as the first of the purely human validators.

The *Leviathan*, like all compact theory, approaches the problem of knowledge through a procedural device. In the *Leviathan*, this is something like, 'We, the citizens, *cannot* know, so we must let the prince decide'. This formula presupposes awareness that true, verifiable knowledge is unavailable, that the citizens know that they cannot know, that there is no external validator to which they can appeal, that therefore the Prince must decide. Put more abstractly, the producer of knowledge is Hobbes's justly famed notion of power. It is Leviathan's power which produces knowledge.

Of course, in Hobbes, all that goes by the name of knowledge must derive from power, the power to enforce that knowledge, since it could result from nothing else. This is as true of a primitive tribe as it is of Leviathan. The difference lies in the fact that the power of Leviathan is a different kind of power from the power of other 'mythically-based' social collectivities. Whereas other social collectivities, such as the tribe or the church, cloak their power in mythical derivations, the Leviathan eschews such mythical derivations. Unlike them, it is pure, 'nameless', uncharacterised power. It is nothing but itself and derives from nothing but the necessity to escape, to compact meaning if meaning is to exist at all.

The concept of nameless or pure power was not Hobbes's invention. That honour must go to Machiavelli who first stripped human action of its moral qualities and made of power a 'quality-less' entity. But in Machiavelli that entity is merely introduced into the service of another ethic, the classical ethic of man confronting his fate. In Hobbes, power is introduced into its own service, it serves itself. Existing for its own sake, it cannot be used to serve anything else. No mythologies can attach themselves to it. Hence, he hopes, it will keep the compact clear of myth.

The demythologising function of 'power' is familiar enough to us in our own time. The use of power by Weber as a grid-concept, the eternal principle moving its way through history, taking on different guises, giving the political scientist a standpoint from which to orient himself as to the true function of those guises, is a case in point. More widely familiar is the New Left whose 'key' to the 'real' explanation of what happens in the world is the notion of quality-less power. The use of power in this way, as the road to knowledge, to what is true, is a direct throwback to its fabrication by Hobbes. He is rather more the father of the New Left than Marx, to whom power was merely epiphenomenal.

But here, of course, is the rub. In Hobbes, power as a purifier, as a demythologiser, only works within the state. It only has such a purifying function when attached to a certain kind of self-conscious *instituted* entity which is aware of its own mechanistic and purposeful function. The hawker of knowledge without such a base is merely a voice in the wilderness. He is merely one more attendant at the court of warring mythologies which is the state of nature itself. It is the state and only the state which can secure the demythologised compact and give it durability.

Here we have the true correspondence and true opposition, the *state* and the state of nature, not the compact and the state of nature. Power without the state is nothing but another compact; it is nothing but mere meaning and ranks equal with all other such compacts in an endless war of all against all. It is the state which in truth opposes nature, which rescues the compact and removes it from the state of purposeless causality to which it would otherwise be eternally condemned.

If we see the concept of the state in this way, as an epistemological principle which was the first expression of the demand for nonnatural, intrahuman validation, we may make rather more sense of what has been called the 'pure theory of the state'. For the pure theory is nothing more than the creation within political theory itself of a series of knowledge-machines, which, turning on themselves, would in the midst of their turning solve the problem of how to validate knowledge, without reference to a source external to or outside of man. As validationist instruments, they were designed to take the place of general philosophical inquiry into 'rights' or 'truth', an inquiry which was deemed to be impossibly 'essentialist' or absolutist in orientation. Hence, political theory gradually broke away from general philosophical inquiry and established itself as a separate autonomous discipline. For once the state provided its own knowledge-system, general inquiry became a luxury, peripheral, and inessential. It became either the handmaid of state theory or inessential altogether.

The structure of a state knowledge-system, deprived of glosses, is simple. It contains a postulated nodule of knowledge, a guide to verification, or a process by which knowledge is produced. In Rousseau, it is the General Will which is the source of truth, of the 'what to do' which will guide community action, which serves as the measure of 'rightness' and to which the state apparatus is subordinated. In Mill, it is Liberty. In second-stage compact theory, American pluralist theory, it is the existence of plurality which ensures truth and interaction which produces it. Truth is said to require 'absence of singleness' in order to fuel the theory. In Hegelian theory, it is the Dialectic which revolving on itself produces knowledge.

These nodules or processes are then set in a frame, the state, which protects them, calls them forth, and without which they would be endangered. It is the state in Rousseau which ensures the existence of *a* General Will, by surrounding the field within which it operates and preventing the emergence within that field of any substate loyalties which would distort it. In American pluralist theory, it is the 'Constitution' which preserves the existence of pluralities, sets them into a relationship with one another and 'processes' their findings. It is the state which in Hegel transcends the Dialectic and makes it more than the random and purposeless movement which constitutes the historical process.

But the relationship of state to knowledge-mechanism goes far beyond that of frame to content. Without the state none of these mechanisms could be said to exist. It is the state which either creates them, as in the case of the General Will, or transforms them, as in the Dialectic, to make them usable. Without the state, their quality is quite different. Until there is a state, the Dialectic *is* simply a process of random historical happenings. It is the frame which, in fact, establishes the content.

This is so because the frame is intended to institute something which none of these mechanisms would have on their own. This something, Hegel called 'consciousness', by which he meant the recognition that the external check does not exist or is non-recoverable. The consciousness which the state institutes is consciousness of that fact, together with a secular, non-mythological order as a replacement. (The secularisation so heralded with the emergence of the state means the demythologisation of the Christian order, the end of the search for the external origins postulated within that particular myth. Secularisation was the Western state's form of its own demythologisation.) It was on that kind of consciousness that the state's legitimacy was established and with it the state itself.

The state is, of course, an historical creation, whose beginnings go back some time in the late Middle Ages and whose course was very much influenced by the experience of one state, the French state, in particular. But if we look at what characterises the 'modern' state, where it took its 'modernness' from, it was from a series of epistemological devices amalgamated with political theory. Our 'state' with its boundaries, its heavy weight of abstractions, its institutions, its demythologised basis, its secularised power, our state did not take on these attributes by virtue of a concept of 'stateness'. There was no such notion in classical or mediaeval political theory. Rather our notion of stateness is an amalgam of attributes which emerged out of an entirely new theory of knowledge, a theory whose key aspect was carried over into the historical, sociological and national revolutions of the nineteenth century, and which has taken, subsequent to its early formulations, many shapes. This is the 'redoubt' or 'frame' theory of knowledge. According to this theory, knowledge not only varies with particular times and places (which is no doubt true), not only is created by those times and places (which may be true), but is created through a symbiotic relationship with a 'frame' which calls it forth and but for which it could not exist at all. State theory is the first version, indeed the source of frame theory.

What the frame creates is not always 'truth'. Sometimes it is mere 'meaning' or 'significance' in Michael Oakeshott's sense. Sometimes, as in Durkheim, it is avowedly myth, but myth which does the work of truth, which is man's particular kind of truth. Sometimes, as in Erving Goffman, what the frame creates is a sort of appearance which does the work of social definition. In the latest version of frame theory–John Rawls's theory of the pure compact–what the frame creates is a very old notion of truth, the Good, redefined as the Fair.

The frame, accordingly, changes shape; from the 'political process', to the 'social bond', to the metaphors of dramatic liturgy, theatres and 'settings', to the compacting process itself and 'changing sides'. But these changes do not act in such a way as to reduce the functional importance of the frame, if politically some of them might make the value of retaining a particular frame questionable. Indeed, they increase its importance. For now it is the frame which creates not only knowledge, but even mere meaning and significance and indeed myth itself, an honour which even Hobbes did not give it. The development of frame theory, particularly through sociological theory, has had the effect of making the social setting the most important definitional influence on all of man's being. Indeed, in some theories, it is deemed impossible for him to get out of it at all.

Taken together, these devices have conferred on our modern notions of real knowledge a singularly locational, bounded or institutional nature. They have conferred on our modern notion of society or state a definite knowledge-containment function. 'State' or 'society' are deemed to have a virtual monopoly not only of knowledge but even of mere meaning or significance, and knowledge itself is deemed to be impossible without them.

As state and society took on such functions, nature was increasingly relegated to the 'outside'; it took on the feel of being non-usable, discontinuous, other and alienated from the social settings which were designed to be discontinuous with it. Accordingly, and in consequence, knowledge of nature became a discontinuous activity, separate from social science.

Here, starting with the intellectual break in the seventeenth century, lie the beginnings of that tension between 'science' and 'culture', of 'the two cultures', which has characterised modern European intellectual life. Each of these realms being knowable in a different way, different methodologies of knowledge were developed. Social knowledge centred on the problem of myth and of turning myth into truth. Nature was subjected to that kind of piecemeal, mechanistic and (from the point of view of knowledge of the whole) ultimately unsatisfactory type of explanation involved in the scientific method.

There was, originally, only one exception to this nature–culture distinction, an exception which, however, proved the rule. It lay in the treatment of social networks which were not institutionalised. These non-institutionalised networks, not having a clearly demonstrable set of institutions which produced 'meanings', began to look very unlike 'societies'. Accordingly, it was felt inappropriate to subject them to the same treatment accorded to 'societies'.

Thus, if the state (by which we may also denote society in a state-framework) generated its political, social, or anthropological theories, so did relations *between* states appear to require a separate, discontinuous type of theory, an altogether different methodology from that to be applied to either states or societies. The very existence of unbounded interaction seemed to make those theories inappropriate for knowledge where no such strict frameworks of control, or origins, existed.

In the first place, state theory gave no theory of how even meanings, much less knowledge, could arise in non-social, non-institutionalised settings. In the second place, if such meanings *did* arise, there existed no 'social' framework within which they could be 'fixed', established and, further, no agreed process by which they could be clarified, no way to work on them either to achieve the establishment of agreed meanings or to refine them into a process of agreed procedures. Hence, the question of whether international law is *really* law, since through state theory, law has come to connote either a system of coercion or, if you prefer Locke to Hobbes, a fixed procedure for reformulation, a frame within which laws can be reconsidered and through which the reconsideration is institutionalised and made to stick.

Without such frames or procedures, international relations began to take on a different aspect from societal relations. They began to be thought of as more like relations in nature, and they began to be accorded a treatment more appropriate to natural phenomena. Indeed, the two went hand in hand. Without 'institutions', the only explanation for regularity must, it was thought, lie in some naturalistic device, some non-societal or mechanistic force. The field accordingly took on the attributes of nature. Secondly, the belief emerged that this particular field was *only knowable* through the description or identification of those forces.

Balance of power theory and systems theory, two of the three classes of theory which have dominated international relations, are both mechanistic theories. Both postulate the system as a field of forces awaiting identification. As such, they could scarcely be in the end very different from one another, as systems theorists with so much labour have discovered. More interesting perhaps is the fact that positivism, the science of society which tries to identify its underlying forces, made its first appearance in the non-society of international relations as early as the latter half of the eighteenth century. Referred to as 'political arithmetic', it was an early attempt to quantify the power which fuelled the balance in order to predict its future forms.[1] Only in the nineteenth century, when in fact the self-sustaining nature of societies began to be called into doubt, was this approach considered appropriate for application to societies.

The only exception to the mechanistic bias of international relations theory is an exception which, again, proves the rule. In the degree to which institutional theories have emerged in the treatment of international relations, they are theories of how to *found* or *establish* institutions, an aim undertaken precisely to make those relations knowable, to make them subject to agreed criteria of what is right. For without such an *institution*, agreed criteria, it was felt, would not be possible. Thus, even these approaches are founded on the belief that it is institutions which distinguish society from nature, and in the degree to which the institutions fail, international relations sink back into a state of nature, to be comprehended again by a description of their underlying forces.

But the very postulate of naturalism, attractive as such a notion seems, is itself autodestructive. It appears to doom international relations to an essential unknowability. For what is it that seventeenth-century men discovered about nature, and why is it pictured as a multiple-field machine? Because its *causality* remains essentially in doubt. Causality can be identified, to be sure. Indeed, multifarious causalities are constantly being turned up. But which cause is prime cause must remain in doubt and, hence, the nature of the system itself.

The difficulties which international theory confronts are not difficulties arising from its subject matter. They are difficulties which arise from the conceptual framework within which international theory developed, and, in particular, from a previous theory which is widespread in its acceptance. This is frame theory, the theory which holds that knowledge, 'true knowledge', derives from frames.

But this theory is itself only part of a wider mind-map, built up from a particular conception of nature itself. For if society was discovered to be a self-contained entity, requiring autonomous intrahuman methods of knowledge, that discovery emerged from a discovery about nature, namely, that it could be structured in any number of mutually satisfactory ways. The fate of systems theory is a replay in microcosm of the fate of nature itself.

The mind-map within which international theory tried to develop, is, thus, a whole with mutually dependent parts. If states were thought to create truths, and societies to create meanings, it was because nature was conceived as being structured by random mechanisms which present an attractive field for exploration but which turn out to be too multifarious in causality to allow for a single structure to be determined.

This thought-structure is not unique to international relations theory. It is endemic in all social thinking. All social thought is, indeed, a round which keeps rediscovering elements on this map. Positivism keeps discovering the problem of random causality, while political and social scientists keep trying to devise alternative and more satisfactory frames. But it has affected international theory most profoundly; it stunted it at birth.

The question is, are the elements of this mind-map true? And it is the central question in any international relations theory. For if they are, then no such theory is possible; not a satisfactory one, at any rate. To successfully devise a theory of international relations, one must begin by refuting these postulates. One must demonstrate that states or frames cannot create truth, or its substitute; that societies do not create meanings; and that mechanisms are not attributes of a random reality such that no mechanistic theory can be really satisfying. A brief attempt will be made in the remainder of this chapter.

The State Reconsidered

The state's claim to our attention, we are told, rests on its special demythologising properties. The state, or frame, or process, maintain the various types of frame theorists, will hold together a truth procedure without which truth cannot arise or will be endangered. But all institutional theory, in the degree to which it is truth theory, depends on truth actually being there somewhere when the state goes to work. Moreover, it depends on this truth being somehow spontaneously recognisable after the realm has been cleared or the truth process begun. Truth must be easy to spot since frame theory gives us no idea what truth looks like, and, indeed, is designed to replace such criteria.

But is truth so easy to spot, and if it is, why, we may ask, is the heavy weight of institutions necessary at all? All contract theory itself begins from the original position that truth in the abstract sense is either unavailable or extremely difficult to locate. The justification of the various frames rests on the difficulty of really knowing the truth when it appears. Here, then, we have a curiosity. Frame theory, to be coherent, is dependent on the existence of that which it denies.

To illustrate this curiosity, let us return once more to Hobbes. Hobbes hoped that by setting up Leviathan, he would clear the realm of mythologies. By elevating power for its own sake, he hoped to ensure that it would be used for the sake of nothing else. But he was also plainly expecting something to be left there when the realm was clear.

This something has been called reality or 'the way things are'.

(Positivists take note. It is this which makes all Hobbesians into positivists.) But we should not be confused. This notion of reality is nothing but a notion of residual truth – truth which mythology interferes with and which will stand revealed when power cuts away the operation of mythologies. Indeed, it could be nothing else, for, unless there is a notion of residual truth in Hobbes's formula, the original problem remains intact. Hence, power creates a field of reality which must be explored, and yet power gives us no guides for its exploration. The only way for meaning to be compacted is on the basis of random mechanisms, but, in consequence and before very long, a state of nature will ensue! Unless there is a notion of residual truth, all the work of Leviathan goes for nought. But what this truth is, how we will know it, all this is left undefined. Indeed, the state is designed to replace it.

The only way in which the theory of Leviathan works is if we substitute Order for the Search for Truth, and Hobbes himself seems to get very close at times to doing so. But he does not succumb entirely and for a very good reason. The truth machine would be converted into not merely a 'peace machine', but a *mythological* machine. For order is an undefined state of affairs. By tying power to the total preservation of order without any other criteria, power would itself take on random definitional rights. It would start to spin off mythic positions. It would not be the demythologiser which Hobbes wants it to be.

Rousseau grasped this gap in Hobbes's theory very clearly. Hence, he gives us the General Will, the 'something' which would be found when the realm was cleared of myths and to which power would be firmly subordinated. The importance of the General Will lies as much in its relevance to Hobbes's theory as to Rousseau's – by filling up the space, it reveals the gap. But the General Will is scarcely more than an incarnate form of Hobbes's aspiration – that aspiration made concrete – not its solution.

Indeed, by Hobbes's discovery of the necessary nature of men, the General Will can barely be deemed to exist. Hobbes's position is, after all, that all men differ or that one cannot count on their similarities by nature. This being the case, the General Will can only be a result of 'socialisation', not the corrective to the socialisation process which Rousseau hoped it would be.

The point is yet clearer in Hannah Arendt's idea of 'the public arena'. She develops Hobbes's position on human difference in her notion of the effects of natality, and promotes a creative theory of knowledge to be discovered through speech and action in the public arena. But what if the Arendtian arena contains Rousseauesque man, socialised with Hobbesian qualities? Her populace must be generally humane, capable of being converted to 'reason' and seeing

the creative or the good when it is turned up. Otherwise what the
arena produces will be justified brutality. But what it is that her
populace must contain is not defined in her theory. Indeed, her
theory is intended to avoid such definitions.

The truth is that if one stares hard enough at the large corpus of
compact theory, one will detect somewhere an empty space trying
hard not to be noticed. In the degree to which entities are named at
its heart, these entities are essentially artefacts or names for things
which simply do not exist. Rather their artefaction, it is hoped, will
create them.

Justice, of course, exists; it is something. But if we knew in all
cases what it was, we would not need the process of changing sides,
postulated by Rawls, to find it. Since we do not know, it is a name
for something which does not yet exist.

It is this quality of emptiness which throws state theory back on
its frame, so that truth can be 'discovered', or created. But, unless we
have a fairly clear idea of what we are looking for, an idea of truth, or
an independent way of checking it, the frame will either turn up
nothing, or whatever the frame turns up will, by definition, be valid.
At the same time, state theory, indeed all frame theory, denies that
such independent criteria are possible. Indeed, it is precisely
because the state provides no criteria, is designed to replace such
criteria, and tells us that they do not exist, that it becomes such a
powerful instrument of random validation, as Rousseau feared, or
its own validation.

Hegel, grasping the dilemma more firmly than Rousseau, found
an independent operator in the concept of consciousness, by which
he meant consciousness of the possible mythic status of myths,
consciousness of the meaning of the Dialectic. But he could only do
so by turning *everything else* into justified myth, which is the meaning of the Dialectic. Further, by tying the Dialectic to the state, he
actually justified the state machine in the role of myth-producer, a
danger which the compact theorists at least tried to avoid.

Compact theory was immensely important. It cancelled out
much fruitless searching for hidden springs. It pointed out the fact
of social derivation. It defined the problem of knowledge as two
separate problems instead of one. It differentiated myth from truth
and created the phenomena of demythologisation. It pointed out
the need for an intramundane validator. But if honour is due to it, it
is because it gave the first and clearest definition of the nature of the
problem, not because it provided the solution.

If frames cannot create truths, what about the proposition that
societies create meanings? This is the more curious statement, both
more convincing and somehow less concrete. Its significance is
plain enough. It was the first way of expressing the realisation that

meanings are *intramundane*. What 'society' meant to our forefathers in this context was: not God, not nature. As such it is a necessary statement and a statement which sets the field for a theory; it is not a theory itself.

For a theory to arise, the myth-creator must be defined. The myth-creator is, for example, 'the *bricoleur*', or 'man-confronting-nature', or the 'means of production'. Each of these is a device for explaining how myths come about. When the myth-creator is defined, however, it is no longer so inclusive or exclusive a term as 'society'. Rather the position is reversed. It is the myth-creator which creates society and not society which creates myths.

Mechanisms Reconsidered
Part of the problem of our compact thinkers lay in their original position. They supposed that myth was a property of mind and mechanism a property of the world 'out there' and, hence, itself unusable. Even those who use mechanisms generally take the same view, seeing their machines as attributes of the world; indeed, for them that is the chief virtue of mechanisms; it is myths that they suppose to be unusable. This view is a mistake. *Both* myths and mechanisms are properties of mind or ways of ordering the world and making it intelligible.

This should become clear if we go back to the search for God in palpable things, 'out there'. How was this search conducted? By mentally splitting up all kinds of phenomena to see if God were in them and then reorganising them. They did not split themselves; they were split and reorganised in differing causal relationships by the agency of the human mind.

The discovery that mechanistic structures are structures of mind and not of nature was the work of Kant, neither a compact thinker nor a positivist in the accepted meaning of exploring reality 'out there'. He had for that reason no clear distinction between myth and mechanisms but saw both as an attribute of something else. The argument has been put in a modern idiom by Ernest Gellner in *Legitimation of Belief*, together with some shrewd analysis of what does distinguish them.

Kant noted, first, that explanation or theory was an entirely human product. It did not exist in nature or 'out there'. Second, he noted that for an explanation to be explanation it had to have a certain structure. There had to be things called 'causes' which led to other things called 'effects'. This, he related not to the world, but to explanation itself. Explanation itself was cause-demanding. Without something denoted as cause, the maelstrom of reality remained in human terms unintelligible, whatever its own structure was. It was explanation which not only sought relations between causes and effects, but which created the idea of cause and effect so as to apply them as grid concepts to the palpable world and bring it into intelligibility.

The feeling must be familiar to anyone who has puzzled over an unknown field of phenomena. Before its decoding, the field resembles a jumble of random happenings, which in themselves, however, do not move. (Hume's minute particles.) They only begin to move, to take on shape and intelligible form when some are classed as causes and others as effects, and a link between the two is established. That small link is a cause-and-effect machine, a small machine without which the world or field would itself be consigned to nothing more than unintelligibility. The world is full of such machines, turning and turning, creating intelligibility out of 'reality'.

As an agency of human mind, this link is assigned to the world or nature to make sense of it, and then appears to become a property of nature. Like myth, mechanism moves from here out to there. Both are properties of mind which are then assigned to the world.

This is often used to make the claim that science is a myth structure and that there is no difference between a creation story beginning with ostriches and one beginning with amoebas. In that both are structures of mind, this is quite true. In all other respects, however, it is false.

As explanatory devices, mechanisms are single-stage causal factors, limited in effect. Mechanistic explanation hovers over an unknown or puzzling field of phenomena and *selects out* particular and specific features which are then inter-related or to which attention is drawn. They generally operate within bodies – human, societal, natural. Myths, on the contrary, explain things in packages. Whole bodies of phenomena are inter-related either by implied parallels, such as the earthly and the heavenly Jerusalem, or by sharp distinctions, such as mental and physical or God battling with the Devil, which, none the less, still coexist within the same explanatory system.

Since mechanisms are single-stage causal factors, they can usually coexist with one another quite happily, each occupying only a small part of the field. Myths, on the contrary, are always, indeed necessarily, mutually exclusive, since each purports to explain the *whole* field.

Because they are particularistic, mechanisms can demarcate happenings. They can put happenings into various classes and sub-classes, call attention to their distinguishing features, or to the way in which, while purporting to be very different, they in fact share similar structures. Myths find demarcations which are not built into their structures very difficult, if not impossible, to deal with.

Because mechanisms do not occupy the whole field, they permit left-overs. This is very important, since the left-overs can be used to check the original proposition. It is the fact that there are left-overs which allows for experiments and for the possibility of refutation. It is because there are none in myth systems that these can only be verified, and if the myth system is too large, not even this is possible. The statement 'God caused the world to be' is not only not refutable, it is not verifiable either.

Mechanisms, because of their shattering and reorienting function, are of themselves, usually neutral; they seldom point directly anywhere. Hence, people are free from attachment to a mechanism for reasons other than the substantive claim the mechanism is making. If a more substantial mechanism appears, they can abandon the first. They are, thus, purely explanatory operators. Quite the contrary often occurs with myths. The very weight and inclusivity of their wholeness make them difficult to abandon.

Mechanisms allow for 'the random'. This should not be taken to mean that nature or history or culture *is* random. It means that there may in fact be few reasons for choosing one structure of causality over another; and that mechanistic explanation does not of itself demand that one structure or the other be chosen. Both can be held within the same overall methodology. Mechanistic explanation identifies such a case as being one where no predominant view can yet be taken. It allows, in short, for non-definition.

Perhaps it is this capability which led nature to be pictured finally as a mechanistic structure. Not because *it* was a form of machine, but because mechanistic explanation was a form of explanation which allowed phenomena about which there was a great deal of ignorance to be explained in more than one way.

Of course, mechanisms can become myths. Freudian psychology and the 'Five Stages of Economic Growth' were each mechanistic theories postulating intraspecific causal relationships which became mythic paradigms, to be applied as total causal factors. More confusing is the fact that since the nineteenth century, it has been felt necessary to base one's myths on the postulation of mechanistic causal properties such as the existence of the proletariat in Marxism and the geographical or blood theories of nationalism. But these are merely inversions in which each, while purporting to remain itself, is in fact taking on the qualities of the other.

First, each is in a sense bowing to the inherently different qualities of the other: to the quality of 'holism' in mythical explanation, while retaining the specificity of the machine; and to the quality of a hard-and-fast machine while retaining total causality. But in doing so each loses its quality and *becomes* the other. No sooner does a mechanism take on holism than it fades from testability and enters the realm of irrefutability and mythological meaning. No sooner does Marxism claim its small machine, than that machine itself becomes amenable to testability and hence refutation.

Taken together, these qualities constitute the most palpable difference of all. Mechanisms demythologise myths. They can even demythologise themselves on the way to becoming myths. Myths, on the contrary, can do nothing in the face of mechanism; nothing, that is, without the addition of that extramythic element, force of arms. Mechanisms, without any external force at all, have the ability to shatter and reorganise mythical meaning.

We may see the irony in the situation of our compact thinkers. What they cast out was what they could have used; that is, small specific machines applied not to the world 'out there', but to meaning. This was after all their problem, the evaluation of myth – not the discovery of truth. What they ought to have done was to bring nature in, to bring the search for causes to bear on meaning itself, to locate its derivations and to reveal its 'false', or arbitrary, or possibly true, base.

They did, however, have one strength which deserves reiteration, and which a lot of machine builders in the new-positivist tradition lack. They did realise that the problem was myths and the continual tendency of reality to take on palpable shapes. Kant's discovery was little more than a logical continuation of their discovery.

The problem of much systems analysis in constructing its machines was that it attempted to avoid this fact. It attempted to attack 'reality' direct without taking into account that all social phenomena are made up of meanings and differentiations which are in fact responsible for the structuring of those phenomena, and that 'structure' cannot be divorced from them. This was a natural impulse. After all, systems analysis theorists are inheritors of that part of the compact tradition which saw meanings as a problem. Rather than frame them, they tried to get underneath them. But to do so they had to convert, on the way, that which *was* structure into just one element of a pre-existing structure, a mythical structure, since it could scarcely have existed without them. They were in the ironical position of creating the random worlds they then proceeded to discover. The real purpose of a machine is to make intelligible a field of meaning, to unpack it, reorganise it and point out certain curiosities about it. Or, to explain why such meanings do not emerge or cannot be generalised.

In doing so, machines do not have to be machine-like. They do not, as Gellner points out, have to be built out of heavy material (money, say, or power). The lightest of matter (ideas, structures of ideas) will do just as well.

The State of Nature Reconsidered

Mechanisms acting upon myths may provide the basis for unravelling social meaning but what does this have to do with international relations? We all know that international relations are not social.

But what does constitute a society? That is the cry of most sociologists. If only they were truer to their own tradition and examined the nature of compacts, and not societies!

The concept of *a* society is an *étatiste* myth, the imposition of state thinking on sociological thinking. What are called societies are in fact series of compacts which inter-relate in a changing magnetic field. The boundaries of this field are impossible to determine without determining or first establishing the nature of the compact itself. What is the society of a student revolutionary? What is the society of a Burkeian conservative? The nature of the compact or the field of meaning itself determines its boundaries, the boundaries of the society.

Second, is not there something very odd about the 'state of nature' which constitutes international relations – namely, the fact that it did not always exist? The fact that it was an *established* state of nature which emerged out of something that went before?

The story of its emergence is usually told through the story of the emergence of the state, and this is, of course, true. But not in the sense of an inward-gathering of forces. That, too, is an *étatiste* myth. The story could just as well and, indeed, rather more accurately be told from the outside in, through the image of a number of princes sitting in a field uttering the words, *cuius regio, eius religio*, words of which they all understood the meaning and some of the implications: a compact, in short, which began the great state of nature.

And indeed, the state of nature did have to be founded. It was scarcely natural to the men of the time that social organisation be cut off from external authority, formed into billiard balls and the space between emptied. The notion of the state as a billiard ball is a convention; it was instituted. That condition of affairs is maintained by other conventions, such as non-intervention and recognition which were also instituted. To say simply that the space between is 'empty' is not true. It is 'empty' in the sense that the state is for certain purposes a billiard ball. But the space is full of the convention which maintains that image. It is also full of the convention that human societies must become states for certain purposes.

As concepts of demarcation, as problems in the progression of knowledge, and as partial or quasi-solutions, the State of Compact or Peace and the State of Nature or War have suffered from being attached to real counterparts in the world and being identified with them, as actual physical areas. Were this the case, international relations would be completely incomprehensible, instead of only mostly so. To the degree that they are comprehensible, they are so because certain areas within them have fallen under the sway of compact or common agreement. 'Meanings' and differentiations have emerged within them, removing them from the completely unprincipled causality of the area of 'nature'.

'War' itself is one of these, and a vital one. F. H. Hinsley makes the point that our notion of 'war' derives from the principle of 'just war' which was first and foremost a principle of demarcation, distinguishing a certain kind of activity, war, from piracy, thievery, brigandage or vandalism and placing it into another area of demarcation, the area of the 'possibly legitimate'.[2] Also, piracy, thievery and brigandage have been demarcated and placed under the relevant authorities. Thus was nature channelled or shattered – 'denaturised'. It is scarcely real nature.

Misunderstanding this, and seeing principle arising from a 'real' state of nature, some scholars of international relations suppose that it is 'real' principle and start chasing around looking for its hidden springs, looking for 'God' in 'nature'.

Even more strange are those scholars who accept that the realm within which states relate is a pure state of nature and assume that, because it is, this particular realm has purer air; in it things are more 'real' than in the realm of the state, as in 'real' power or 'real' interest. But the chief attribute of reality is unintelligibility. If 'real' power existed in international relations, we would not be able to speak about it, we would not be able to understand it. Its reality would be of the same nature as the random act of an undiagnosed psychotic; that is, unintelligible. And indeed the advocates of 'real' power or 'real' interest do have difficulty defining what they mean. For power like anything else changes its content through the differences of its context and can only be understood contextually, through the agreements or disagreements on its meaning, through the social and 'mythical' context in which it arises. What the advocate of 'real interest' means is that he is establishing a cause-and-effect relationship concerning the state's use of its power other than the relationship claimed by the state, a relationship of greater explanatory power perhaps, but none the less a created, artefacted relationship.

If international relations do appear to be more palpably real than the tamer stuff of civil society – and they do – it is because of the continual view they provide of men confronting the prospect of unprincipled causality and rushing to compact it. We may look at the 'rationality' of deterrence as such an instance – the shattering, to the degree possible, of the unprincipled nature of nuclear confrontation by making and attempting to enforce agreements on its meanings. (This is also why deterrence theory seemed to provide such a powerful model through which to comprehend the relations of states.)

In that the field of international relations is different from the state, its difference lies in the distinguishing features of its compacts. It lies, for instance, in the fact that its compacts are legitimised or brought to full agreement by states, who try to keep that legitimating power as their prerogative. This is not to say that nothing else operates within the same field. Multinational companies may operate in it, as do guerrilla fighters and some 'civilians' (all of Eric Ambler's heroes, for example). It is merely to say that states are the agents of the legitimation processes of the field.

One should avoid the confusion which replaces 'agents' by 'actors' or puts the two on the same plane. The main reason for the founding of the original compact was precisely to distinguish between agents – legitimate members – and 'actors' – anyone else. The present policy of the Palestine Liberation Organisation is precisely to turn itself from an actor, just anyone, into an agent, a legitimate member of the society.

To say this is not, of course, to solve the problem of the true, right, good or 'fair'. The state is, by the compact of the states-system, the only agent of moral action in the community of states, but that does not solve the problem of what constitutes morality. Whether or not this problem can ever be 'solved', it can, however, at least be more clearly demarcated from the question of the state's formal standing, and thus the confusion which has plagued our subject can be somewhat dispersed.

Theories about international relations, to make sense, should be historically specific 'sociological' theories. These are theories about the derivation of meanings in international relations, the accretions to those meanings and the causes of their withering away. They are descriptions of the myths which structure international relations through the unravelling of the mechanisms of those relations. Knowledge of international relations can only follow from unwrapping these packages. It will not arise from the assumption that no packages exist.

NOTES FOR CHAPTER 6

1   See Moorhead Wright, ed., *Theory and Practice of the Balance of Power, 1486–1914* (London, Dent, 1975), p. 139.
2   In *Nationalism and the International System* (London, Hodder & Stoughton, 1973), pp. 88–93.

7

International Society and International Theory

JAMES MAYALL

The difficulty of distinguishing between what we know and what we believe lies at the heart of contemporary international theory. Until recently, many held that the distinction was basically clear-cut and that it was possible to develop scientific theories insulated from normative concerns. In the past few years, we have seen the collapse of this 'value-free' social science, and it is now understood that values must be accepted into international theory. There has as yet, however, been little discussion of what this involves. In this chapter, I seek to contribute to the groundwork for a discussion.

As a start, I reassert the concept of 'international society' as central to international theory. When so much theorising has been concerned to avoid explicit argument of a normative or moral kind, it is not surprising that this concept should have fallen into disuse. After all, the writers who traditionally employed it were directly concerned with ethical questions, most notably about the derivation of rights and obligations in political affairs. Nor is contemporary scepticism at their efforts difficult to understand. One can even sympathise with it. On the one hand, the natural law tradition of an international community of mankind, despite its apparent universalism, is very largely a product of Christian philosophy and theology and seems oddly inappropriate in a secular age which demands demonstration of its laws 'in the world' rather than by reference to a metaphysic. On the other hand, the positivist conception of an international society of states, designed and maintained by men for their own purposes, while clearly less ambitious and consequently more acceptable to contemporary tastes, has also seemed to many to neglect certain positive evidence, namely, the evidence that suggests that in international politics it is not law, custom or convention that determines what happens but the clash of powerful wills.

There is another consideration behind our reluctance to continue the traditional debate between the natural law and positivist positions on international society.[1] It is clear that both sides of the argument belong within the Western intellectual tradition. In our world, possessed as it is of extensive documentation of the diverse cultural, political and intellectual conditions under which men actually live, it seems only prudent to avoid universal moralising altogether. Even within Western society, attempts to ground political action on secure moral argument are notoriously question-begging. Pascal still provides what is probably the best defence of the modern antipathy for moral theory. 'Larceny, incest, infanticide, everything has at some time been accounted a virtuous action.'[2] Political morality, in other words, is humbug. We may well share his view of the absurdity of mankind's moral pretensions, 'true on one side of the Pyrenees, false on another', and join him in deploring the demands on our loyalty made by those in authority in the name of such absurdities; but if human morality *really* is so fickle, what more is there to say?

But persuasive as these arguments against universalism undoubtedly are, they do not in fact dispose of the concept of international society. The dangers of adopting a particular moral standpoint cannot properly be used as an argument for amorality, particularly if, as I wish to argue, this is not really an option at all. Nor can the empirical diversity of the world, any more than the evidence of conflict within it, be used as an argument against international society. No doubt all baselines for intellectual inquiry are inadequate but some are less inadequate than others. The case for adopting this particular baseline for international theory rests on the commonplace observation that human relations always and necessarily take place within a social setting which can be specified and rendered mutually intelligible by those involved. What would clearly invalidate it, then, is not the possibility of misperception, conflicting beliefs or even error, but the absence of any common standards for comprehending or evaluating human actions. The world of international relations often seems menacing and out of control but it is not as incomprehensible as all that.

Despite its current unpopularity, a strong case could be made for reviving the traditional debate about international society. Certainly both contending positions have their modern echoes. There is an obvious, if unrecognised, link between natural law and the widespread demands for a just world-order, where justice is made to sound as empirical or utilitarian as possible, but turns out on inspection to rest on some fairly metaphysical conceptions of human rights. And on the other side, the enormous expansion of treaty and administrative law bears witness to the continued vitality of the international society of the legal positivists. But it is not with a revival of this debate that I am primarily concerned. Rather, it is my contention that, whatever the situation may have been in the past, we now *know* that we live within a single worldwide society and that discussion of relations within this society must start with the attempt to describe and understand its nature.

Such an attempt requires both an historical and a sociological perspective. The description of international society, no less than of any social group, involves, that is, a double focus. We need to look at the external boundaries of the society, the demarcation lines which separate those within from the excluded outsiders; and we need to look also at its internal 'constitution', those formal and informal arrangements which determine what Maurice Keens-Soper rightly called in beginning this book its 'identity'. The central part of the argument in this chapter is concerned accordingly with these two aspects of the matter.

But, right at the outset, there is a formidable problem. How are we to view what we describe? The boundaries of states, no less than their constitutional arrangements, are not given by nature but represent human and therefore moral choices. Consequently, any attempt at description raises issues which bear directly on the place – and status – of ethical considerations in political and social theory. I shall reserve these issues as such until the end, but since my entire argument reflects the view that the moral basis of international society is built into its historical development and contemporary structure, it is clear that I am claiming a cognitive basis for morality which runs counter to the conventional divorce between positive and *n*ormative in Western thought. It is to the justification of this claim, therefore, that I wish to turn first.

I

The observation that presuppositions, including moral pre-suppositions, colour our view of the world, is common enough. But in the attempt to approximate the human to the physical sciences, the hope has generally been that these contaminating presuppositions could be either eliminated or at least neutralised by stating them unambiguously at the outset, bringing them out into the open and thus separating them off from the subsequent 'objective' analysis.

In this genuinely laudable ambition, the possibility that the knowledge we can have of the human world differs in kind from our knowledge of the physical world, is largely ignored. In saying this, I am not making the old defence against a charge once levelled by the behaviouralists against other writers on international relations that their work lacked 'rigour' and therefore 'scientific' value. It is not the process of knowing which is different when one is confronted by human as opposed to natural phenomena. To know is, after all, to know. In both cases, the object is to explain the world by establishing, so far as is possible, what is true. The distinction lies not in the different nature of the explanations we seek – the point that generally emerges from arguments about method – but in *what we cannot help knowing* in the case of human affairs. Here we are doubly endowed (or constrained, depending on one's point of view): first, we cannot but assume that we are dealing with beings in some fundamental sense like ourselves; second, the fact that we are helping to make our own history even while we study it and that the laws, institutions and conflicts that we study also bear the imprint of human design, inescapably creates a different relationship between observer and observed in the one case and in the other.

What I am suggesting here is also fairly familiar. This is simply that one cannot divorce an explanation of human relations, in this case international relations, from their history. A history, however many behaviour patterns it may embrace, remains a sequence of events, a story which we ourselves tell and of which we do not know the end in advance; and this enterprise imposes on us a moral viewpoint in the going, rather than as an optional extra before or after the event.

I can best illustrate this by discussing a specific issue. The one which I wish to consider, first, by analogy as it arises in human affairs generally, and then, in connection with the development of international society, is the question of intervention across frontiers.

Few images are so compelling as the 'frontier', at once a challenge, a problem and a point of reference. A 'frontier' guards the known from the unknown, protects those within and supports their identity and beckons the impatient, the curious or the hungry to whatever may lie in the empty space beyond. A 'frontier' is first and foremost an intellectual category, a region of the mind, rather than a territorial or political fact, whose demarcation can be exactly, let alone timelessly, charted. In international relations its significance is obvious (indeed definitional) but the idea exercises almost as strong a hold on the way we think about other areas of human activity, for example, about science. When we talk of scientific discovery and of scientists extending the frontiers of human knowledge, the idiom is at once prescriptive and expansionist.

This parallel is not idly drawn; the common imagery in fact suggests a set of common concerns. It is a convention, no more, that divides mental from physical activity and which regards the one as self-evident, the other as requiring both explanation and justification. If one assumes that human beings have in the first place a propensity for action, and that thought is one kind of action just as the movement of armies is another, then a rather different set of questions emerges to those we are normally accustomed to ask. In particular, it becomes more relevant now to ask negative questions – to inquire of knowledge as of other kinds of action about the constraints rather than the stimuli, to ask, in other words, why states do *not* more frequently intervene in each other's affairs or why wars are *not* fought more often than they are? And so on. The frontier suggests one kind of answer to such questions. Soldier and scholar may occupy different territory, but they both take up and defend positions along their respective frontiers. They both also stand ready to press the attack when the opportunity offers. That is how both discoveries and conquests are accomplished.

Nevertheless, in one critically important way social and political frontiers differ from those to be found in other areas of human activity such as the natural sciences. They divide not the present from the past, true knowledge from false, the classical from the romantic, and so on, but people from each other. In science, imperialism or at least expansionism is essential to the enterprise; there are no ethical problems to be faced in crossing the frontier – indeed, what other justification for the life of a scientist could there be? On the other hand, expansion notoriously is a problem in politics. Here our epistemological and moral imperatives do not obviously run together. The point is not that political frontiers are in some way natural and inviolate and hard, whereas cognitive frontiers are always temporary and problematic and soft. In principle, as in practice, there are no permanently inviolate frontiers; an attack in any area is likely to be met by resistance, and the degree of hardness or softness can in the end only be measured by its success or failure. The point is that an attack on a political frontier raises inescapably a separate moral question. By what *right* is intervention across a political frontier carried out?

II

When we turn to the historical description of international society, it is clear that this difference between cognitive and political frontiers has not always and everywhere been recognised. Europeans, notably, acknowledged the problem of intervention at home, as in their Westphalia settlement of 1648, but denied it in the world beyond Europe. Historically, it was always possible for them to defend the double standard by invoking what one might call 'the barbarian option': the rule which applied in relations between 'civilised' peoples did not automatically apply beyond the civilised world. The procedures and institutions which were finally codified to deal with the consequences of Europe's political fragmentation, did not, in the first instance, apply to Islam, because the Westphalia settlement was among Christian princes or at least among statesmen whose moral vocabulary had evolved from the experience of mediaeval Christendom. Not, of course, that knowledge of barbarian peoples always led to demands for annexation; in the history of the European states-system, its first consequence was a preoccupation with defence.

But it is easy to see how a set of principles which apply within territorially defined limits, among those who in some sense have agreed to be bound by them, may fall away in dealings with those with whom no such compact has been made. The regular contacts with alien peoples, with Orientals, American Indians, and Africans, that followed the European voyages of discovery, raised the question of the moral basis of uninvited intervention in the affairs of these peoples, if not always of outright annexation. In this context 'the barbarian option' operated in reverse. It was no longer a question of defending civilisation but of extending the frontiers of the 'known world' and bringing the benefits of enlightenment to peoples whose condition could be regarded as a function of their ignorance. It was as though men had been forced to acknowledge that the exercise of power within international society raised moral problems which arose precisely because those involved (that is, the states) were cognitively equal, in possession of the same intellectual equipment for interpreting the world. The legal doctrines and diplomatic conventions (sovereignty, non-interference, recognition, and so on) which were developed in the European states-system were thus not an attempt to provide a solution to a moral problem, but a way of acknowledging its existence. Beyond the frontier, especially where resistance was weak, this problem did not arise. In this *terra incognita* there was no pressure to prevent political and epistemological expansionism marching together.

Of course, as an account of Western expansion, this will not quite do. The attempt to codify and articulate the rules and conventions governing the relations of European states may have required the recognition of a moral problem attendant on the exercise of political power, but it was also the outcome of experience, in particular the experience of prolonged fratricidal conflict between rival powers. It would have needed an extraordinary (and even by European standards unjustified) self-confidence to assume that their forays into the wider world need pay no attention to the prudential considerations which applied in relations among themselves. So it is not surprising that the double standard did not immediately or always assert itself. At the beginning of the nineteenth century, for example, formal relations between European and African 'states' were still conducted on the basis of theoretical equality on the grounds that whatever paramount political authority existed in the non-Western world constituted a 'sovereign state'.[3]

Perhaps contact bred contempt. In Vattel's writings the barbarian option is already foreshadowed by his extension of the legal right of annexation of *territoria nullius*, limited at first to unpopulated regions, to include predatory peoples, hunting and gathering tribes and nomadic herdsmen who were a danger to their neighbours or pursued an 'idle mode of life' and occupied 'more land than they would need under an honest system of labour'.[4] In any event, it was the argument that the European powers were the purveyors of enlightenment, of true knowledge, that eventually prevailed in Africa as it had in America three hundred years previously. The scramble for Africa was the last occasion when this particular option could be exercised. There is, so far as I know, little evidence to suggest that by the time of the Congress of Berlin the powers were constrained by any feelings of legal, let alone moral inconsistency. Indeed, on this score the argument must surely have been on the side of intervention. In many cases, treaties of a sort had been concluded. And while on the coast of West Africa the power of the state had been invoked to substitute legitimate trade for slave-trading by unscrupulous Europeans, in East and Central Africa moral consistency could be held to require that the policy be directed against a similar trade carried on under the auspices of Islam, whose moral and territorial encroachments had been resisted for so long in Europe itself.

But if intervention could be justified, an argument which rested on the unity of moral and cognitive considerations offered an obvious hostage to fortune. What was to happen later on when it would no longer be a case of true knowledge confronting ignorance but of a shared enlightenment? Would it then be necessary to concede the legitimacy of resistance to imperial rule and to extend the principles of the Westphalia settlement beyond the limits of the European states-system? In a sense, of course, this was more or less what happened at the time of decolonisation. But (and this is perhaps even more interesting) the answer was implicitly provided by at least some of the imperial powers long before they were confronted with demands for independence or self-determination. There was an important difference between the conquests of

America and Africa: the nature of the light had changed. The mandate of the *conquistadores* was conceived within the unitary scheme of Christendom; whereas the conquest of Africa – notwithstanding the missionaries – had finally to be justified in terms of European state theory.

Faced with apparently stateless societies, whose cohesion often seemed to rest on a jumble of unsavoury customs, the European conquerors had no alternative to direct rule. But sometimes, as in Buganda or among the emirates of northern Nigeria, the social and political world was more recognisable. Once one had got used to the fancy dress, the kabaka and his court were not so different from the group of Victorian gentlemen who ruled at home, and in northern Nigeria the emirs, with their elaborate horse culture, took to polo, 'as to the manner born'. Their conquerors, like most of us in our daily lives, were no doubt naïve empiricists, looking simply at 'facts'. But had they been pressed, they would have had to concede that they were viewing the world and judging it in terms of European state theory. Thus, was a shadow from Western thinking about the state cast over the spectacular progress of imperial expansion. For the outcome was the theory and practice of indirect rule, the recognition throughout most of British Africa of traditional authority, and sometimes, as in Buganda, the preservation of a political community with special privileges within the colonial superstructure, a state, as it were, within a colony. When African nationalists were demanding independence they accused the imperial powers of using traditional authority to divide and rule. However accurate this diagnosis, it overlooks the way in which the theory of indirect rule constituted a first and fatal weakening in the intellectual defences of imperial power.

Weakened by indirect rule, the frontier of international society was finally closed by decolonisation. If, in the future, the barbarian option were to be revived it would no longer be able to rely on any distinction based on appearances. For, formally, 'out there', there are no more barbarians; both the right to independence and the right of all independent states to participate in international society have been universally accepted. And if it is protested that this point about the formal acceptance of international society ignores the more basic fact of cultural diversity, one may legitimately point to the way in which the significance of culture itself has changed in Western thought. It is no longer respectable to make points about 'lesser breeds without the law'; the belief that cultural diversity is an inescapable fact and is indeed desirable is now firmly embedded in our contemporary world-view. Hence, for example, if the great powers were to protect their access to Middle East oil by military intervention, they would hardly be able to justify their action on the grounds that their enemies were not fully paid-up members of international society, or by the absence of any recognisable pattern of social or political order. Two checks would immediately operate against such a defence. They would be acting against a duly constituted and internationally recognised group of states; and they could not defend their action on the ground that the culture in these states was different, beyond the pale – barbarous.

III

But what of the inside? How have the inner workings of the traditional society survived the incorporation of so many new members? Any attempt to answer such questions involves an encounter with certain relativist arguments which seek either to repudiate the legacies of Western expansion or to defend the inner core of Western values from internal subversion or corruption by contact with the new membership. Adda Bozeman, for example, comes close to advocating a redoubt theory whose aim is to restore the intellectual and moral coherence of the 'West' by leaving other parts of the world to their different, although no doubt equally authentic, arrangements.[5]

The European states-system was the product of European civilisation. The present situation, on the other hand, has been created by the collapse of European imperial power and the absence, on a worldwide basis, of any body of shared historical experience. On this ground the relativist retreats from the idea of a global international society. His attack on the universalist pretensions of the contemporary order is advanced on two levels. First, he questions the credibility of the Grotian idea of a society of states with the argument that the state itself is a European invention without firm historical roots in other parts of the world. Second, he questions the credibility of common standards, let alone ultimate values, and therefore the possibility of fully human relations such as are possible between members of a genuine community.

But on neither level can the attack be sustained. Consider, first, the state itself. Whether or not it lacks indigenous historical roots in some parts of the non-European world, it has been successfully exported everywhere. And this success is now firmly rooted. It stems from the universal and enthusiastic acceptance of the Western theory of sovereignty. This theory has always been sufficiently elastic to accommodate a wide variety of régimes since, in the last analysis, only *de facto* control is regarded as proof of legitimate authority. No wonder that in the wake of Western imperial withdrawal the doctrine was embraced with such enthusiasm by leaders who were often short on legitimacy in their own societies and felt themselves threatened by external forces whose command over resources was generally greater than their own.

Legitimacy is, indeed, the crux. For, in the end, what did the European theory of the state amount to but the assertion of an authority, supreme by virtue of its power, uncluttered by any mythological explanations of its mandate and beyond which there could be no appeal. Because it extracted from European history an abstract theory of authority, state theory was necessarily scornful of 'culture', and so, for the same reason, capable of universal application. The theory seems ideally suited for export. In any event, its success in non-European markets has been overwhelming.

In the past, it is true, there were rivals to this doctrine. Moreover some of these less absolutist systems of political authority, such as the ambiguous status of Tibet *vis-à-vis* imperial China or the traditionally acknowledged *de jure* suzerainty of the rulers of Morocco over Mauritania, have left a cultural and political imprint on the countries concerned. But while the past has complicated the attempt to recast the present, it is the theory of state sovereignty which has prevailed, not the more subtle but culturally exclusive systems which distinguished between types of international political authority, and which presupposed not a simple division of the world into separate states, but a series of inner and outer boundaries, some political, some religious and some no doubt narrowly social and cultural. Despite the inclusion of Tibet in the buffer system by which the Raj secured the northern frontiers of British India, Britain never formally disputed the Chinese claim to suzerainty, and in the event neither Britain nor India was prepared to back the Tibetan case for recognition as an independent state by the United Nations. Such independence as Tibet had sometimes enjoyed had depended not on legal recognition by other states, but on the weakness of imperial China. The re-emergence of a strong government in Peking was followed by the reabsorption of Tibet. However troublesome to liberal consciences, this was not inconsistent with the theory of state sovereignty, since the distinction between suzerainty and sovereignty had not been carried over into the contemporary international system.

Unlike China, Morocco did not possess the power to enforce its claim by force of arms. But the king was, in any case, forced to abandon it by the strength of African diplomatic opinion in favour of the doctrine of state sovereignty. Although Morocco was one of the few African states with a usable pre-colonial past, for the majority it was imperative to recognise the statehood of Mauritania.

If Mauritania was not a sovereign state, then on what basis did their own claims to sovereignty rest? Against this compelling argument no appeal to Islamic political tradition could prevail. Culture was at a discount, the principle of the state paramount.

The institutionalised diplomacy of the European states-system has proved equally adaptable. No doubt the modern diplomatic system developed within a specific cultural tradition which was shared by the princes of Christendom. But the idea of representative privilege, which grew out of the conventions concerning the treatment of heralds and those charged with plenipotentiary powers, was entailed by the doctrine of sovereignty, not the culture of Christian Europe. The reason is simple. Long before the Westphalia settlement, the common Christian culture was fragmented into particular and often hostile cultures. The state preceded the full development of state theory. Diplomatic privilege was necessary to protect, on the basis of reciprocity, the symbolic representation of sovereign power. And what distinguished a sovereign prince was not what he shared with his subjects, his cultural or national identity, but what he had in common with other princes. Substitute state for prince and the argument holds.

Once the scale of international transaction had reached a point requiring a permanent diplomatic establishment, it also seems 'natural' that a transnational profession of diplomats should have developed. The common conventions of this profession in part serve the function which language performs in national cultures: they act as vehicles for communication, hold and transmit the values of the profession and provide an effective barrier between those within the charmed circle and the uninitiated outside.

Diplomats, like the sovereigns they represent, have access to a concrete international society, which to some extent protects them from the pressures and mutual incomprehension which might otherwise arise from cultural diversity. Within this society, the primary values of the modern international system, independence and the sovereign equality of states, are formally upheld by the fact that all diplomats have equal rights and privileges, while in so far as the diplomatic corps is required to act corporately and may therefore require a titular head, this position is filled not by the representative of the most powerful state, but by the ambassador who has been *en poste* the longest, a point to which new states as well as old appear to attach considerable importance.

The relativist's second challenge to contemporary international society doubts the existence of general standards. (I postpone the question of ultimate values.) To meet this, it is necessary to move back from the conception of a legally constituted society, whose members are states, to consideration of the social and political ideas which move freely across state frontiers. Such a perspective is provided, I believe, by what may be called without undue exaggeration, the imperative of modernisation. Unfortunately this notion has become so discredited by liberal optimism about the end of ideology that it is necessary to guard against misunderstanding. I am not offering a watered-down liberal determinism in which economic laws will lead necessarily to a world of like-minded states capable of living in harmony by virtue of their commitment to rationalism. What I do wish to suggest is that, whatever the eventual outcome, a modernising mythology is now very widely diffused across the globe. This new world view involves a set of shared positions and aspirations, which regulate or at least support participation in international society. They include a rather specialised notion of national self-determination as the basis of legitimate authority; a secular and materialist approach to social and economic affairs; a belief in and a desire for technological advance, and an ethical position which is, notionally at any rate, egalitarian.[6]

There is much evidence to suggest that this myth of the modern industrial state transcends even quite deep ideological differences about the route to be taken to the earthly paradise, as it does the cultural and other barriers between the industrial or 'developing' states. To this latter group, indeed, modernisation is a vital support. It is difficult to think of any Third World régime which does not at least buttress its claim to legitimate authority with an official commitment to economic development and industrialisation. And in many cases it appears to be the sole basis of their legitimacy.

There are four components of this world-view which together constitute the shared experience of all modern states and thus create the possibility of society among them. First, modernisation is everywhere a necessary, if not a sufficient, justification for the exercise of political power. Even where traditional authority survives, as for example in Iran, it does so by monopolising the modernising role and commanding the loyalty of those who possess the new (scientific and technological) knowledge. Diplomatically, such attempts to direct change from above are not problematic because, despite the egalitarianism of much contemporary ideology, it is still the equality of states that counts in international relations. But whether change comes from above or below, whether it is substantive or merely part of the political rhetoric of the new élite, it is the old, culturally exclusive order that is under attack, the objectives and values of modern secularism that are upheld. No doubt cultural legacies continue to muddy the waters, but the general outline seems clear.

Second, nationalist ideology has been variously described as an exotic and pernicious European export to the rest of the world, and as a quasi-objective phenomenon, which arises at a given point in the great transition from traditional to industrial society.[7] Either way, nationalist ideology is destructive of traditional forms and beliefs, even when it takes on the protective colouring of some secondary aspects of traditional culture. In any event, Asian and African nationalism has not produced many specifically non-Western ideas about international politics. Possibly non-alignment makes marginally more sense when interpreted in the light of Indian traditional philosophy, but it is equally accessible, like the rest of Nehru's policies, to anyone familiar with the basic ideas of Fabian socialism.

It is probably true to say that most of the ideas on which the foreign policies of the non-Western states are based have little independent life in the societies on whose behalf they are advanced. To this extent Adda Bozeman's scepticism about the contemporary international order may be justified. But again one may question how widely they are understood in our own societies. It is hardly in dispute that there are everywhere discontinuities between popular sentiments in favour of industrial society, or at least its material benefits, and the technical arguments employed by those charged with the execution of public policy. On the other hand, such arguments are common currency in the concrete international society of diplomats and experts which embraces Western and pre-industrial societies alike. Some opposition movements in the Third World – the Indian Jan Sangh is one example – have based their appeal on a rejection of Western values and a reassertion of the indigenous or the authentic. But such movements seldom generate any substantial ideas about the external world (they preach isolation or expansion according to circumstances) for the simple reason that to operate in the international arena at all, it is necessary to use the universalised language of Western diplomacy.

Third, in relations between 'developing' countries themselves, there is no departure from the general diplomatic standards which form part of the modernising mythology. For example, in the Charter of the Organisation of African Unity, the principle of non-interference is prominently enshrined, and forms the basis of what little co-operation is achieved. In the Nigerian civil war arguments were advanced, allegedly deriving from African traditional philosophy, in favour of mediation in disputes between brothers. But the majority of African governments did not in fact intervene, and the federal government successfully defended its policies in the name of the same principles and with the same arguments that had been employed by the Union in the American Civil War a century before.

Within the general commitment to modernisation, almost any kind of régime is eligible for membership of international society. If it is illegitimate to interfere in domestic affairs, it is certainly illegitimate to question the basis of the state itself. Nowhere is the principle of self-determination regarded as open for debate (in the way that at least in some societies the idea of the national interest might be accepted as open). On the contrary, it is accepted as a once and for all episode, of central importance to the founding and legitimacy of a new nation-state, but irreversibly tied in space and time to the withdrawal of European imperial power. All attempts to use the OAU to censure African régimes, other than those in the 'white' south, have failed. This general acceptance of the *status quo* differs in only one respect from the mainstream tradition of Western thought.

The difference is the absence of a countervailing tradition, either indigenous or imported, concerning the justification of intervention under special circumstances.[8] Historically, the absence of such a tradition is not surprising. For many African and Asian statesmen, their only previous experience of the international society in which they now find themselves acting independently, was as disenfranchised subjects of the European powers. Their careers were devoted to reversing European intervention in practice and repudiating it in principle. But conceptually, the absence of this tradition does indicate a tendency to treat second-rank principles as if they had first-rank status, to confuse, in other words, prudential arguments with arguments about cause and value. I shall return to this confusion shortly, but it is important here to emphasise that it is not confined to Third World states but constitutes a general problem in contemporary political debate.

Finally, the 'modern' world-view contains its own reformist 'tradition'. The positive claims that are advanced by Third World states on the international community have nothing at all to do with inaccessible cultural traditions of thought or alternative non-Western conceptions of justice. Revisionism abounds but it is not revisionism in the name of cultural synthesis. It comes in two versions. The first attempts to derive an ethic of redistributive justice from the institutions of the Western international economy; the second maintains, more uncompromisingly, that the capitalist West has maintained, by its very nature, a structure of imperial exploitation despite the formal transfer of power. In practice, in most Third World pronouncements, these views, the one liberal and normative, the other radical and structuralist, are conflated in a populist version.[9] The merits of these arguments do not concern me here. What is important is their ancestry. Wherever demands are pressed for positive change in the international environment, both the direction in which it is proposed to move, and the arguments which are used to justify change, are chosen by reference to universalised Western models.

The argument may now be summarised. It is that a worldwide international society exists: first, by virtue of a powerful negative, namely, the absence of outsiders; second, by virtue of the successful export to the non-Western world of both state theory and the formal structure of the states-system; and third, as a consequence of a widely diffused modernising mythology, which in practice links the institutions of the formal order with the aspirations and justifications of men in society, or at least of their leaders, and provides at least a surrogate culture within which it is possible to communicate across boundaries.

In this sense, boundaries in international society, as in less elevated social groups, unite as much as they divide. Those on both sides are capable of mutual understanding and reciprocity. I argued earlier that the perpetual crossing and recrossing of international frontiers – and this applies to all international transactions, not just to the limiting case of armed intervention – raises unavoidably a question of right. Within the world of international diplomacy, in other words, there is no *a priori* reason to suppose that moral arguments are any less universally accessible than technical arguments about, say, commodity pricing or expropriation.

IV

Such are the negative and positive supports for the idea of an international society as a necessary baseline for international theory. But while the description of some of our contemporary arrangements, or rather of some part of their inner logic is complete, the argument cannot be left there. I have suggested that contemporary international society is sufficiently coherent in terms of a commitment to a generally shared cognitive ethic to allow for an intelligible and cross-cultural debate about 'right' in the matter of intervention. But to say so much is not to say much. The question of 'right' may be logically unavoidable, but in practice states succeed in avoiding it most of the time. Or, to be more accurate, they often raise the question but also answer it in their own interest, without reference to any wider obligations to international society. The frontiers which men choose to defend may be arbitrarily drawn, their defence in terms of a parochial moral imperative may be absurd (and there is no difference in principle here between my right to continue a reign of terror or summary executions or a particular pattern of racial or sexual oppression and 'my country right or wrong'), but men do in fact continue to defend them, absurd or not. In such cases, the principle of non-interference in domestic affairs can easily be read as building a degree of moral blindness into the constitutional arrangements of international society. Pascal, after all, was not complaining about the different moral schema of Islam and Christianity (which were never themselves mutually incomprehensible) but of the much nastier relativism which begins nearer home.

In taking the argument about 'right' across the frontiers of states, the difficulties are largely practical. To the extent that particular boundaries support the identity of the insiders, arguments which question the legitimacy of this identity are bound to be met with continuing resistance. In what is a practical and in the end psychological problem, the best that can be attempted here is a clarification of some of the issues. If positions based merely on a particular way of life cannot claim any special privilege or immunity from criticism, and if at the same time we must acknowledge the impossibility of escaping from our diverse cultural inheritance (where, after all, could we escape to?) it becomes extremely important to distinguish between malignant and benign forms of relativism.

It is possible, I suggest, to distinguish between three areas in which moral questions arise. There is, first, the area where variety can safely be accepted as the spice of life; second, areas in which the question of 'right' is genuinely ambiguous and where the precepts and conventions of the states-system may provide a framework for bringing it under control, or at least for discussing it intelligibly; and finally, that dark region, the area of ultimate values, which may in the end, have the most decisive influence on human society but which lies beyond the reach of the states-system and possibly of any system of authority. These three areas can be roughly separated but are in no way radically discontinuous with one another. Indeed little sense can be made of any of them unless the implications of each for the other are kept firmly in mind.

The region in which diversity raises no substantial moral problem can be fairly easily sketched, although its frontiers remain hazy. It would be as absurd to intervene in the affairs of another country merely because in outward appearances its social customs seemed odd to us, as it would have been to persist in the demand that Birmingham's Sikh bus drivers be required to abandon the turban in favour of a corporation cap. Indeed, it would be more absurd: at least in the latter case the issue could be represented in terms of the conflict of loyalties implied in wearing the wrong uniform, while in the former intervention would amount to the denial of the right of the other state to sport a uniform at all. It is true that the 'rationalising' procedures of modern society have everywhere played havoc with the traditional cultural props of our identity, all those devices from harvest festivals to national costumes, which, we are constantly reminded, gave life 'meaning' in the past. But we all hang on to some cultural furniture, we are all in some measure beachcombers among the wreckage. No one could seriously argue today that nakedness is a sign of sin and a just cause of intervention. In this sense, then, cultural diversity is not currently an international problem.

Cultural diversity could pose, however, two kinds of problem which it is important to distinguish if we are to understand contemporary international society or to see what is and is not possible within it. The first would be where a particular social custom was both (let us suppose) proscribed by some future and expanded version of the Convention on Human Rights and so deeply embedded in a culture that the identity of those involved would be compromised by its abandonment. A notorious example of a custom rooted in this way is female circumcision, which has implications for the perceived integrity of persons of both sexes. A second sort of problem would arise if one state attacked another in the name of God or Allah or any other principle which claimed privilege but at the same time had no general currency among the community of states.

Both kinds of problem would arise from granting cultural practices an absolute status, seemingly at odds with the wider cognitive ethic which has been generally endorsed in the name of modernisation.[10] But their implications for international relations would be different. The former (the female circumcision type) raises questions, which can finally be resolved only by a change in the nature of human consciousness and hence identity. The latter (the Crusade or *jihad* type) bears directly upon, in that it blatantly repudiates, the compact of convention and procedure which represents the only available framework for discussing the question of 'right' in international affairs. It is no doubt because this is in fact recognised that such old-time justifications of war, while still sometimes threatened (United Arab Republic, 1967; Morocco, 1975) are seldom used.

The distinction lies, in other words, between issues which can be discussed within the compact and those which must be handled outside it. Now that it is no longer a merely European arrangement, the compact would need to be defended – if necessary by force – against any revival of the holy war, just as it had ultimately to be defended against the challenge mounted by the Third Reich. In the past force has also been used to suppress cultural practices which seemed to those in power peculiarly inhuman or obnoxious.

(Female circumcision was never effectively suppressed by the European imperial powers, but suttee was.) However, now that there are no 'barbarians', a problem such as female circumcision which obviously raises deeper issues than can be handled by diplomacy, can certainly not be solved by force. On the other hand, unlike *jihad*, such problems need not threaten the compact provided its implicit rules and limitations are understood and observed.

These can best be illustrated by referring back to the original model – the Peace of Westphalia. The Westphalia settlement was the final acknowledgment in European politics of a failure, not the solution of a problem. In it the princes accepted that ultimate values (in their day, religion) should not be a *casus belli*. That this was what they acknowledged is clear in as much as within their own societies they were in no position to say that religion was unimportant, while, as we have seen, their new commitment to restraint did not apply to infidels or 'barbarians' whose ultimate values were condemned by them all.

The settlement had two momentous implications, one recognised at the time and repeatedly since, the other still working itself out today. Necessity was recognised as a legitimate reason for restraint, for the avoidance of war over ultimate values. On the other hand, the princes retained the right to go to war among themselves over secondary questions, that is, in support of another kind of necessity, reasons of state. And yet, if ultimate questions, by definition the most important, could not be settled by war, how could it be possible to sanction war at all?

The seventeenth-century answer to this question was to make war itself a part of the compact, an answer which allowed the development and codification of the laws of war. This entailed the adoption of a morality of consequences, and indeed, in a compact of the kind agreed at the Congress of Westphalia, the only kind of morality which makes any sense at all is a morality of consequences. But so far as war is concerned, this answer is no longer fully credible. To fight a war nowadays, the belligerents must satisfy two conflicting demands: on the one hand, fear of the probable consequence of unlimited warfare demands that they do not upset the central nuclear balance, that they fight for limited political ends, in other words that they stick strictly to the consequentialist spirit of the Westphalia settlement; on the other hand, experience of the human and moral costs of modern warfare has led to the demand that they fight only in self-defence, that they be sincere and above all not be guilty of aggression. No matter that these concepts are all ambiguous; no other justification for fighting is any longer available. Nowadays, it seems, states must only fight over fundamental questions, which they cannot safely do for the very reasons that were recognised in the Peace of Westphalia. Ultimate values, whether located outside the system or, as now, 'in the world', cannot be regarded as negotiable.

The contemporary consequence of these implications is both paradoxical and confusing. It is that survival increasingly depends on the acknowledgment by states of the compact and its rules, while at the same time there is no longer any moral justification for the use of force *within* the compact. Faced with this confusion, states have tended to react, as noted earlier, by elevating the principles and procedures of the international system, especially the principle of non-interference, into something more than conventional obligations. The result of this tendency is disastrous for the states-system. Quite apart from the fact that words cease to bear any close relation to deeds, non-intervention cannot be taken seriously as an *absolute* principle once it is accepted that frontiers, on the ground as well as in the mind, are in the end arbitrary. But if intervention by force can no longer be properly regarded as part of the compact, there are many areas of international life where consequentialist principles of the kind embodied in the Westphalia agreement still apply. Such principles first lead to a baseline agreement and then permit derogations as a result of further debate about consequences. To take an example from the recent past, the idea of non-discrimination in international trade, which forms the basis of the General Agreement on Tariffs and Trade, was important because it established a baseline of agreement rather than for its connection with the progressivist programme which aimed at recreating the worldly paradise of free trade.

It should not be imagined that this account of the implicit meaning of the Westphalia settlement ignores history or disregards some historical time-bomb, whose explosion may one day shatter the whole edifice. The argument offered here does not deny the importance of history, but suggests that the framework of ideas relating to international society has survived because it is procedural. The European states system bequeathed to the world a compact based on the articulation of a need: the necessity of accepting, as it were under duress, renunciation of armed conflict about absolute values. This principle has survived, not the particular rendering of necessity or the particular view of the Absolute on which the compact was based. If the idea of moral progress is to be defended, if a case is to be made for holding that men are now capable of creating an international community in which ultimate values are derived neither from mere social tradition nor from an external Absolute, then no doubt it can only be done by showing that human consciousness itself has a history. In this chapter, I have argued that the myth of the modern industrial state (and it is the common frame of reference, the idea, not the material base which is important) provides the necessary prerequisite for such an enterprise. I have also acknowledged the continuing relevance of one outcome of the Thirty Years War, that a community of mankind cannot be accomplished by the sword. But it does not seem to me to follow that it cannot be accomplished at all, or that progress in this direction requires that rulers should be able to claim immunity from criticism under a spuriously absolute principle of non-intervention. Whether the idea of a community of mankind can be envisaged, however, is a question I leave for discussion in the chapters that follow.

NOTES FOR CHAPTER 7

1   This debate is discussed by Martin Wight in *Systems of States*, ed. H. Bull (Leicester, The University Press, 1977), ch. 4.
2   Pascal, *Pensées*, vol. III (292), trans., A. J. Krailsheimer (Harmondsworth, Penguin Books). p. 46.
3   P. D. Curtin, *The Image of Africa* (Madison, Wisc., The University of Wisconsin Press, 1964), p. 279.
4   ibid., p. 280. The quotation is from Vattel's *Le Droit des Gens*, bk I, ch. VII.
5   Adda Bozeman, *The Future of Law in a Multicultural World* (Princeton, N.J., The University Press, 1971), pp. 161–86.
6   cf. Ernest Gellner, 'Our Current Sense of History', in *Contemporary Thought and Politics* (London, Routledge & Kegan Paul, 1974), pp. 113–33.
7   For these two views, see Elie Kedourie, *Nationalism in Asia and Africa* (New York, The World Publishing Co., 1970), pp. 1–153, and Ernest Gellner, *Thought and Change* (London, Weidenfeld & Nicolson, 1964), pp. 147–78.
8   The nearest to a sustained African defence of intervention is contained in *Tanzania's Memorandum on Biafra's Case*, a document which President Nyerere circulated privately to his fellow Heads of State at the 1969 OAU Summit Conference. It failed to win further adherents to the Biafran cause, but made sufficient impact to persuade the Nigerian Federal Government to make an official refutation. For both documents, see A. H. M. Kirk-Greene, ed., *Crisis and Conflict in Nigeria*, vol. 2 (London, OUP, 1971), pp. 429–38.
9   President Nyerere's speech to the African trade ministers involved in the negotiation of the Lomé Convention with the EEC is a good example of the *genre*. He suggested that their efforts 'should be directed towards obtaining that which rightfully belongs to us, remunerative trading arrangements in a dynamic context, through a scientifically worked out built-in mechanism, within the framework of international trade and exchange, and full reparations for past neglect imposed upon us by colonialism'. (Quoted in *West Africa*, 15 October 1973).
10 On the ironic nature of contemporary nationalism, see Ernest Gellner, *Legitimation of Belief* (London, CUP, 1974), esp. ch. 9.

8

Justice in International Relations

CHRISTOPHER BREWIN

'Every statesman must attempt to reconcile what is considered
just with what is considered possible. What is considered just
depends on the domestic structure of his state; what is possible
depends on its resources, geographic position and determination,
and on the resources, determination and domestic structure of
other states.' (Henry Kissinger, *A World Restored*[1])

Probably most scholars of international relations would endorse
this quotation from Dr Kissinger as clear, firm and accurate. It
gives prominence to the concept of justice in world affairs, and it
must be admitted as an empirical fact that the sentiment that right is
on one's side is immeasurably important in international conflicts.
British resistance in 1940, the Arab-Israeli wars, any other conflict
one names, alike testify to this fact. At the same time, the heart of the
quotation is that the sense of justice of states depends on their
domestic structures. There is no agreed standard of justice
worldwide.

If there is nothing more to be said than this, if 'justice' is merely a
powerful expression of 'sacred egoism', then it is philosophically
uninteresting. The absence of much theoretical discussion of it in
our books and journals of international relations is to be applauded
rather than regretted. For the maxim that others should co-operate
in advancing the egoist's view of his good cannot be universalised.
Dr Kissinger may not imply in this quotation that there is nothing
more to be said, but without doubt there are many who reject or at
least take little interest in the long tradition – classical, mediaeval
and modern – which declares the possibility or even the actuality of
certain common conceptions of justice and law.[2]

This rejection is an understandable consequence of historical developments which seem to have done more to undermine than to strengthen any material basis for a common standard of justice. Reverting to the arguments of the last chapter, many will still wish to insist that the enormous cultural diversity of the nations in the modern world makes the idea of a common myth of modernisation uniting them feeble in comparison. Again, the universalisation of the concept of the sovereign state has been accompanied by common concepts of diplomacy, law and the like as developed in the West; but these still seem weak restraints on the egoism of the states. Politically, the ideologies and ideological conflicts that have developed in pushing through rapid social and economic change have resulted in deep divisions only precariously restrained by the common fear of involvement in a general war. Militarily, the rapidity and distance associated with modern weaponry have reduced the sentiment of pity as the psychological basis of justice, and blurred the old distinctions between combatant and non-combatant or between peace and war.

So far, then, the history of this century offers on the face of it no alternative to the view that such order as exists is determined by force or force of circumstances. Whether one thinks of the political division of Europe between East and West, or the world economic division between North and South, both have been determined by force and could not possibly have been willed as just by the parties concerned.

Yet one is also uneasily aware that, in both these cases, demands for 'justice' and for a deliberate change in the present order are not merely constantly voiced but seem to have some small common element among the states concerned, even if it is only the common intelligibility of what is being urged. Moreover, to the small extent that order between nations depends on a worldwide structure of political and economic co-operation, just dealing is conceded to be the most efficacious foundation of the liberty of each state and the well-being of all.

I am struck by an analogy with Greek history. As with Greek heroes, the virtue of states traditionally lies in their ability to defend their territories and citizens by the fear in which they and their allies are held. But so soon as the Greeks lived in the co-operative framework of the *polis*, heroic swaggering became intolerable. It was this material transformation that explains why Socrates could perplex the citizens, who read heroic poetry but lived in a *polis*, with the question of what they meant by justice.[3] If we are in an analogous transition from competitive to economically co-operative frameworks, this may help to explain our comparable unease. Of course, we are not living internationally in a *polis*; but there seem to be sufficient small makings of an analogy to justify a discussion of this topic of justice.

I shall look first at the three main kinds of reasoning which are used by contemporaries in justifying international institutions and actions, and then at the claim of contract theory to provide a better foundation for what will remain our hazy judgments.

I

The first kind of reasoning has the merit of greatest clarity. Justice is adherence to established law. Since none of us know what is right, it is the job of the duly authorised politician to declare what is right, as much in foreign policy as domestically. Whatever the state decrees is right, and whatever a number of states decree by treaty, or accept by convention, is right for those states. Proper authority, not reason, is the only basis of international obligation. The ground of any protest must be limited to the objections that a state is breaking a treaty or ignoring an established convention. And protesters must recognise that, like Acts of Parliament in England, the latest decree takes precedence over earlier decrees or precedents. It may well be that this positivism is the realistic condition of order where men are not agreed that there are rationally defensible and commonly acknowledged principles. On the other hand, it removes any ground for objecting, for example, to the actions of an Eichmann where he was following orders.

II

A second favoured approach lays more store by rationality. The good of a state in the world is first defined by reference to its domestic structure, as Dr Kissinger said above. This is called the 'national interest'. This has to be calculated over time. It will be different according to whether it is defined as the sum of conflicting particular interests or whether it is brought forth by some Gaullist incarnation wedded to an undying national princess. The statesman's job – what it is right for him to do – is then to maximise the good of the national interest, by whatever means he thinks will achieve his purpose. What is right is limited pragmatically by the good of the cause – the Right is contingent upon the Good.

To maximise the national interest rationally requires that the statesman correctly calculate the national-interest sums of a hundred and forty countries, or of the most influential and proximate of them, in order further to calculate how they will interact over time so that the policies to be followed will maximise his own country's interests. Using the same utilitarian logic, one could substitute the good of some other cause – International Communism, the Free World Family, Muslim Fraternity – for the national interest. A just action is one that furthers the good of the cause.

Less commonly, the good is defined in universal terms. For example, the good is the advance of mankind in mastering nature. It then becomes justifiable as well as usual for the superpowers to appropriate a disproportionate share of the world's resources. 'Mankind' is enabled thereby to land on the moon, settle on the ocean bed, develop electronics or the like, more speedily than would otherwise be the case. Another conceivable variation would be to postulate a 'world interest', a sum of all human happiness to be maximised.

The main drawback to the utilitarian 'national-interest' approach is not the difficulty of calculation, but rather that it is not unjust to do great harm to others if this will benefit one's own. To take a topical example, it is right for the statesman to appropriate as much food as his nation wants if he can manage it, even if this means that other nations starve. If it is in the national interest that the pressure on food resources by other countries be reduced, then it would be right to permit unnecessary famine, or worse. The trouble with the universal versions, apart from their self-serving or utopian connotations, is that again the least advantaged have no protection if their elimination or reduction would increase the sum of total or average happiness. On such grounds, we feel intuitively that justification by utilitarian methods is inadequate.

III

The third kind of reasoning might be described as 'intuitionist'. States and individuals hold to a number of maxims which they consider to be right, but have no priority rules for deciding which takes precedence where these conflict. The only guide is intuition.

Part of the attraction of this approach in its many guises is that it seems to accord with the diversity of peoples involved, the haziness and contingency of judgments in this field. The weakness is the reverse of the attraction. Commonsense intuitionism, relying upon the more or less specific precepts of everyday morality, is itself highly various and arbitrary when taking into account the variety of national moralities. It is not as bad as sacred egoism, in that it recognises claims which would limit behaviour by applying to a state's actions abroad the maxims which limit it domestically; but there is no basis on which to recognise claims. It is too easy to choose in any particular case the maxim that most favours one's interests.

IV

I shall now try to sketch the argument for justice based on the social contract tradition in so far as I understand it. I shall try to illustrate the difference it would make to current controversies, using the examples of conscientious objection, the European Common Market, international trade, and jurisdiction over the ocean bed, the moon, outer space and the air. The inspiration comes from the work of John Rawls.[4] His subject was justice in domestic society, where strict compliance with the precepts of justice is conceivable. It may well be that the problems posed in applying his concept to relations between states (where the question of dealing with injustice – what Rawls calls the realm of partial compliance theory – more obviously arises) are too great. Other chapters in this book discuss the peculiarities of international society, so I shall content myself with listing at the end what I see as the principal objections to this approach as applied to international relations.

The main idea is that the justice of any social order, of any international institution, of any act of foreign policy, is determined by the extent to which it could have been agreed irrespective of the contingent interests of the parties. It is characteristic of this approach that it tries to set out the rules for deciding claims before describing what each party thinks is in its interests. The Right is prior to the Good. In international society, where the parties can be expected to have very different conceptions of what is good, this method is potentially advantageous.

Traditionally, the way to establish what the rules would be has been to postulate a 'state of nature'. In Rawls's exposition, this is called the 'original position'. The parties are held to know the historical facts about the world as it has developed. But they do not know what their particular place in that world might be – whether rich or poor, populous or not, endowed with a coastline or not, and so forth. The reason for this procedure might be expressed hypothetically as follows. If one is to accept the social order as just, then the rules for institutions and behaviour must be rules to which one could have agreed from the standpoint of any social role in which one might find oneself.

When seventeenth-century theorists used this method, it accorded with the new social phenomenon of 'masterless men' after the breakdown of the all-embracing formal ties of service in what can loosely be called the mediaeval hierarchy. They assumed, in accordance with the then historical reality, that the parties would be men, or heads of households. Today all women and all servants would have an equal claim to be considered parties. In the same way, we can assume that the parties in international relations would be masterless or sovereign states. We need not assume that the parties will always be states as now understood. And, of course, this assumption that the parties are existing states does not help where the issue is about which nation should be sovereign over a particular territory, as in the Arab-Israeli dispute.

Assuming that states are the parties, what political and economic principles would it be reasonable for them to accept, knowing the world as it is, but not their own immediate or future position in it? Politically, the important principle would be that of equal liberty. No state could rationally choose to give up its independence to become a client state or satellite for the sake of possible material or ideological benefits. The only justification for restricting liberty is where this is for the sake of liberty itself. It might be necessary to the long-term preservation of independence to accept alliances that limit one's liberty. Or it might be that to enter close co-operative or federal or new unitary state arrangements best expresses the liberty of those freely participating. Plainly this kind of argument is open to differing interpretations in some cases. But the principle itself provides a universalisable foundation for the familiar insistence of states on sovereignty, and for the fact that it has been in defence of national independence that the sentiment of being in the right has been most efficacious. The principle accords with the precepts of the law of nations and in certain instances deepens them. Thus, it is clearer that war is only just to the extent that it is to preserve independence, and not for glory, or resources, or for ideological motives that deny the independence of others.

The economic consequences are much more radical. Statistically, the chances of ending up as a poor state – or worse, as a poor state in the foreseeable future denuded of raw materials by exploitation – are too great to be ignored in any rational calculation. Self-interest, therefore, demands that one protect oneself in this respect and adopt the standpoint of the less advantaged. For if the criterion of a just framework were the maximisation of average or total welfare of mankind expressed in gross national product, a state might find itself consigned by the system to the role of supplying soya beans or copper at low prices for the good of all. It would not be rational to agree to that. Again, if the criterion adopted were the perfectionist ethic suggested earlier, where one or two states are right to appropriate disproportionate resources in order to land men on the moon, this too could not be rationally agreed. The chances of being one of those states are too remote, and states do not have the altruism necessary to agree to this course.

From this radical standpoint of the less advantaged, frameworks and policies would be just to the extent that they would be acceptable if a state found itself in the worse-off position. It does not follow that an equal distribution would be to the advantage of the worse off: if the system is destroyed, it would not be to anyone's advantage to have an equal share of nothing. Just schemes would have to benefit the less advantaged more than they would benefit from an equal distribution. In other words, all advantages of power and wealth would have to be justified as contributing more to the interests of the less advantaged than a more equal division would have done. On this basis, those better endowed could reasonably expect others to collaborate with them when some acceptable arrangement is a necessary condition of the good of all.[5]

Ideally these principles would be strictly complied with on the security of a well-ordered society. If the rules are not to be unfair to the would-be just state, one needs guarantees that others will also respect them. In the absence of an authoritative interpretation and enforcement of the rules, it is easy to find excuses for breaking them.

This is the condition in which the ill-ordered society of states finds itself. Once having determined whether a proposed policy is just, states are only under the obligation to comply to the extent that they can expect others also to do so, or where they do not put their existence and perhaps their welfare at risk by their compliance. Since states are highly organised societies, recognising laws and some notion of justice within their boundaries, it is more likely that they will comply than in the case of individuals in a state of nature. Nevertheless, the law of nations must fall into the partial compliance part of the theory. The degree of compliance would be decided by intuition, realism and a respect for established law – the methods outlined as already in use. And of course, since most states are less advantaged in the present very unequal world, it will be in their interests to invoke justice, and to try to secure compliance. As they become better organised, perhaps around the banner of contract theory (!) and find that the threat of germ warfare is as fearsome and cheaper than the threat of nuclear warfare, then force as well as reason will induce compliance with this new distributive principle. (I have in mind here the analogy with the domestic implementation of what began as the doctrine of socialism.)

To illustrate the effects of the general political and economic principles that I have outlined above, I shall now briefly try to apply them to some current problems. Conscientious objection to military service is a good example in that I can refer those interested by this approach to Rawls's own account. Also it can help the individual make up his own mind on a difficult issue that requires an appeal to reason in refusing to carry out a properly authorised law. As such it exemplifies the 'partial compliance part of non-ideal theory'.

The three grounds on which Rawls[6] proposes to ascribe to individuals the right, and on occasion the duty, to refuse to comply with a conscription order are (1) that conscription for this war contravenes the principles of domestic society where individual liberty is being restricted by the conscription order for motives that are other than for the protection of that liberty, (2) that the ends of this war contravene the law of nations, and (3) the closely related argument that the means likely to be used in the conduct of the war could not be countenanced from the standpoint of states in the original position. Rawls suggests that since the aims of states are often predatory, acceptance of these limitations would help to keep them in check.

My second example of an application is the European Community – chosen to illustrate the workings of the principles in an international framework where the states are culturally close. At present, the workings of the Community are justified in ways that accord with the modes of contemporary thinking set out earlier. Thus, institutions and policies are justified by reference to the Treaties of Rome and subsequent interstate agreements. Second, the so-called 'Community method' is supposed to be a confrontation between national interests and a common interest which in theory the Commission is supposed to express. Third, obligations like Community Aid are adopted in a somewhat intuitionistic manner.

Although at first sight, the federal aim of a United States of Europe seems to contradict the principle of national independence, on reflection this is not so. Co-operation or federation are to be freely chosen, and if it is to be federation, this new state would then be the party to the social contract.

Economically, the standpoint would be that of the least advantaged. This would be a big departure from the present national compromises or Community method. There would be far less haggling about policies. The policies that were most acceptable to the country with the lowest gross national product would be those which states in the original position would want adopted. If the Community had existed in 1950, the Federal Republic of Germany would have been the key country. However, the weakest country would have to use its intuition in not pressing the richer countries so far that the whole set-up became unacceptable to them. Even more radical would be the consequences for adopting this approach in a new Lomé Convention.

This brings me to my third application, to the question of

international trade. I shall argue in terms of the present system of international trade, without however suggesting that it is the only possible system. How far could the present system claim to be just according to the criteria of contract theory? From that standpoint, the present pattern of benefits is not the best available to a rational state ignorant of its eventual position in the order. The only conceivable line of justification is that it is better than no system at all. A just system would be impossible to establish tomorrow. However, it would be reasonable for states to expect that terms of trade at present determined by power be tempered by the demands of justice. This would mean at least the deliberate favouring of the industrialisation and commodities exports of the less advantaged.

My fourth example relates to the problem of jurisdiction over the new 'territories' of the air, the continental shelf, outer space and the moon. In the case of the air, the concept of territorial sovereignty was adopted as likely to provide the most orderly basis of division. In practice this led to many absurdities, with immense difficulties of establishing routes. After 1945, the power of the United States enabled these problems to be circumvented by conventions allocating routes according to complicated formulae allowing for the national interests of those able to establish airlines. The same principle of sovereignty is now being applied to the attempted reinterpretation of rights over sea-fishing and the ocean floor. It is hoped that the divisions of interest between landlocked, littoral and imperialistic states will be overcome by some formula achieved by diplomacy between them.

Offhand, it would be simpler to adopt the solution that was the best possible for the least-advantaged state under the circumstances. In this instance, there might be a question whether the poorest landlocked or the poorest littoral state was relevant. The answer would depend on whether one would regard it as fair to be excluded if one were the poorest landlocked state. A hundred years ago, the answer would have been that exclusion was fair. Today, when it is a question of sharing the benefits of mineral exploitation and preserving fish stocks, I think the answer is that it would not be fair. Further, there is the question, which the diplomats now debate according to disparate national interests, which form of exploitation would best meet the case – free enterprise or national quotas or an international agency or some mixture. Any of these might satisfy the criterion of the economic principle of justice that it be rationally acceptable to the poorest. In all cases, the efficiency of economic exploitation must not infringe the prior political principle that safeguards the equal sovereignty of all.

I hope that these four illustrations will suffice to show that the contract approach deserves serious theoretical consideration as much as the positivist, utilitarian and intuitionistic thinking on which we currently rely. It seems to me that it makes more precise the extent of the gap between an international order imposed by force and one that could be voluntarily willed as just. It provides a useful test of our ordinary judgments by suggesting a new method of specifying problems and solutions.

However, it must also be said that the difficulties to be surmounted before one could expect states to act on these principles still seem overwhelming. I shall note some of them briefly under three heads.

In the first place, contract theory shares with all theories of justice the difficulties consequent upon the fact that the role of justice in 'international society' is necessarily much less important than its role should be in domestic society. It is not yet obvious that some arrangement acceptable to all states is necessary to all. Thus, the presently rich states might well not be more secure either internally or externally after redistribution than they are by spending the world's resources on arms. A related point is that the number and equality of states is not sufficiently analogous to the number and equality of citizens. As there are only two superpowers, for example, it would be hard to formulate general principles without the use of what would be recognisable as proper names or rigged definite descriptions. Again, if justice is not the first virtue of 'international society', as it could not conceivably be, then considerations of justice would by definition be subordinate to other aims. For example, the need to preserve the ideological purity of some neighbour might then be held superior to the claims of justice. In this situation, it might be said, liberal contract theory is a petty-bourgeois idealistic refusal to commit oneself to the cause either of the big capitalist or of the big proletarian countries.

Second, contract theory places much emphasis on rationality. The cultural diversity of the present world makes it likely that there would be much dispute on what would be rational from the standpoint of states in the 'original position'. It is also arguable that the approach is over-rationalistic in not allowing sufficient weight to the conservative nature of justice in the sense of giving established expectations their due. To decide what is just on the basis of human reason, is to put a heavy burden on that poor faculty.

Finally, the approach might well be attacked as unrealistic– rather as the doctrine of socialism used to be attacked. No state, it might be said, has adopted the tradition of Rousseau, Kant and Rawls on its domestic constitution; *a fortiori*, one cannot expect states to adopt this approach internationally and certainly not without the assurance that others will also act justly. States arguing about justice would find it impossible to agree, and like the Greek city-states, would end by getting orders from a Roman hegemony.

Whether such criticisms are enough to stop any further discussion of the application of the contract theory of justice to international relations or indeed any discussion of justice in international relations at all, is a question which I now leave with the reader.

NOTES FOR CHAPTER 8

1   New York, Universal Library, 1964, p. 5.
2   See M. Wight, *Power Politics* (London, RIIA, 1964), final chapter.
3   See A. W. H. Adkins, *Merit and Responsibility* (London, OUP, 1960).
4   J. Rawls, *A Theory of Justice* (Oxford, The Clarendon Press, 1972).
5   ibid., s. 17.
6   ibid., s. 58.

9
Obligation and the Understanding of International Relations

BARRIE PASKINS

The problem of explaining what, in the deepest sense, we are trying to do in studying international relations is a philosophical one. I believe that it is Hegel who speaks to us most clearly on this problem and that J. Glenn Gray provides the best account of Hegel's renewed importance for the English-speaking world. In his introduction to *G. W. F. Hegel on Art, Religion, Philosophy*,[1] Gray links Hegel's appeal to the fascination with existentialism and to the search for a more humane Marxism. Thus far he agrees with other commentators, but he goes on to cite 'perhaps a third cause' for the recent revival of interest:

'Hegel's deepest longing – amounting to a passion – was for a reconciliation of the conflicting forces which in his age the Enlightenment and subsequent Romanticism had set in motion. His passion . . . could be satisfied only by a comprehensive system in which every legitimate source of conflict and division was incorporated as an organic part of the whole.'

'By now we should be safely past the compulsion to be either Hegelians or anti-Hegelians. Perhaps the best one can learn is to become more reflective about the interconnections and unities this nineteenth-century thinker saw in what have since become separate and warring disciplines.'

Among the many merits of this statement is the way it enables one to see how deeply Hegelian were two other nineteenth-century philosophers who haunt twentieth-century culture: Kierkegaard and Nietzsche. Their frenzy and distress sprang in large part from the frustration of an Hegelian passion for order, for that reconciliation which Hegel thought himself able to obtain and which they found agonisingly unattainable.

The quest for Hegelian order and reconciliation involves many things, including the need for an understanding of international relations. It is impossible for us to stop short at the state as Hegel did. The search for reconciling order is the only available alternative to an ultimately trivialising positivism. Some of the most acute contemporary sources of conflict and division are to be found in international relations. Hence we are driven back to Hegel, and the Hegelian is driven to the study of international relations.

Now, even if these ambitious philosophical assertions are granted it might still be doubted whether the student of international relations is thereby compelled to interest himself in Hegel. To consider such doubts, let us turn to the specifics of international relations.

An example of a kind of difficulty that currently plagues the study of international relations; a proposed philosophical remedy

An acute problem facing all students of international relations can be illustrated by reference to *Essence of Decision* by Graham Allison.[2] The undoubted merits of this book are its careful exposition of the three models of state action with which it operates and its circumspect relating of these to some of the available data on the Cuba missile crisis of 1962. What concerns me is the overall thrust that Allison plainly sees his work as having. He is trustful that it will be illuminating for the study of 'similar phenomena' and is content to bring forward his three models *ad hoc* with no explanation of why they are favoured when an indefinitely large number of other models are possible.

What is meant by 'similar phenomena'? To avoid vacuity the words must mean something more than 'phenomena which can be discussed interestingly in terms of the three models'. Are we meant to read 'all crises'? All interstate crises? All crises between nuclear superpowers? Within the kind of inquiry to which Allison is committed, it is impossible to answer such questions. Such obscurity is remarkable in a good book purporting to advance our understanding. Our understanding of what? Advanced in what direction? The silence is deafening.

Once one notices this, it seems strange that so many political scientists are willing to study the Cuba missile crisis in a spirit that makes Allison's three models look the most natural thing in the world. Questions that receive no analytic attention in his book are: Who were the people, what were they like, who could go through with such a thing as a fifty-fifty chance of nuclear holocaust? To what inhibitions, if any, were they subject? How would other sorts of people with different values have been permitted by their different value systems to behave? How does the participants' sense of values compare with our own? And: How did the threatened non-participating world receive the event? What place does the crisis have, or not have, in the contemporary mythos? Has it altered our perceptions of value in any way?

If one reinterprets Allison's book as part of a wider inquiry which includes such questions, it can be seen as a contribution to a humane understanding of ourselves and our world. As it stands, the book is deeply unintelligible despite its surface lucidity. It gives the appearance of a study in terms of three arbitrarily chosen models of an arbitrarily chosen set of events. The inevitability of our interest in the Cuba missile crisis is totally hidden.

The book's natural effect on, say, an intelligent research student is to make him or her into an anti-theoretical historian. I have seen such a student select an arbitrary period in the United States' bombing campaign in Vietnam and scrutinise it in the light of Allison's three models. Finding that none of them quite 'fits', the student searched for other models. But noticing that this is a game without rules – for there is nothing except the finitude of human intelligence to preclude the insertion of all the past history of all 'the participants' – the student concluded that 'models' are neither more nor less than the statement of arbitrary assumptions articulated by the historian for the convenient handling of arbitrarily chosen data. This is not a student blunder but a clear-headed perception of the true thrust of such a work as Allison's taken out of a wider humanising context.

In what terms, then, are we to frame a humanising context which may rescue theory from the self-stultifying positivism of mere arbitrariness? One of the key terms available to us is the word 'obligation'. It is my subject in this chapter.

My way of using the word may be somewhat unfamiliar. Despite the many treatises on political obligation, I may seem to be suggesting that international relations fall within the realm of ethics not politics. But in fact I shall be arguing that moral and political obligation are one and the same thing.

What I have in mind can be indicated perhaps most clearly by reference to Plato's *Republic*. In Book II, Glaucon asks Socrates to prove that it is better to be just and suffer for it than to be unjust and get away with it. This sets Socrates on the long haul towards a definition of justice. He begins with the state – why? His explanation at the outset is an obscure joke: it has something to do with the state being larger and therefore easier to read, like a book with bigger print. What he is really doing becomes apparent only in

Book IV. Having satisfied Glaucon about the nature of justice and injustice in the state, he puts forward a thought which F. M. Cornford's translation renders as follows:

'The discovery we made [in the state] must now be applied to the individual. If it is confirmed, all will be well; but if we find that justice in the individual is something different, we must go back to the state and test our new result. Perhaps if we brought the two cases into contact like flint and steel, we might strike out between them the spark of justice.'[3]

Socrates's proposed procedure makes sense only if it is assumed that there is something common to state justice and individual justice, underlying both. I argue in similar vein that moral and political obligation are identical. But where Socrates finds harmony among our obligations, I see conflict and division.

Examples of obligation 'political' and 'moral'; necessity of understanding the state in terms of obligation

Let us take, first, a textbook example of 'a moral problem'. What should you do if you can rescue from a burning building either Sir Alexander Fleming who is discovering penicillin or your own mother but not both? According to classic utilitarianism, you must rescue the great bacteriologist because that is what the greatest happiness of the greatest number requires. But some people feel that this is the wrong answer, while others think that it should not be obvious where one's duty lies – the situation is a dilemma, and utilitarianism makes it seem too easy.

Peter Singer, in an article on the relation between those of us who enjoy relative affluence and the victims of famine and poverty, propounds a closely related problem: how much should we give to the needy?[4] The answer that Singer appears to favour is:

'that we ought to give until we reach the level of marginal utility – that is, the level at which, by giving more, I would cause as much suffering to myself or to my dependents as I would relieve by my gift. This would mean, of course, that one would reduce oneself to very near the material circumstances of a Bengali refugee.'

The driving force behind his argument appears to be the Benthamite assumption that in the promotion of the greatest happiness, each person is to count for one. If we have more than our share, we should give until our giving becomes counterproductive of general happiness.

There are, of course, many questions to be asked about the

wisdom of Singer's proposal. Most salient for my argument is to ask what the moral significance is of having dependents. It is a widely shared maxim that one's own family must come first, and it is not at all clear that Singer's perfunctory 'or my dependents' takes this seriously enough. Singer does not discuss the point explicitly but his view is plain enough: the victims of famine must take precedence 'if we accept any principle of impartiality, universalizability, equality, or whatever'. He 'takes no account of proximity or distance': 'The fact that a person is physically near to us, so that we have personal contact with him, may make it more likely that we *shall* assist him, but this does not show that we *ought* to help him rather than another who happens to be further away.' If this seems a bit hollow, that is presumably because it depicts all distance as spatial. The nearness of those who are near and dear to us is not a matter of geography but involves a moral force other than Greatest Happiness and Fair Shares. It is the same force which impels one to think that perhaps one ought to save one's mother from the burning building even at the expense of the Greatest Happiness.

Although Singer's paper is concerned with dealings across frontiers, he confines his attentions to the private citizen. But it requires no great mental leap to shift our attention from the obviously 'moral' issue he is discussing to certain 'political' issues in international relations. 'The prince,' one might say, 'like the private citizen has to consider how much to give, and how. When he does so, he is subject to that force which utilitarianism seeks to ignore: just as the citizen may have dependants, so the prince necessarily has subjects who are his special responsibility. His affluence is not his to give – those who are his special care take precedence.'

This formulation might be challenged as anachronistic and question-begging. There are no princes any longer, only states and governments. To personify these as princes is to beg the question about the relation between ethics, which is concerned with individuals, and politics, which treats of states and governments. Such an objection would be misconceived.

In the world of the princes, politics had a triune structure. The prince stood between God *to* whom he was responsible and the people *for* whom he was responsible. The prince had servants, the legitimacy of whose activity flowed from God through the prince to the servant. Despite the massive upheavals of the post-mediaeval world, this structure has remained intact. There is some person or persons (for example the Führer, the president) responsible *to* somebody or something (*das Volk*, the people) *for* somebody (the citizens of the Reich, of the United States). When we speak of 'the state' or 'the government', we assume this structure.

Any attempt to think outside it results in intellectual chaos. An example: it is a commonplace that the military often exerts a strong 'influence' on foreign policy. How are we to express this fact? Some of what we say will vary from case to case but there is one interpretation that can be rejected with confidence. It is never right to say, without severe qualification and special explanation, that people 'influenced' by, say, the 'interests' of the officer corps are trying to meet their obligations to their fellow officers in submitting to such 'influence'. For there is a deep and inescapable difference between, on the one hand, the state and, on the other, such organisations as the officer corps (or air force).

What is the difference? An insight for which Hegel is rightly famous, and which largely explains the neo-Marxist interest in him, is his realisation that human beings find or fail to find such happiness, fulfilment, true self, and the like, as is attainable in this world within life in the state and life in the family, life in the air force and life in the officer corps. Once it is granted that happiness and the rest are to be found only in the life of concrete institutions, a sharp distinction emerges. To find oneself and happiness in the air force and officer corps is to discover oneself in the pursuit of an organised activity for which there is a deep need in the world. If the world does not need armed forces, then the self to be discovered through military service is a shallow thing; at most one will obtain merely psychological returns, be they 'job satisfaction' or the gratification of bloodlust. Without military service being a service to somebody channelled through some such mediator as the state, the manifest universal appeal of the military to our respect would not be what it is.

And if this is still denied, notice that the alternative to the view of the military as an organisation lodged in the triune structure of the state is a view in which a soldier's obligations to his fellow soldiers could in principle be such as to require that no one be sent to death in battle except for the good of the service!

Hence, although it is of course possible that someone might be 'influenced' by the thought that his over-riding obligation is to his fellow officers, there is good universal reason for viewing such a person as intellectually misguided. He is moved by a perception of the importance of his fellows or service, but takes a view of the same which entails for it not importance but triviality. In any such case, a special explanation is required of the fact that he is acting upon an incoherent outlook.

This is but one example of a very general point about 'the state' and 'the government'. Readers of *Essence of Decision* will be aware of the inadequacy of any attempt to understand states as impenetrable atoms of rationality (the rational agent model). For much of the data can be made sense of only in terms of bureaucratic politics; we are forced to delve into the state. Such delving can and should be guided by the systematic understanding that what the state is must be understood in terms of obligations: the soldier's and civil servant's obligations to obey, their superiors' obligations towards 'the people', and so on. The alternative is a chaos which would render it quite unproblematic if soldiers refused to fight because their first duty was to one another. As a register of this general fact, I shall continue to speak not of 'the state' or 'the government' but of 'the prince'. The prince is shorthand for those who, as I put it above, are not free to give to the needy as utilitarianism requires because 'the prince necessarily has subjects who are his special responsibility. His affluence is not his to give – those who are his special care take precedence.'

According to classic utilitarianism, you must abandon your mother to the flames and reduce your dependants to 'very near' the material circumstances of a Bengali refugee. But there is a very well-entrenched view, straddling ethics and politics, which holds that a person must put his dependants first, and a prince his subjects. It will be useful to have some names for this conflict, so I shall speak of general obligation (the obligation to all human beings, maybe all sentient beings) and special obligation (for example, to one's mother and dependants, or to one's subjects if one is a prince, or to one's prince if one is his servant and thereby his subjects' servant).

Concentration on general obligation strengthens the feeling that our obligations transcend all divisions between human beings. Reflection on special obligation tends to give moral and political force to those divisions. People who doubt whether any kind of obligation is fundamental to international relations are usually impressed more by the divisions than by any residual humanity. So let us look at special obligation more closely.

In morals there is an impressive division within the realm of special obligation. Many of one's special obligations are consequent on one's will – one has entered into them. For example, I have given my word and thereby undertaken a special obligation to my promisee. I shall call such obligations 'voluntary'. Not all special obligations are voluntary: I have my parents to thank for my existence and pre-rational life. My obligation to them derives at least partly from this. To the extent that one's obligations derive from things independent of one's will they are 'involuntary'. Note that the difference arises from the source of the obligation and not from the extent to which one welcomes or rues it. There is no implication that involuntary obligations need be more onerous than voluntary.

Contract theory views all the obligations of which it offers theoretical analysis as voluntary, tracing them to a compact, a mutual promise. In *Obligations*, Michael Walzer recalls that Blackstone takes a view of obligation opposed to the contractarian.[5] Blackstone explicitly likens political obligation to filial obligation. And it is in terms which anticipate Blackstone that Socrates explains the compelling power that the Laws of Athens have over him: he does not say that he has promised the Laws anything, still less that General Happiness requires his loyalty to the Laws. His claim is that he has the Laws to thank for his being the person he is since they have given him social life as his parents gave him biological life. Hence an involuntary special obligation (which he welcomes) to obey.

Before we limply accept the divergence between contractarians and Socrates–Blackstone as Just A Difference Of Opinion, let us look more closely. An instance, first, of 'individual morality'. I have assumed so far that the burning building problem represents a clear-cut clash of obligations, special against general. But it is possible that my mother and I have agreed that the public interest shall come first in situations like that of the Burning Building. If we have come to such an agreement, the decision may be no easier emotionally (she is still my mother) but morally the problem is no longer a dilemma. For, after all, my mother and I are both responsible moral beings with the power to enter, granted good moral reasons, into binding new moral agreements to forego the most elementary claims on each other.

What light can we get from the Burning Building on public issues? Contract theorists have always been interested in the freedom to move from one state to another, so let us consider a special case of such movement. If a person's services are needed in the state in which they were born and educated, are they nevertheless free to emigrate? In contract theory this is a hard and complex question unless the person has explicitly contracted to stay or contracted freedom of movement. In the absence of such rare contracts, the problem will have to be examined in terms of tacit consent, a notoriously difficult notion, or through some such device as John Rawls's initial position – the implications of which for the problem are obscure in the extreme. I have no wish to suggest that the issue is always simple but one strand seems to unravel readily enough if one accepts, as contract theory does not, the importance of involuntary special obligation.

Has a citizen whose services are needed ever an involuntary special obligation to stay and not to emigrate? Suppose there are certain people, citizens of the home state, whom the emigrant has to thank for his existence and social and intellectual being. Suppose these would suffer if he leaves. He would then appear to be under an involuntary special obligation to these people to stay and serve. To affirm this is not to preclude the possibility of a clash of duties: perhaps in addition to the obligation to stay the person is under a general obligation to leave and continue the fight against an unjust régime, or a special voluntary obligation to protect his family by exile. But the *prima facie* obligation to stay rules out certain courses of action. If a person not wholly self-taught is in a position to profit from his special skills abroad, then *ipso facto* that person has certain teachers to thank for that from which he is in a position to benefit. Whether the fact is inconvenient or not, and regardless of whether the person 'feels' grateful, the fact abides of an involuntary special bond.

The foregoing remarks can be subjected to various kinds of questioning. Perhaps most directly relevant is a kind of doubt characteristic of much political philosophy: if I want to talk about politics, will I kindly confine myself to the state and not ramble away into merely sentimental ties between would-be emigrants and their families and teachers!

Such a challenge is closely related to the earlier objection to my practice of speaking of the prince in preference to the state. It merits a closely related reply. In the world of the princes, the individual's obligation to obey his prince was neither more nor less than a channel through which the individual's relation to God flowed – it gave practical form to the individual's supreme duty of loving God. A prince who blocked the flow was unjust and could be justly removed. In the contemporary world, the individual's obligation to obey the state is the structurally similar channel through which the individual's relation to his fellow men flows. There is no reason whatever to suppose that on all occasions the same relations to the same men are given practical form by this channel. One's obligation not to obstruct the course of justice is a forming of one's relation to those who need justice, presumably all of one's fellow citizens. But it by no means follows, nor is it true, that obligations 'to the state' always channel relations to all of one's fellows. The obligation not to frustrate the state in its support of, say, the arts or sport channels one's relation to those of one's fellows with an interest in the arts or sport.

This general and, no doubt, controversial view sheds light on the difficult subject of patriotism. The obligation to die for one's 'country' is a leading instance in all theories of political obligation. Very many people, if they recognise this obligation at all, experience it as the involuntary special obligation to certain persons from whom good has been received. (Not: Nazi Germany is threatening the vital interests of the United Kingdom, but: Herr Hitler is *hitting the East End*.) Patriotism, loyalty to the *patria*, is the sense of being bound to a certain place experienced in personal terms as the place where *we* did this and that and where one received, independently of one's will, the literal ground of one's being on which one literally stands. Such 'feelings' might be dismissed as merely inarticulate and incoherent emotions on which the government must work in the state interest or national interest. But such dismissals fail to explain what the work of manipulation will have to consist in, and why patriotism is so important – both as an instrument and as an obstacle – in nation-building and the 'legitimising' of states. The view which begins by seeing the state as something wholly different from the *patria* inevitably tends towards the conclusion that the state must rout all rivals for loyalty, stamp out all local pieties and become the only god. Such conclusions naturally outrage one. My argument is that the starting-point is wrong: the state is not a rival to patriotism but a channel through which, if things go well, the articulate passion for one's own place and one's own people can flow and find their legitimate position in – if there is a God – the love and worship of God.

To affirm that there are involuntary special obligations which are channelled by the state is not to say that such obligations cannot be qualified. Just as my mother, as a moral being, has the power to release me from special obligations towards her for good moral reason, so those to whom I am bound through the state can release me for good moral reason. To the extent that the state is entitled to speak for them, it can release me. Not, of course, that this makes it possible to see how a moral being could have serious moral reason to put before his own legitimate moral interests the merely private profit, in the form of higher pay and lower taxes, accruing to a would-be emigrant. Some good moral reason for release will be required, perhaps that the intending emigrant is caught in a genuine conflict between, say, the advancement of medicine or astronomy and the need in the home state, among people to whom he is bound by involuntary special obligation, of a certain doctor or astronomer. I conclude, *pace* contract theory, that a citizen whose services are needed may on occasion have an indissoluble involuntary special obligation to stay and serve.

So far in this chapter, I have tried to sketch the notion of obligation. I have distinguished special from general obligation, and voluntary from involuntary special obligation. I have argued that the state is to be understood in terms of obligation, and that moral and political obligation are one and the same thing. I turn now to certain problems in the study of international relations and to the question of how the concept of obligation can contribute towards reconciliation.

Reconciling certain conflicts and divisions in the study of international relations

The study of international relations is subject to several divisive tendencies. Among them are: the inherited quarrel over the use of natural science as a model; the rift between practical men and scholars; the doubt about the relationship between personal, state and system perspectives; the sense that in teaching and studying international relations one is attempting to handle competing theories whose interconnections are obscure; and the grand divide between those who see themselves as studying the community of all mankind and those who think of international relations as solely a matter of interstate transactions.

Is any kind of reconciliation possible between such warring factions and coalitions? In this section I suggest that it is. In my final section I shall try to indicate the underlying tension of which these divisions seem to me to be manifestations.

Science as a model. Many different aspirations motivate the desire to employ mathematical or natural (including biological) science as a model for the study of social phenomena, and the use to which the model is put varies in ways that are partly determined by the relation between the various possible underlying motivations.

If I am right to say that the state is fundamentally a nexus of special and general obligation, then there is at least one very good reason for striving to obtain the kind of independent assessment of state action which appears to be the desire of many people who are impressed by natural science as a model for the understanding of international relations. We are under inescapable pressure, if we care about obligations, to look beyond the realm of a person's or state's *words* to see what in their *deeds* speaks for and against the sincerity and integrity, or cant and humbug, in their professions of obligation. It is all very well for the developed states to express concern about the developing states in language so vague as to preclude criticism in their own terms, but what do they *do*? *Under No Circumstances Take Any Decisions*? Unless it is possible to identify and describe their behaviour in other terms than those which they themselves apply in their bland statements of goodwill, it is impossible to convict them of insincerity. I often doubt whether opponents of the effort to employ natural science as a model take the full force of this simple point.

To say merely this, however, is to leave something very like classical political science still very firmly in the saddle. For no vindication is being conceded to the heroic pragmatism of (to choose a figure above present battles) a Quincy Wright, bent on construing international relations in terms which make no concession to the supposed deep differences between human and natural phenomena.

In fact, however, my argument is far from robbing behaviourism of all initiative in international relations. To take what seems to me the leading possibility, there is no guarantee built into history that one will not radically alter people's perceptions of their obligations by making them conscious of their bad faith. Suppose that someone working with one of the natural or mathematical sciences as a model brings to light massive discrepancies between the obligations that princes acknowledge and patterns which can be read in their conduct. It may happen that this demonstration of hypocrisy will be seized on and elaborated into a new doctrine of obligation (for example, a new 'theory' of the state and interstate system). This new doctrine will perhaps strike some as a charter for wickedness and licence, others as a heroic revaluation of all values or a new Moment in the Absolute. Machiavelli and Hobbes are best understood as such revolutionising scientists, students of hypocrisy with an essential place in the forging of new values. Freud's psychopathology of everyday life and Marx's sociopathology of Hegel are somewhat more distant examples. It is hardly a slight on contemporary adherents of the models of natural and mathematical science to suggest that they might join such company.

A very important item in any peace treaty between the 'natural scientists' and others relates to 'values'. There appears to be a wider consensus at present than formerly on the importance of taking values into account in the analysis of international relations. Some people still desire to make the concession only by treating values as part of the data. Such a desire is foredoomed to failure. In thinking about international relations, one is working within a world of values which guide one's thought and attention. There is no way of attaining a world in which this is not the case. The best way of bringing this ineluctable fact to consciousness is through an articulation of the obligations that appear to be relevant to the problem in hand.

We want, of course, in the sciences of man as elsewhere to be disinterested and to obtain as comprehensive a view as possible. So far as I can see, the only way to do this is through the articulation and comparison of the values of those concerned, including one's own values. The latter, being one's own, cannot appear solely as data. People and situations differ too much for us to be capable of any usable general typology of values, employable on all issues of social concern. Take as an example Einstein's remark, quoted in the Introduction to this book, that it is impossible to refute someone who sincerely thinks that it is right to extirpate the human race. It is not at all clear that there is any practical issue to which this remark is relevant. What possible point could there be in essaying a refutation?

If the practical question is whether, say, the Allies were justified in punishing Nazi war criminals, then it is necessary to pay attention to Nazi values, and to ponder our own values (for example, to ask what we think we are trying to do when we *punish*). But from this it does not follow that it makes sense to think of proving, from our standpoint, to the sincere and unrepentant Nazi, with his standpoint, that he is wrong. The role of proof in science is potentially misleading here. If, contrary to much evidence in the history of science, we see the scientific community as a body of people proving things to one another, then it is tempting to see the moral community likewise, as a community whose limits are determined by the limits of proof. The trouble with such a view comes at the very beginning. At fault is the implicit picture of punishment as making sense only where proof is possible, to the offender, of his fault in the terms in which he committed the crime. It is necessary to labour this point because many adherents of the scientific model appear to think that there are no other options than a mere pragmatism which treats all values as data and a 'fully worked out' moral system with proofs ready for all possible reprobates.

In this chapter, I have spoken repeatedly about how *we* think of morality and politics. By far the least misleading picture of what I intend by 'us' is as follows. Imagine a changing population of moral–political beings having to discover again and again through practical discussion of the ever-changing agenda of international relations who *we* are, we who agree and disagree, who understand and fail to understand. The Socratic sense of dialogue as self-discovery is inescapable for the human sciences. It represents a third option distinct from both mere pragmatism and the system with proofs for all seasons.

Speaking within the grand Socratic dialogue (where else?), I am suggesting that 'we' can understand 'ourselves' better through the concept of obligation sketched above. Some of 'us' are in traditions of sympathy to the natural science model, others in traditions of antipathy. What I am arguing is that the employment of the non-human sciences as a model for the study of international relations can have great utility but is subject to certain limitations: the limits of our intellectual world are fixed by our understanding of obligation. If there are conflicts and tensions among our obligations, these will pervade our world and no amount of 'science' can properly eradicate them. In particular, if there is an inescapable tension between general and special obligation, then this polarity will necessarily polarise all our thinking about international relations, however much we may hanker after the undivisive uniformities of the natural and mathematical world.

Statesmen and scholars. In the difficult business of dialogue with politicians and officials, scholars appear to be torn between two kinds of approach: to accept the official questions and premises and do a narrow advisory job of problem solving; or to insist on a non-official agenda which is apt to make the man of affairs rather bored and perhaps intellectually uneasy. The notion of international relations as a Socratic dialogue is readily suggestive of the kind of reconciliation that is and is not possible between statesmen and scholars.

There is just one good systematic reason why officials and politicians cannot accept the academic characterisation of public issues: they have a job to do. 'All very well for academics to play intellectual games with the international economic order but we at the FCO have a job to do!' There is something true and something false about such an argument. It is true and important that the official or politician has his special responsibilities in that the doing of his job is a necessary channelling of relations between human beings. But it is obviously untrue that a job is to be contrasted with an obligation – among the most important obligations of a person's life are the things which it is his responsibility to do in virtue of having a certain job.

As a consequence, the relation between statesman and scholar is an orderly one. It is for the scholar to bring to mind (including the public mind) that vast network of obligations that includes the obligations which determine the official's job specification. The concrete realisation of this network involves both those whose jobs give practical form to interpersonal relations (for example, officials and politicians) and those whose special responsibility is to strive for a disinterested view, 'scientific' in being orderly and synoptic, of the whole. The scholar who is content merely to do an advisory job on commission and then to return to something less than active dialogue about the structure of international relations is committing a very elementary blunder – he is failing to do his job.

The kind of reconciliation that is possible between scholar and statesman is, thus, that each should speak to the other out of his own special responsibility on the subject of joint concern, namely, what is obligatory in the concrete situations which each will identify at the outset in the different terms of his special interest. A clash of views is to be expected. But mutual incomprehension or indifference indicates that one or both sides fail to understand what international relations are.

Person, state and system perspectives. Kenneth Waltz in *Man, the State, and War* develops a typology of approaches to the specific topic of the causes of war which is readily transferable to international relations generally.[6] Waltz, of course, argues that we need to think in terms of human nature, the state *and* the interstate system if we are not to fall into oversimplified because one-sided explanations. He is surely right that international relations can be characterised in personal terms, in terms of the state, and in terms of the international system. But it can often appear, as it does in Waltz, that such characterisations represent three independent, inter-acting factors whose connection is mysterious. Granted that we do think in these three sets of terms, what guarantee is there that we are all the while talking about the same thing?

This question is readily answered if it is agreed that international relations is a manifold of obligations. Personal, state and system language represent three aspects of the manifold. An example: one important sustaining cause of war is that citizens have such thoughts as 'I am a soldier so I must obey the call to arms', 'It is going to be such an adventure that I owe it to myself to participate', 'It is my duty to go, so I shall say my goodbyes and join up'. Whatever one thinks about the supposed 'instinct' of individual aggression, it is plain that without a dependable widespread perception of the duty to fight, there would not be the orderly preparations for war which are one fundamental characteristic of the international system. The relation between the state and war is, thus, essentially the same as that between the individual and war: in personal discourse one stresses the individual's perception of certain obligations, in state discourse the relation to those same obligations of the prince and his servants. These are but two ways of representing the same complex relation.

The ways in which the international system is predictable and unpredictable confirm this. In training people to practice international relations (as princes, diplomats, soldiers, and so on), one trains them in their duty. It is predictable that they will do what they are trained to do, apart from backsliding, and that they will cope or fail to cope according to the similarity or dissimilarity between the problems envisaged in their education and those which they face in practice. Accordingly, it is natural that we find ourselves permanently locked into a situation of knowing that the practitioners of international relations will do what they take to be their duty, or will fail to do so in one of a relatively small number of ways. By the same token, we naturally find ourselves at a loss to generalise systematically about what they will take their duty to be, and whether they will seek to do it or to evade it.

There is, then, a reconciliation possible between three major perspectives on international relations: wherever one starts among them, one finds oneself talking about the same thing.

Competing theories. An important part of our perplexity in international relations arises from our familiarity as teachers and students with a plurality of competing theories. We find ourselves with several seemingly incompatible sets of ideas and no well-established way of understanding what we are doing with them. To reply that we are modestly striving to consider all sides of the problem would be merely an evasion, for the competing theories give no agreed meaning to the notion of 'the problem'. Each theory addresses its own 'problems' in its own way. If one is teaching *Hamlet*, there will be vast divergencies of approach for the scholarly to accommodate but there is an unexciting yet crucial way of explaining what one is doing as a whole: one is teaching *Hamlet*. In international relations we lack this secure anchoring-point since there is no publicly identifiable object, independent of the theories about it, which corresponds to *Hamlet*.

My response to this unsettling problem is that one can divide theories of international relations into two: those that manifestly address themselves to obligation, and those that fudge the problem of values and therefore the question of how thought and action are related. The latter require reconstruction. The former can be seen without difficulty as the articulation of different perceptions of obligation to be examined in the usual variety of ways – for internal consistency, for relation to one another, for relation to 'our' sense of obligation.

If it is true that there is an irresolvable tension between special and general obligation, then this will survive the solution of the problem of conflicting theories. At the end of the day there will still be conflict in our ideas about our obligations.

World community or system of states? The clash between these two views of international relations is ancient and well-entrenched. The reconciliation is this: there is a world community and the practical form thereof is the states-system. There is a world community in that what makes the world go round is obligation. The practical form thereof is the states-system in that, regroup the obligations as we will, we keep running up against the state and the interstate system as the significant pattern to which all other patterns have to be related.

Here we encounter a mystery. It is to be expected that the interstate system should be fuelled by obligation, but it would seem to require explanation if every regrouping of obligations leads back to the interstate system. What is it about obligation, or about the world in which obligation is located, that explains this patterning of obligation around the state? Without an answer to this question, the concept of obligation effects at best an incomplete reconciliation of the divisions in the study of international relations.

Explanation of the Stubborn Rock of the state

I want to try and explain the stubborn rock of the state in terms of our felt obligations. I am not going to attempt to deduce history *a priori* or to claim that the state is somehow an invariable part of the human condition. I propose only to address myself to our current historical predicament and to draw attention to certain historical features of it.

When one says that the state is a stubborn fact of experience, that the state's central importance is a brute fact, there is often a philosophical picture at work bewitching our imagination. It is a pre-Hegelian picture. In it, our moral–political aspirations and good will flutter across boundaries. The state is a kind of ogre, seizing the beautiful butterflies of our hopes and dreams and smashing them on its wheel. We are full of good will to all men, but the state is the obstinate fact that gets in the way of our benign values. Hegel would have dismissed such thoughts as unphilosophical, as mere edification. In his terms, they are to be condemned for lacking concreteness: our butterfly hopes have no concrete in them. I want to try and make the point plain in the language of obligation.

So far as I can see, we find ourselves at the present time besieged by the three types of obligation distinguished earlier in this chapter. We are unable to accept a utilitarian view of the world because we recognise the binding force of special obligations. We are unable to accept a refined utilitarianism modified only by the devices of contract theory because we accept that we are under involuntary special obligations. Special obligation blocks the kind of thinking exemplified by Peter Singer's article, discussed above, and involuntary special obligation sets limits to the promise of the kind of contract theorising discussed in the previous chapter by Christopher Brewin. Singer and the contractarians offer two different keys for unlocking the state and freeing our butterfly hopes and good will to range over boundaries, maximising happiness and universalising justice. But involuntary special obligation, in tension with general obligation and voluntary special obligation, structures our obligations and therefore structures international relations. A special case of involuntary special obligation is patriotism, and it is true that patriotism is not enough. But patriotism is more than enough to render utilitarian and contract theories of international relations untenable.

This fact about the moral standing of the state shows how misleading it is to view the state as a mere obstacle to our moral aspirations. The state is indeed a rock on which our hopes break but the simple fact is that our operative moral convictions include the state. In our historical situation there is no alternative. Our sighing after a moral community in which all are fed is the unreal, ghostly part of our moral life: for our sense of obligation makes it imperative, but our obligations render it systematically impossible for the foreseeable future. Without real obligations, moral aspirations would be unreal. That which gives reality to our desire for a world transcending the state also calls the reality of that desire into question.

This explains why, try as we will to reshake the kaleidoscope of obligation, we run up against the state and the inter-state system. The best understanding of international relations that we are currently capable of is our own, and to the best of our (moral–political) understanding, the state is an inescapable rock.

Our situation is not that of Hegel, because we are unable to stop with the state: our best aspirations cross the frontier. But equally our situation is not the tormented, criterionless one of Kierkegaard and Nietzsche, for a vast network of obligations gives direction and meaning to our activity. That which saves us from existential torment also makes impossible a Hegelian calm. The state channels our moral life, and if that were all that required saying, then we could attain to Hegel's reconciliation of the conflicts and divisions in our political life. But a necessary part of our moral life is a ghostly part, in which we are haunted by impossible aspirations. To know that we are driven by a necessary ghost is fundamental to a contemporary understanding of international relations.

NOTES FOR CHAPTER 9

1   New York, Harper and Row, 1970.
2   Boston, Little, Brown, 1971.
3   Oxford, The Clarendon Press, 1941, p. 127.
4   'Famine, Affluence and Morality', *Philosophy and Public Affairs*, vol. I, no. 3, Spring 1972, pp. 229–43.
5   Cambridge, Mass., Harvard UP, 1970.
6   New York, Columbia UP, 1959.

10
The Justification of the State

PHILIP WINDSOR

When Virgil is sent to guide Dante on his journey through Hell, he is sent on the instructions of Beatrice, who, from her celestial seat, has seen Dante wandering into mortal danger below. All three belong to a universe whose laws do not change. She from Heaven, Dante from Earth, and Virgil from the infernal region, all know these laws and are bound by them.

Equally, Dante is able to judge – in every sense of the word – the nature of events in Florence because he can judge them from the vantage point of Hell. History, even political history, is a series of decisions, not a series of developments. Since the laws of the universe do not vary, history, however tumultuous, remains static before the transcendent. The interest of history lies not in the nature of historical change but in the necessity of moral choice before these laws. Florentines who have transgressed them are liable to meet Dante as he passes from one circle to the next.

Dante's position is more difficult than it might appear at first sight – and I shall return to that in a moment. But what is immediately striking is that he was living through a period of immense political change – and towards the end of a long period of technological change in Europe[1] of which the religious import had been exhaustively discussed – and that he was yet able to assume an unchanging moral order. More than that, he asserts that politics has an unchanging moral content. Because he enjoyed (so to speak) the vantage point of Hell, he was able to weigh the Florentine Republic by a transcendent measure. For him, the transcendent was timeless; it was therefore also immanent. And I suggest that the assumptions derived from this approach underlie much of the Western democratic tradition.

In that tradition, the state is a Republic because its citizens are responsible, individually responsible, for their own choices and actions. The state provides the framework of moral choice, and the law the framework of action. Even the dilemmas inherent in such a tradition – as for example between obeying one's conscience and breaking the law – are readily recognised as dilemmas because of the powerful assumption that the state is a moral arena.

But, as I suggested, there are difficulties in Dante's position, and these in the end evoked a contrary tradition. His very certainty lands him in a number of artistic and moral problems. For clearly, at one moment, the nature of history – if not the laws of the universe – *had* changed. That moment was the Incarnation, through which, since God had become human, humans were brought into direct relationship with God. They were offered salvation, but also had to know what they were rejecting if they refused it. The artistic difficulties arise from this fundamental change: namely, how to treat all those who had lived before the strict point of time at which the change occurred.

Dante's solution to this is simple. All those who had been precursors of the new human condition, in other words those heroes of the Old Testament who had had a direct relationship with God, are rescued by Christ during the Harrowing of Hell. And those who were not, the noble pagans? They, of whom Virgil is the representative, live in the globe of light of the first circle, deprived of access to God, but able, even in this new transcendent universe, to realise their own nobility. The artistic solution is quite satisfactory – at least in the sense that it is the stoic comprehension of Virgil which makes the poem possible at all.

But morally it is awful. It implies that God has made his saints indifferent to the sufferings of those who were born at the wrong time. Indeed, Dante is quite explicit about this:

> *Io son' fatta da Dio, sua mercè, tale*
> *che la vostra miseria non mi tange,*
> *nè fiamma d'esto incendio non m'assale*
> (God in his mercy made me such
> that your wretchedness can not touch me
> nor flame of that furnace do me harm)[2]

says Beatrice to Virgil. And Virgil knows it full well, as he suggests when he takes leave of Dante at the wall of fire at the end of the 'Purgatorio'. I do not think Dante was able to resolve this question – nor the many other Christian writers before Dostoievsky who spent their energies trying to justify Hell. For if the universe is ruled by love, and if that love was realised in time, how can one ignore the fate of all those who fell outside its temporal revelations but are still subject to the same laws?

I do not know enough to be able to say whether Dostoievsky *began* another tradition when he did confront this question, but he certainly gave it a particularly powerful expression. Indeed, he does not merely confront the problem of what happens to those who did not have the chance to know; he meets head-on the question of what Hell does to Heaven, simply by existing ('Ivan's Rebellion' in *The Brothers Karamazov*). He does so in the context of a novel, not a poem, a debate and not a cosmic explanation; and from the inside standpoint of his different characters. Even so, it is clear that the prospect of eternal punishment, even for knowledgeable sinners, is intolerable to him; and that while the eternal laws are a necessity, they had better be changed at some point if they are not to betray their own nature.

For Dante, the implications of the cosmic order were that for even the noblest of people there was no escape from their moral position precisely because the moral order can not change. That is why, in the framework of choice which is the Republic, there is no escape from responsibility. But for Dostoievsky, the nature of the moral choice is a cosmically awful burden laid upon the shoulders of humans, and they are quite inadequate to cope with it. It is laughable to think of the state as a framework for such choice; on the contrary, the very nature of the state is bound to imply that it presents a perpetual challenge to the transcendent.

Since the transcendent has realised itself in time, and thereby changed the nature of time, it can also change again when time ends. (Or rather the other way round: the point at which time will end is when the transcendent achieves its full realisation; and there is no way from inside time of knowing the full nature of that transcendence which will abolish time. Hence, perhaps, the importance of the eschatological tradition in Christianity.) In any event, for Dostoievsky, the state is no more than a temporal holding operation, one which can only acknowledge the transcendent but can take no account of it. And if it is challenged by absolute moral values, it must dispose of them ('The Grand Inquisitor'). In consequence, the state does not exist to provide a framework for moral choice but to ensure that temporal – temporary – laws are observed. It is, therefore, a framework of purely secular and public behaviour. But beneath the cloak of every individual, the cosmic struggle must go on.

In moral terms, Dostoievsky's state is minimalist; in public terms, it is – and ought to be – authoritarian. For the very nature of the moral conflict and of human inadequacy to cope with it imply that human beings, from their different inside standpoints, can make different choices: some clearly reprehensible, others perhaps justifiable within a limited context, and few clearly right. Morally, humans are engaged, not by desire but by necessity, in a war of all against all. Even the choices made within the limited frame of context can be totally incompatible; and if one attempts to elevate these choices to a *political* status, one is in danger of creating, politically as well as morally, a tyranny (*The Possessed*). It is the function of the authoritarian state to guard against such emergent tyranny. Soul and state can be confused only at the peril of both.

This view of the state which Dostoievsky articulated so powerfully is among the ancestors of an alternative Western political tradition. Just as Dante exemplifies the kinds of Western asssumption which underlie belief in the moral dignity and necessity of democratic choice, so Dostoievsky emphasises an alternative view: that humans are too weak to cope without the existing framework of the state. His successors, acting on this belief, but with the added assumption that the different circumstances in which people are born so complicate the issue that they cannot choose freely anyway, now go further. The state shall cope on behalf of humans with the dilemmas of living in society. They have become the spokesmen of the welfare state.

So far, I have been trying to suggest that the roots of Western thinking about the nature of the state are to be found in the conflicting traditions of Christianity. There are also reasons, which I shall indicate later, for taking works of art as a starting point. For the moment, the question that I wish to raise is how we can think of the functions of the state when we are living in what is fundamentally a post-Christian period. For it seems to me that Christianity was able to suggest a manner of approach to the question of the state precisely because a moral order, far anterior to and more important than the state itself, was deemed to exist. The state could be judged, and its role and function spelled out, in the light of a transcendent order which was always immanent. Now that the view of this transcendent order has been lost, many assumptions which were once so painfully made explicit have reverted to the pre-articulate.

What has happened, for example, to the 'welfare state'? It has come to acquire the dimensions of moral authority. These are seldom made explicit, but I will illustrate their nature by two examples from contemporary Britain. The first lies in the tendency which is visible in public policy and debate on the universities to suggest that scholarship should be at the service of the state. In attempting to make scholarship 'useful', such an approach is of course self-defeating, since no one can tell the eventual uses of free inquiry; and such a utilitarian approach can only have the effect of depriving society of future flexibility in choice. (Did anyone, including Rutherford, foresee the consequences when he split the atom? He himself declared that it had no practical use at all.) But the point here is the basic assumption that the state is fit to declare what the purposes of scholarship should be.

The second instance is the dispute over private treatment in National Health Service hospitals. The crucial aspect of this dispute is that, while arguments over the use of national resources can cut both ways, much of the fury has been directed at the principle whereby private patients have hitherto been allowed to co-exist with Health Service patients in the same hospital. Yet who are these private patients? They are people who have paid their National Health Service contributions along with the rest, and are therefore entitled in any event to the medical treatment they receive. Beyond that, they have chosen to invest a portion of their income in insurance schemes against the eventuality of illness, rather than, say, buying consumer luxuries. It is this, apparently, which their opponents find outrageous. In other words, the class origins and values of the patient become the criteria for moral action. Beginning with the same assumptions as Dostoievsky's – that human beings are weak and need help – Mrs Barbara Castle and her like end by turning the welfare state into a form of tyranny. Yet they do so in the name of democratic values! Dostoievsky's nightmare is fulfilled in such a case.

Dante's successors, on the other hand, who believe that the purpose of the state is to provide a framework for individual choice, are in an even worse case. For how can the laws of the state provide such a framework if they have no relation to the laws of the universe? The American Republic, for example, claims to provide its citizens, just as if they were latter-day Florentines, with a framework for moral choice and moral action. But such a Republic explicitly abjures any official religion. University chapels which can be converted at the touch of a switch from a synagogue to a Catholic oratory; restaurants which bear a printed card to guide Catholics, Protestants and Jews to their respective forms of grace before eating; these are not merely expressions of the principle of toleration: they represent the reduction of religion to a civic act. In such a situation, the Republic has lost any meaning which Dante could recognise and at the same time extended its own moral claims. The United States is not subject to the laws of a moral cosmos, nor is it a mediator between the citizens and the moral cosmos; it has had to *become* a moral cosmos. It is precisely this arrogation of moral value which makes moral judgment about the behaviour of the state difficult – so difficult that for years the citizens of America acquiesced in the atrocity of Vietnam.

The state, which was founded within a Christian tradition of transcendence, has lost the tradition but thereby vastly expanded its own claims to moral authority. This is a sad and potentially tyrannical confusion. Two particular historical moments helped to create it.

The first was the profoundly anti-Christian Peace of Westphalia. If one endorses the principle *cuius regio, eius religio*, the transcendent is banished from politics, and politics becomes a trivial calculation of advantage. The second was the emergence of the theory of toleration towards the end of the seventeenth century.[3] In Locke's form, this theory reduces the state's role to that of a guardian of property, on the basis of which those privileged enough to enjoy a good life can work out a set of morals which have little more import than a code of manners.

These two principles came together in the American Constitution. Indeed, the original formulation in the Declaration of Independence referred to the *pursuits* of happiness – a Lockean enough notion, but at least one which comprised some sense of social dignity and communal understanding. But it was subsequently amended into the concept of the *pursuit* of happiness, which, while sounding grander, was not only inherently more trivial but also suggested a perpetual pattern of individual conflict. It is a leading example of the way in which the demise of transcendent authority led to a condition in which the state's claims grew bigger but their content became more petty.

The idea of toleration makes it impossible for the state to act as mediator between the citizens and the transcendent – for it depends on the assumption that all citizens have their own version of the eternal laws. Yet, at the same time, this banishment of the transcendent was necessary. It was necessary in the sense that the only alternative was the indefinite continuation of a European civil war, fought to establish a single eternal law.

The theory of toleration was not only necessary; it also led to a new view of human intellectual activity. It led to a picture of the mind set against the world rather than operating as part of the world in a divinely ordered natural schema. This independence of the observer raised new sets of questions. They were to prove of the utmost importance in the development of ideas about the state.

The beginnings unfortunately were not promising. In the first place they led to the eighteenth-century detour through rationalism and enlightenment. This was the detour in which physical science became the paradigm of thought, and as a result of which it is still impossible today to say anything about the nature of the state, or about moral choice within it, without incurring shallow questions about value judgments, subjectivism and the like.[4] But the immediate outcome of this detour was a split between the idea of truth and the idea of sincerity, between classicism and romanticism.[5] For rationalism produced no significant work of art, nothing that said anything worthwhile about the human condition, human choice or human society. Perhaps it was in response to the need to be able to speak again that a new pattern of symbols was invented: a pattern of significance as opposed to fact, of experience as opposed to science, of romantic sincerity as opposed to the 'laws' of nature. Not the least of Goethe's achievements was that he was able to create a schema within which a new unity was achieved between science and poetry, truth and meaning, experience and reason. But the *Geheimrat* had few ideas about the state.

Still, the concerns and question of politics, and the necessities of judgment imposed upon the state, underwent a fundamental change arising from the new ways of thinking in the eighteenth century. During Goethe's lifetime the newly-independent observer was able to ask a number of new and fundamental questions. Not only that, the questions took a particularly significant form. It is surely striking that the foundation of the Society for the Abolition of the Slave Trade, Mary Wollstonecraft's *Vindication of the Rights of Woman*, and Babeuf's Conspiracy of the Equals all occur within ten years of each other. In historical terms, these movements of thought can be said to have been simultaneous. And the components of all three – race, sex and class – haunt the political and social thinking of the modern world. But it is interesting to note the order in which they made their impact.

The effective movement for the abolition – first, of the British slave trade, then of slavery throughout the British dominions – was the first to be successful. This was, however, a comparatively simple question. Slaves were 'other', a group 'out there', an alien race, black. The imperishable Charles James Fox was the first to point out that the reason that the British corsairs did not carry off French captives for sale in the Indies was that they were white and of our kind; but he was nevertheless making a point which was (comparatively) rapidly understood. The state could revise its attitude, and behaviour, towards those 'out there'.

The second movement to achieve some degree of success was that directed towards changing relations between the classes. Pressure for an instalment of political and economic freedom for the lower or exploited classes began to find a political form in Britain in the fourth decade of the nineteenth century – and the pattern was followed elsewhere in Europe. Gradually (and partly, of course, through the work of the rationalising neo-Hegelians, the Marxists) the problem of class was acknowledged as a *problem*. It was understood that class raised questions as to how society sees itself, of how human beings see themselves in relation to one another, of how they acknowledge 'the other' among themselves. This is harder for the state to grasp as a problem than the question of race: for race refers, by definition (in Europe, at least, until recently), to others 'out there'. With the question of class, the state has to come to terms with others *among us*.

In both these cases, I am clearly halfway equating the notion of the state with the notion of society. But this is less illegitimate than it looks, in that, since the rise of the idea of toleration, the Western state (of which the United States is in this respect the paradigm) has constituted the moral cosmos of society, and done much to justify Durkheim's famous, if erroneous, contention that every society worships itself and calls that God. (Could Durkheim possibly have read Dostoievsky?) But the real crux is that in my first two cases, it was relatively easy for the state, as the moral cosmos of the society, to react to the problems raised: race and class are concerned with recognisable others. The case is different when it comes to sex.

This question, which was raised simultaneously with the other two at the end of the eighteenth century, has, until recently, had practically no impact on the nature of thinking about the state. Mary Wollstonecraft is an historical footnote in books which treat Wilberforce at length. (And the explanation is not merely one of political effectiveness – though even were that the case, it would be strong evidence of the priorities of thinking involved. In the end, it is that race has been regarded as an important question and sex has not.) The question of sexual exploitation was important to Engels but virtually ignored by Marx.[6] It was the one portion of Mill's work which his disciples did not take seriously. Why?

If one considers why it was easier to begin to deal with the question of race than that of class, it is perhaps possible to see why it was easier to deal with the question of class than that of sex. Each represents a movement inwards: from the other 'out there', to the other among us, to the other *within ourselves*. Start tampering with the sexual order of society, and you no longer know who *you* are any more, even in your most intimate relations. And this question which, in its modern form, is already nearly two centuries old, has only been taken seriously as a criterion for the judgment of social morality in the past ten years or so.

In other words, the revolution of self-discovery which began late in the eighteenth century has been characterised by a slow process of zeroing inwards. The first revelation of the revolution was: 'Good Lord, we've been racist all this time!' To my knowledge, as I say, the first man to declare this was Charles James Fox. The second revelation was that we have been classist all along, a revelation of which the principal prophet was Karl Marx. And the third, which achieved its resonance not with John Stuart Mill but with Kate Millett, was that we have always been sexist.

Each of these revelations took the slow and cautious and conflict-ridden form it did because each of them demanded an entire re-evaluation of human history. What had been taken for granted as right – or to put it more strongly than right, as natural – was suddenly seen to be wrong, monstrous, unnatural and therefore unjust. And they had all been uttered before Hegel lectured or wrote.

Even before Hegel embarked upon a new philosophy of mind, the questions asked by the independent, observing mind of the eighteenth century had begun to prompt a perpetual process of self-discovery in which not only did human history have to be rewritten continuously but the human consciousness itself was continually remade. As opposed to the legitimising principles of Natural Law, as opposed to the certainties of immanent transcendence, the mind that asked the questions had to change itself by changing history.

This change of mind (literally of mind) demanded a new philosophy of human consciousness. For what did it imply? First, surely, that the more we know about our history and about ourselves, the less we know. Old certainties become injustices; old institutions demand a new revolt. But it also implied, second, that the less we know, the more we know. History is seen, not as a self-validating exercise in the comprehension of a proper order which finds its expression in the right forms and institutions, but as a continuous act of negation. And this very negation, conflict-ridden as it is, increases our understanding of ourselves. When we know that slavery is based on race we understand that our minds have been racist. And so on.

Now the fact that the less we know, the more we know, means that from now on we must approach an understanding of history and of the external forms it takes – as, for example, the state – not through a study of these external manifestations themselves, but by an understanding of the human mind. And this is what Hegel attempted to do.

I am not suggesting that Hegel was merely concerned to incorporate the three revolutionary questions I have sketched above into a new scheme of things – though I would regard these three as determinant for our understanding of the mind in the world. Hegel, in the development of a complex, and indeed omniscient, philosophy of the mind and spirit, implied a revolution in the consciousness of history and also a revolution in the consciousness of consciousness. This implies, of course, a new transcendence.

The transcendence that follows from the Hegelian schema is no longer immanent, no longer operates outside time, and yet it reveals itself in time. It is now seen as a function of time itself. Not only is history time-bound (that is to say, it develops over time and changes its very nature over time); the mind too is time-bound. And not only does mind develop over time, it continually transcends itself. In turn, this implies that history has nothing whatever to do with the laws of the universe (if any) but can only be understood as thought. Above all, no state of consciousness can apprehend that which transcends it. Hence, the dominant mode of society or state at any given historical moment is condemned to a static consciousness and is, thus, incapable of working for the more just society which will take its place; and correspondingly, only the oppressed, the weaker, are capable of transcendence.[7]

The continuing form of transcendence in time, therefore, enjoins not only that history has always to be rewritten; it also means that moral laws are now laws only in a limited sense. They are the codification of what we have achieved so far. They are open to transcendence as we go on discovering. Discovering how the moral order has demanded victims whose own potential for transcendence has been sacrificed to the maintenance of a social framework. In other words, society becomes inherently oppressive.

This raises a number of questions. First, it almost banishes the concept of truth. Truth, if not exiled from the kingdom altogether, is at least confined to the borders. That is, truth can only be apperceived at the point where the social framework meets other considerations: either, those of science or else those of an immanence which is clearly seen to depend on sheer faith, not on revelation or on Natural Law. And, second, what of meaning? Meaning too has lost its meaning. The constant process of discovering that *we are other*, the constant becoming in which we are caught up, is bound to invalidate the individual perception of the world and the individual ability to act out oneself in the world – the ability, as it were, to create a nexus of meaning between individual significance and social significance – which had characterised the earlier attempts to allow Meaning to take the place of Truth. Hence two opposite but almost simultaneous processes come about. The first concerns art; the second, the social sciences.

Art had earlier been deemed to have a social significance. Even the 'rebellion' of the Romantics had taken social significance for granted. For they had continued to draw on a long and scarcely spoken tradition in which the ordering of art revealed that essence of human nature in human society which might otherwise have been drowned by the noise of human activity. But art now – at the end of the nineteenth century and increasingly in the twentieth – began to peel away from society.

The evolution of art has been the opposite of biological evolution. In biological evolution, one watches the emergence of increasingly complex and coherent forms of life from out of the random soup. Culminating in our sapient selves, the evolution we perceive is one of increasingly ordered significance. Art, on the other hand, begins in the forms of maximum significance. It starts as myth and from there it works its way through poetic truth to 'significant form' and finally out into the random. Today, for example, in order for art to maintain its validity as Art – that is, still to bestow on us a perception of freedom – it must strip itself of any pretensions to significance. The random is a necessary element of contemporary art.

The reason for the split that we seem to have perceived between the nature of artistic evolution and its true paradigm, that of biological evolution, surely lies in the fact that as we realised that human scope which was the culmination of the biological evolution, so we also realised that the latent powers of the cortex and the increasing demands that we made in consequence upon our human selves and our human society, prevented us, progressively, from endowing that society with any fixed meaning. And therefore art, in order to retain its meaning, had to lose its significance; that significance of which human evolution in human society should, in a properly meaningful world, have provided both the model and the justification.

If art, then, reflects the new prevailing view of the meaninglessness of society, what room may there be for any attempts to find a scientific order for the development of society? None. Where the grand (and, in many cases, fascistic) views of social evolution that follow upon the paradigm of biological evolution fail, those who cling to the idea of a scientifically ordered society are forced into one of two impossible moulds. One depends on a somewhat iron view of historical law – which I shall revert to. The other consists in empiricism.

Many British and American scholars still cling to the methods and beliefs of empiricism. They believe that somewhere 'out there', there are such things as hard facts. They believe that these facts exist prior to and independent of any act of interpretation which makes them facts in the first place. They have not yet recognised, in so far as they belong to the empirical tradition, that there is no such thing as an uninterpreted fact. For Anglo-Saxons such as these, Galileo's experiment from the Leaning Tower of Pisa either established facts or it did not. If one drops two lumps, one ten times as heavy as the other, from the same height and they both hit the ground at the same time, what this shows is that lumps of whatever weight will rush down to hit the ground at the same time if they are dropped from the same height.

Within the schema of Newtonian physics, that is, of course, perfectly 'true'. But in the schema of Einstein's physics, it is just as 'true' to suggest that the earth rushes up to meet the weights; and, even more fundamental, there can be no such thing as 'the same time' anyway, since each weight exists in virtue of its own function of energy over time. So what on earth (or anywhere else) are 'facts'? In brief, empirical observation which makes no attempt to establish the interpretative framework within which facts can be said to exist and have a meaning is condemned to the random. Natural scientists are perfectly aware of this. It is their country cousins, the social scientists, who are reluctant to see it. They still operate, for the most part, on the set of eighteenth-century assumptions which made science the paradigm of thought. They seem to have paid little heed either to Hume's criticisms in the eighteenth century or to developments in the philosophy of science since.

Social scientists, in other words, and especially those social scientists who are in the forefront of 'behavioural' thinking, have done no more than create an artificial codification of what is at best random observation. They do not explain the grounds on which they perceive their own perceptions. But once having decided on the perceptions they perceive, they frame them into facts, and use these 'facts' as heuristic criteria. In doing so, they condemn themselves to a form of causal explanation which is doomed to remain merely positive.

Yet, at the same time, they are fond of using cybernetic analogies, borrowing the authority of cybernetics to substantiate their claims to 'knowledge' and 'method'. But cybernetics proper never offers a positive explanation; the cybernetic explanation is always negative. Cybernetics considers what alternative possibilities might conceivably have occurred and then asks why they did not. In doing so it establishes its own negatively defined interpretative schema of the nature of fact.[8] Its social science imitators merely draw correlations between one set of observations and another: 'Let us measure the intimacy of relations between different states by measuring the density of postal traffic'! After all, why not? Let us decide that there is a correlation between smoking and lung cancer.[9] But once we have established that there is a correlation, let us not, for Heaven's sake go on to ask any questions about whether the correlation also provides a positive explanation; and above all let us ask no questions about the validity of positive explanation itself. If we did, we could not call ourselves scientists any more.

Randomness in selected fact, lent a spurious authority by the correlation of observations, and preserved through philosophical ignorance: this is the staple of behavioural analysis. And even when this question-begging observation has been acknowledged to be unsatisfactory (that is, when it has been acknowledged that observation is only satisfactory in so far as it sets epistemological frontiers, so that, for example, observation of animal behaviour is known to be no more than observation of animal behaviour whereas with humans one has to draw on a whole set of historical assumptions to *account* for the way one is observing human behaviour and for the human behaviour one is supposed to be observing, and the observational mode is thereby demonstrably inadequate even as a notation of human behaviour while remaining by definition incapable of grappling with history), even thereafter, the post-behaviouralists cannot get away from the weakness that their method imposes on them.

Conflict researchers, for example, are forced to posit a concept of 'conflict' of which their research is seldom more than a taxonomy of forms. How are they to account for a 'conflict situation' in which no conflict exists, for example, that of the Happy Slave? They find themselves obliged to posit a situation of *inherent* conflict: the slave is *really* in a position of conflict with his master but he does not know it. In other words, they have to assume a model of Hegelian transcendence if their methodology is to make any sense.

But if what I said earlier is true, it is useless to try to evaluate forms of social behaviour in a continuing context of transcendence. Such evaluation implies a comparison of comparable with comparable; and the notion of transcendence inevitably implies that stage two supersedes stage one, namely, that the two are incomparable. This makes a nonsense of the principles of conflict research. The whole empiricist school of observation finds itself, in short, in an ineluctable dilemma. It has to assume transcendence in order to rationalise. If it assumes transcendence it cannot predict. If it cannot predict, it cannot rationalise. *QED*.

If the empiricists provide one example of a latter-day attempt to create a scientific basis for the understanding of the social world, and if that attempt is based largely on ignorance, the available alternative is also inadequate. This alternative involves the notion of the laws of history. At least, this has the merit of building transcendence into the framework of intellectual understanding. Indeed, the laws of history, ever since Hegel, have been assumed to *be* the methodology of transcendence. But problems arise.

A preliminary point to notice is that which I have suggested a moment ago: namely, that the revolutions in human self-perception which were concerned with questions of race, class and sex, all occurred through the questions asked by the independent observer of the eighteenth century before Hegel. Hegel's attempt to provide a philosophy of the mind implied a rationalisation – or at least a method for thinking – which could re-establish a continuity with history instead of making a break with history. He was not so much concerned with the rewriting of history that these revolutions entailed as with showing how such revolutions were implied in the history of consciousness.

Now this initial point has a corollary: namely, that one can only write about history – that is, consciousness – if one stands outside the historical consciousness. Hegel was bound to operate, conceptually, from outside history, for he was speaking not only of consciousness becoming conscious of itself, but of the consciousness of that process too. *His* statement could not be time-bound, as consciousness itself, according to him, had to be. But if consciousness could not be independent of time, and if history is consciousness, where could he stand? He could not stand like Dante in Hell for Dante had assumed an immanent transcendence, working from the start (so to speak) outside time. Hegel's only recourse was to assume that history had already come to an end.[10]

Alexandre Kojève suggests, indeed, that Hegel's argument that the state had now become the appropriate vehicle for the World Spirit necessitated a prior assumption that the dialectical conflicts of history had finally reached their culminating point (that is, their stopping point) in the state which proclaimed itself to be founded on the universal principles of liberty, equality and fraternity. In other words, for Hegel, the state as embodiment of the World Spirit already meant that the final forms of transcendence were available to all – at least 'like the red outline of beginning Adam'. Thereafter, history was merely a struggle – between states – for the realisation of this already apperceptible form. The fact that Hegel knew that his work implied a revolution in the consciousness of history merely confirmed his understanding of what had been historically achieved.

For Hegel, the state was therefore both a framework in which these historical revolutions could find their true fulfilment, and also – because the struggles between states themselves helped to bring about the fulfilment of these revolutions – a vitally necessary element of future activity and future understanding. *We* might be living in an appendix to history, but it is in the appendix that history fulfils itself – and the state is the form in which it can do so.

Now this Hegelian argument at least gives the state an importance within a scheme of rationality which can be readily understood. But in fact, Hegel lost the argument, historically. To refer again to Kojève: a *total* theory of history demands an outside standpoint from which one can see it when it has already achieved its end. But the successors of the man to whom Hegel lost the argument, have claimed only to be living in the middle of a period of transcendence, and yet to be able to foresee the end of the whole process. I am speaking here, of course, of the official successors of Karl Marx: the socialist states and governments which confidently predict their own demise and the conditions which can bring this about. How do they get away with such a confidence trick? The answer lies in the iron law of historical materialism.

Put the dialectic and the nature of transcendence into material terms, and you can prove practically anything – because you have the authority of measurement, of quantifiable analysis, of '*reine wissenschaftliche*' data on your side. Of course, one still has to be a good dialectician and to spot when a quantitive change becomes a qualitative change, and all the rest of it. But at least it looks real, unlike the World Spirit. And it also enables one to extrapolate material conditions, so that even in the middle of transcendence it becomes possible to talk about the future.

But what does this amount to? The only conclusion of such official Marxist transcendence is that the state *must* wither away. The one attempt to view the state in a mode of thought which would not demand the eternal criteria of immanence, but would be compatible with historical transcendence, has been lost. All that is left is the competition among different models of transition. No wonder that the internal politics of officially Marxist states are both brutal and meaningless. Or that every attempt to rethink a scheme of values within a scheme of relationships is suppressed; or that the state proclaims itself to be merely a form of transition hurrying as fast as it can towards its own dissolution – but meanwhile does everything in its power to prevent the transition from ever coming to an end. If relations in production are the sole criterion of *all* forms of human relations, the transitional state, by the very partiality of the Marxist analysis, has set itself insoluble problems. It had therefore better continue in being, like a ruthless Micawber, in the hope that something will turn up.

It might be reasonably objected that these remarks are all very well, but they apply only to the Soviet Union and kindred governments, which are, after all, betrayers of Marxism; and that the Marxist mode of thought can hardly be adjudged thereby. In one sense, such objections would clearly be justified, but certain difficulties remain. First, to suggest that anyone is a betrayer of Marxism would imply that Marxism had an essence. But the idea of essence derives from a positivist way of thinking; and whatever his other faults and in spite of his *rein wissenschaftliche* pretensions, Marx was at least no positivist. But that is perhaps only a logic-chopping objection. There are two more serious difficulties. The first is that, as the history of Western Marxism indicates,[11] Marxist thinking can be assimilated into almost any mode of philosophical undertaking. For Gramsci, for instance, Marxist praxis was a lateral descendant of the principles of Machiavelli; for Sartre, Marx provides a methodology for the existential questionings of Kierkegaard; for Althusser, he renders a similar service to Spinoza. And so on. If such be the case, Marx might have provided a valuable stimulus to many acute or generous minds – but he hardly provides a method for thinking about the state and human relations within it. Unless – and here the second difficulty follows from the first – that method is one of historical materialism. One could well argue that it is only within the context of historical materialism that many of the perennial problems of human experience can be thought about today. But if this is so, it means that of the three revolutions in human consciousness which had occurred before Marx was even a gleam in his parents' eyes – that in race, that in sex and that in class – he fixed on only one as the key to the understanding of history. He regarded the other two as epiphenomena of the class struggle without bothering to say why. Or, to the extent that he did say why, he reveals a still greater inadequacy than even this single-factor explanation might suggest. For his method depended entirely on a positive explanation. In this way, he was hardly capable of fulfilling the requirements of systematic thinking. Systematic thinking demands negative, and not positive, explanation. (Marx, of course, was always negating. But his negation was an historical exercise which still depended on positive explanation.) This is a point I shall return to shortly. In the meantime the followers of Marx are left with a series of dilemmas. Either the state fulfils the brutal and meaningless role which is the form taken by official Marxism, or the liberal followers of Marx elsewhere have to claim that somehow a class analysis of society and the state will help to deal with such other questions as those of relations between the races and the sexes. Arguments of this nature tend to be both convoluted and thin. The victory of Marx over Hegel has not in fact done much to clarify the issues involved in judging society and the state; and historical materialism is either an iron law with all the limitations that that implies or else the vehicle for a vague idealism which needs filling out from other sources.

At this point I should like to summarise the argument I have been advancing so far – if only because I am going to find the rest more difficult. I suggested, first, that the traditions of Western democracy are based upon a number of Christian assumptions, but that these have now reverted to the pre-articulate. In the process they have created greater moral claims for the state but have at the same time made it more difficult to articulate, at any given moment, the nature of moral choice. Further, they are open to the temptation of moral tyranny.

I suggested, second, that after the tradition of Christian immanence had been lost, the 'rational' independent mind of the eighteenth century began to ask a number of questions which have revolutionised the nature of historical consciousness. Further, these questions were characterised by a slow process of zeroing inwards through a number of political and social conflicts. In each case, in order to apprehend the nature of the question, humans had to become 'other'. This implies that the less we know, the more we know. The full implications of this I have not yet taken up.

I suggested, third, that the revolutionary process necessitated by such questions was organised into a new philosophy of mind by Hegel: and that this new philosophy was capable of suggesting an articulate role for the state within an understanding of human transcendence.

Fourth, however, transcendence over time created a fundamental challenge to what had hitherto been conceived as truth – and this has affected both the evolution of art and the understanding of social science. Art can no longer, as it could in the case of Dante and even in that of Dostoievsky (in whose country the Christian tradition had taken a different form from that of Western Europe and had survived the Age of Reason), suggest a significant framework of social and moral questions. At the same time the dominant modes of social scientific thinking depend either on philosophical and scientific ignorance, as in the case of behaviouralism and empiricism, or on an unwarranted assertion as in the case of historical materialism.

So how can one think about the nature and functioning of the state today? Apart from the short and obvious answer, where do we stand on this? How, for instance, can one discuss what, at any moment, is the nature of justice with the random empiricists who do conflict research? There is neither a moral tradition nor a philosophical language. The reductionist approach of the behavioural school implies more than that the state is no longer a useful concept; it implies, first, a static unhistorical understanding, and second, that there is no framework in which on can even discuss questions about the relationship between the political and moral order.

The main problem for anyone concerned with the questions of political order and the articulations of moral choice (and the world teems with such questions) is how to devise a language in which these questions find their context. I would like to suggest the beginnings of an approach to doing so.

The approach implies, clearly, that before one can see the state in its relations with other states, one must first consider it as a self-regarding entity: that is, a social form which comprises the framework for the relations of its citizens. It is, indeed, only in this sense that the state itself or the study of the state can be justified. For I suggested earlier that all society is inherently oppressive. Can the state be more than the custodian of such oppression? A prevailing view among many students of politics is that it cannot: that the state and its power are responsible for the 'authoritative allocation of values' and that is all. Can one get beyond such static pessimism?

The way forward is, in the first instance, the way back – to Hegel. I suggested earlier, following Kojève, that Hegel could only write from a position outside history because history had already come to an end. But, of course, Hegel was wrong. The state, for all the universalising ideals of the French Revolution, was a terrible framework for the World Spirit. After the experiences of the twentieth century, who could possibly suggest either that history has come to an end, or that it makes sense? But I do wish to suggest that we are approaching the end of history.

Before doing so, I think it is necessary to tackle a preliminary difficulty. This difficulty arises, perhaps, from the attempt to clear away the moral wreckage of European totalitarianism and European imperialism. It arises, even, from the very process by which Western states have degenerated into moral authority. This process consists in emancipating the areas and peoples over which the West once claimed not only political rule, but moral suasion. The emancipation has been held to be a moral act; and the claims are now seen as immoral. They have been replaced by a kind of universal and mindless tolerance. Moreover, this Western attitude coincides with a tragi-comic parody of Hegelian transcendence – the transcendence which the slave was capable of achieving, but not the master. It is now the new states of the Third World, especially in the international forum of the United Nations, that lay claim to moral suasion. And their claims are met either by an emphatic but barely articulate rebelliousness, as for instance in the case of Daniel Moynihan, or else by the enthusiastic acclamations of the neo-Liberals who believe that they can now emancipate themselves from their own history.

And yet these new states are, for the most part, not only inherently but blatantly oppressive. So far, the Moynihans are right. But the real difficulty lies not in the contradiction between the claim and the actual nature of the post-colonial societies (that would be easy enough to deal with), but in the confusion of concepts and language on the part of those who would wish to see a moral order in the world.

Perhaps one instance might indicate this confusion, and I have picked, somewhat unfairly, on Julius Nyerere. Nyerere is, admittedly, not as bad as some other dictators; but the point is not one of relative moral standing, but of the confused admiration which is lavished upon him by the Trevor Huddlestons, the *Guardian* liberals, and the bright-eyed radicals. Nyerere has been guilty of appeasing an exceptionally cruel island dictatorship; he has, in the name of racial equality, sanctioned institutionalised rape; he has in the name of nation-building and state unity passed a marriage law which is unspeakably sexist. Now the point is that if one has nothing to say about these things, except perhaps to murmur *autres cultures, autres moeurs*, one has nothing to say at all. There are no criteria by which one can say racism bad, sexism therefore good. At this level, one is reduced to the bleat of the sheep in *Animal Farm*. Equally, one cannot easily adopt what might be called the conservative Western position: that which asserts that *we* are, somehow, 'free' and are charged with a moral authority which those without the law will never possess. That would merely be to adopt the attitude of Beatrice to Virgil, and forget our own recent history in doing so. Both these attitudes ignore the historical revolutions of the past two hundred years, and in their common ignorance, are distinguished only by the mindless relativism of the one and the mindless authoritarianism of the others.

If one wishes to do better, two questions are involved. The first is that which I have already suggested, namely, that of negative rather than positive causality in a scientific system. If we are concerned to frame some kind of heuristic criteria in a world which operates through the relations of states, we have to know what we can understand about the nature of the states-system. And this is where negative criteria are all-important. What one has to explain is not why states behave as they do, but why they don't behave as they don't. This follows from the present understanding of scientific method, as argued in particular by Karl Popper.

Now, in the present context, the importance of Popper's work might appear somewhat paradoxical. After all, if one has been at pains to emphasise that attempts to turn the study of the state (and of relations between states) into a form of science are ignorant in their basis and misleading in their conclusions, then surely one should have the grace not to adduce the methodology of science at this stage of the argument. But the Popperian criteria of refutation do appear to me to have important implications for the manner in which one can think about the state.

For refutation depends, as a working principle, on the situation of controlled experiment. But in such a situation, refutation actually means that it is the control group and not the experimental group which is the better known about.[12] If, for example, one can show that metals expand with heat whatever the time of day, one has not perhaps said very much about thermodynamics or the nature of metals, but one has certainly shown that the time of day doesn't matter. In other words, even refutation might be said to include a negatively defined principle of verification. (Similarly with Galileo's lumps: at least we know that it doesn't matter how much they weigh.) I would argue, indeed, that behind some of the controversies in the philosophy of science that have taken place in recent years lies a not always explicit dispute as to whether one is making propositions about a control group or an experimental group.

But what, one might reasonably ask, does this imply for thinking about the state? I wish to suggest that the answer lies in the fact that one is dealing with situations where experimental control is not possible – situations involved in the historical understanding of the nature of the self-regarding state, and of the development of its relations with other such self-regarding entities. And it is here that refutation really comes into its own. It can say nothing about a control group because between such entities none can exist. But in consequence refutation can do more. It can, in the absence of any such group, show that 'laws', either those which derive from generalised assertions about history or those which derive from generalising propositions about the way states behave, are meaningless. They cannot be refuted because there is no criterion of control; equally, nothing can be verified, even by implication, about a control which does not exist.

Now the interesting thing about this is that if there are no 'laws', there is no certainty. If there is no certainty, there is no baseline. The baseline merely extends indefinitely backwards into how we decide to think – that is, into myth. The state in this sense is essentially mythic. That is why I decided in the first place to approach the problem of the state through works of art rather than through the *post hoc* rationalisations about its functioning which constitute the main body of writing in the subject of international relations. But if art no longer serves a generalised function, it can hardly be a valid model of approach to the state. And yet it provides the approach to a subsequent understanding.

The argument is in two parts. First, the key to the valid model lies in understanding why states don't behave as they don't. If it were true that all states tended to behave the same way; if it were true that states share an equal preoccupation with different questions of justice like the triad I have suggested, we would have few problems. But if we know that Chinese, South Africans, Saudis, Tanzanians and Israelis all behave in different ways, have different views about the nature of the state and the obligations of relations between states, at least we have problems. We might even have a subject in studying relations between them. And in my view this subject consists in framing criteria by which we can judge the behaviour of states.

The difficulties, and the subject, arise from the way these mythic entities regard each other. On the one hand, each recognises in the rest its own mythic character: hence, the inability to judge the internal behaviour of one country by the criteria formed in another, the principles of non-interference and of Augsburg and Westphalia, and – to confirm the circular legitimacy of the myth – the acceptance of sovereignty. On the other hand, every student of international relations, every intelligence service, every foreign office, knows that there is no dividing line between the internal and external behaviour of a state; and that sovereignty in its universal form of non-interference does not provide an adequate answer to the problems raised by sovereignty in its several forms of internal morality. (If it did, the questions that continuously exercise statesmen when they contemplate Eastern Europe, or the Middle East, or Southern Africa or Northern Ireland, would never arise.) In consequence, and precisely to the extent that they accept the universal myth of statehood, states bring themselves ineluctably to judgment. But how?

If they matter at all, if they are anything more than a pretty random way of organising society, they must come up for judgment. If they can't come up for judgment, international relations doesn't matter – in any of the modes available for talking about it. But if the state does matter, that is not because it's all we've got to deal with, still less because each state constitutes its own legitimation. (Consider Amin, or consider Stalin's Russia; that would only be another way of saying that we have nothing to say.) The state matters because it is the only available, and still perpetual, mediator between (to go back to Hegel again) the objective and the ultimate. As such, it is not only, in a truer sense than Marx suggested, always transitional; it is not only, as all societies are, inherently oppressive; it is also the framework in which society can seek continuously to transcend its own oppressive nature. Only the state can provide the possibilities of a continuing debate which does not degenerate into a murderous conflict; but in so doing it is continuously driven to abnegate its own authority *qua* state. If it did not, if it were content merely to rest upon the 'authoritative allocation of values', if it proclaimed that statehood is enough, it would be impossible to distinguish at all. Hence, it is the very justification of the state which makes the judgment of states a necessity.

At which point it might appear that Hegel was right after all. Is not then the state the vehicle for the World Spirit? Rather, the contrary. *His* history has not come to an end, and it is precisely because it did not that the necessities of judgment are so acute today. But can one, in that case, suggest, as I have suggested, that the end of history is in sight?

I would argue that Hegel–though at times he implied omniscience and even implied that his method could not begin unless it *were* omniscient–was restricted by the fact that he wrote before the study of psychology. It is the study of psychology, perhaps, and not of the Hegelian state, which provides the beginning of the end of history.

Psychology clearly is a term of so many different meanings that it will take a long time yet for history to accomplish its task. I wish here only to suggest that the very notion of psychology implies the universal study of the human mind. Within the study of psychology, many of the arguments that have been rehearsed here would have to be entered upon afresh–as, for example, between a Jung and a Skinner. It is, one hopes, clear from the foregoing that I have no great sympathy for Skinner's methods, let alone his conclusions,[13] and that I would regard the study of myth as more important and more appropriate to an understanding of the human mind. But the main issue at present is that the emergence of this universal mind can create a principle by which the workings of history–and of the state within the context of history–can be judged.

In other words, it is not the state which creates the universal principle so clearly envisaged by Hegel's end of history. It is rather that the end of history lies in our approaching understanding of the beginning of history: the transcendent fuses with the static in our study of the human mind. For the changing nature of our minds at work in society also serves to emphasise the unchanging nature of the psyche which lies behind them–and it is precisely out of the conflict between the two that we can increase our understanding. In such a context, the state is still the vehicle for the realisation of the Spirit, but only in the sense of that which can be *said*. It can, however, now be judged by that which can be *shown*.[14] That, of course, is the second part of the argument whereby the consideration of works of art might provide the approach to an understanding of the state.

It is because the less we know, the more we know, that we can understand the workings of the human mind. And this understanding can create the rationale for the consciousness of transcendent consciousness in a fuller sense than perhaps even Hegel could envisage. It might mean that we can never transcend *ourselves* in quite the way that he imagined; we will always know now that we are stuck, individually, with the reptilian brain below the cortex; the more we know about the unconscious, the more perhaps we are condemned to poking about for elbow room in the 'foul rag and bone shop of the heart'. But it does not preclude us from criticising and changing societies, in which the scope for elbow room can be created; societies in which the understanding of oppression can defeat oppression, or in which an emerging agreement on the nature of justice can harmonise the relations between the states. In which states can be judged, condemned and encouraged by the common understanding of the human mind; and in which humans can become more than themselves.

NOTES FOR CHAPTER 10

1 See Arnold Pacey, *The Maze of Ingenuity* (London, Allen Lane, 1974).

2 *Inferno*, c II, l. 91. It should be added that in the end the noble pagans are in Paradise. But as the indifference of Beatrice indicates, there is an unresolved tension about them in the poem as a whole; and Hell itself remains.

3 Of course, in one sense, the principles of the settlements of Augsburg and Westphalia already implied toleration. '*Cuius regio, eius religio*', after all, suggested toleration at the international level. But it meant that, if peace was not divisible, toleration was. Tolerance outside one's borders was accompanied by intolerance within. Hence the dual conception of sovereignty and the confusion it has given rise to. I shall revert to it later in the chapter. Meanwhile, to do him due credit, Locke did formulate a more comprehensive theory of toleration.

4 See Cornelia Navari's chapter in this book for a fuller discussion of these questions.

5 To the best of my knowledge, the first person to point to the romantic ideal of sincerity in opposition to the classical ideal of truth was Sir Isaiah Berlin.

6 Except in *The Holy Family*, where he welcomed such exploitation, apparently in the name of sociological tidiness. See Igor Shafarevich, 'Socialism in our Past and Future', in Alexander Solzhenitsyn, ed., *From Under the Rubble* (London, Collins, 1975). One wonders what the 'Young Marx-ists' of Eastern Europe, who try so hard to equate the earlier works of Marx with a scheme of human values, make of *The Holy Family*.

7 See *The Phenomenology of the Spirit*, s. A, ch. IV, 'Autonomy and Dependence of Self Consciousness: Master and Slaver'.

8 See Gregory Bateson, *Steps to an Ecology of Mind* (London, Paladin, 1973).

9 I am not, of course, suggesting that there is *no* correlation between smoking and cancer of the lung. What I am suggesting is that correlations of this nature are virtually useless as a form of scientific research. As far as I understand it, almost anything, if taken in sufficient quantities, could induce a cancerous reaction. But (again, to the best of my knowledge) this fact does tend to leave us in a situation in which most people produce small cancers all the time. In which case, the crucial question would *not* be that of what provides positively explained stimuli to cancer, but what it is that prevents us at some point from suppressing the cancers that we produce. In other words, the negative explanation might have a great deal more to offer than the positive explanation.

10 See Alexandre Kojève, *Introduction to the Reading of Hegel*, trans. James H. Nichols (New York, Basic Books, 1969).

11 See Perry Anderson, *Considerations on Western Marxism* (London, NLB, 1976).

12 At this point, and for much of the following argument, I wish to acknowledge my debt to Roger Holmes, Senior Lecturer in Social Psychology at the London School of Economics and Political Science. I am indebted to him for the many insights that discussions with him have provoked, and also for his outstanding book, *Legitimacy and the Politics of the Knowable* (London, Routledge & Kegan Paul, 1976).

13 For a brief criticism of Skinner's methodology, see Morton Kaplan, *On Freedom and Human Dignity* (Chicago, The University Press, 1973).

14 The implied quotation is from the conclusion of Wittgenstein's *Tractatus*.

11
International Relations and Philosophy of History

PETER SAVIGEAR

The study of history and the study of politics may be said to differ in one main respect. The study of politics centres on the conflict between the world as it is and the desire to change it for the better. The European tradition of politics is about the Good Life, the tension which exists between the 'is' and the 'ought'. This theme has run not only through thought about the state, at least since the time of Machiavelli, but also through thought concerned with international relations.

With the study of history, on the other hand, it has been different.

'Oh, shut up arguin',' said William. 'How d'you think things d've got done in hist'ry, if people kept on arguin' an' making objections like you?'
  'Some things didn't get done in hist'ry,' said Douglas.
  'I could tell you lots of things that didn't get done in hist'ry.'
  'Well, we don't want to hear 'em,' said William.[1]

The study of history has accepted that the 'is' and the 'ought' have come together in events. This is true anyway of the approach to the study of history that emerged from the eighteenth and nineteenth centuries. Tolstoy captured the point in *War and Peace*. He wrote of the dichotomy between 'freewill' and 'inevitability': 'History surveys a presentation of man's life in which the union of those two contradictions has already taken place.'[2] The events of history have, in some way, resolved the conflict inherent in politics.

My intention in this chapter is to examine some of the implications of this philosophy of history, articulated within the last two centuries in Europe, for thought about international relations.

These implications move the study of international relations in a particular direction, that is, an historical direction which imparts to it at the same time a moral element and a purpose.

I

A philosophy of history which reconciled the apparently contradictory elements of political action was quite new. Thought about history before the end of the eighteenth century, with the great exception of Vico's *New Science*, published in 1725, was based on a dualism between the world as it is, recounted by the chronicler, and the world as it ought to be, expounded by the pedagogue, using the past as a pool of examples of conduct for imitation. This last was the humanist tradition of history-writing, principally directed at statesmen. Much the same approach was adopted by those who wrote teleological history, whether of a religious kind like Bossuet or of a rational and secular kind like Voltaire. In their eyes writing history was purposive, it was telling a story of the past which revealed a truth that was imported into history from outside, from Faith (Bossuet) and from Reason (Voltaire), and which established examples of how to conduct oneself. The change came with the acceptance of an approach, similar to that adopted by Vico in his *New Science*, by authors at the end of the eighteenth century, notably by French and, to a lesser extent, German historians.

The new philosophy of history did not rely on criteria taken from outside the historical discipline in order to explain the direction and meaning of historical events. On the contrary, it believed so firmly in the discipline of history that Collingwood, a later exponent, was able to assert that all knowledge whatsoever is historical knowledge. Every kind of knowledge had a history which alone enabled it to be fully understood, even the knowledge of the scientist. Thus, he argued that Einstein could only be understood in the historical context of Newton and the other scientists who were his predecessors.[3]

All knowledge was, in the view of Vico and the historians of France, Germany and Italy of the nineteenth century and, later, of Collingwood and Croce, a history of mind and its thoughts. Vico grasped the significance of 'a truth beyond all question ... that the world of civil society has certainly been made by men and that its principles are therefore to be found within the modifications of our own human mind'.[4] History, as the story of events, was intelligible through the working of the intellect; 'since men have made it [the world of nations] men can truly know'.[5] The study of history was the study of mind, of its thoughts and responses to the human situation. 'Our science comes to be at once a history of the ideas, the customs, and the deeds of mankind',[6] and 'proceeds by a severe analysis of human thoughts about the human necessities or utilities of social life'.[7]

This philosophy of history gave mind (reason) itself a history. Reason had not been always and everywhere the same but had varied according to time and place. Above all, reason progressed through history so that, wrote Vico, 'when our human reason was fully developed, it reached its end in the truth of ideas concerning justice, determined by reason from the detailed circumstances of the facts'.[8] On this basis, the study of history could claim to show how mind (with its desire to change and improve human life) and observable action in the world (at first sight a lamentable record for the most part) were in fact reconciled in past events. These events were manifestations of mind, and therefore the study of the history of mind could claim to resolve the tensions and contradictions between the way men wanted to make their world and the way it actually was. The events were themselves the living evidence of the reconciliation between the world and the desire of men to change it.

This philosophy of history claimed, then, that the only way in which to understand the world of politics, as every other aspect of the social life of man, was historically. This was not an easy task. It required that one think one's self back into the minds of the men of the past, not only their conscious minds but also the total circumstances in which their minds had worked, in order to attempt to understand the nature of mind at that moment in the past. The task required humility not arrogance.[9] The detailed knowledge of the past served solely to help in this process, to assist the historian in placing his mind in the context of the past.

The process of rethinking the past provided the purpose of the study of history which earlier writers of history had sought outside the story of events and the evidence. They had found meaning only by importing criteria from theology or a non-historical Reason. Now the acquisition of knowledge about the past created a link between the historian and the past which was understood as the history of the changes of human mind. A story has both a beginning and an end (said Virginia Woolf) and for each historian this particular story of the past ended in his own mind. He traced the continuity between his mind and those that went before him. The continuity and common element was that all phenomena other than those of the world of nature, all human phenomena, were in this special sense products of mind and manifestations of thought. History which 'has hitherto lacked beginning' henceforth has both beginning and end through the account of the 'modifications of our own human mind'.[10]

The climax of the new philosophy of history was the work of Hegel. It was also expressed, however, by other historians in their accounts of the evolution of institutions, such as those of the French as described by François Guizot, in which the *ancien régime* and the events of the Revolution were brought together and shown to be consistent with the whole history of France. It was also expressed in the realm of international relations. Here perhaps the greatest contribution was made by Leopold von Ranke in his history of *The Great Powers*, published in 1841.

Ranke examines events, from 1648 to the nineteenth century, in terms of developing mind. To be a Prussian in the eighteenth century and to look at the affairs of Europe was to be affected by the history of France in a special way, a way that demanded an intellectual response quite different from that of a Prussian in 1640 or in 1830. Ranke tells us about the powers in terms of the history of the European mind. Their actions are the product of thought in this new, historical sense. The story is not one of 'chaotic tumult, warring and planless succession of states and peoples'. The 'secret of Western history' lies in creative forces, 'in their interaction and succession, in their life, in their decline or rejuvenation'.[11] 'Out of separation and independent development will emerge the true harmony', that peculiar Europe where the 'union of the whole which grows firmer from decade to decade, has happily preserved the freedom and separate existence of each state'.[12]

There was at the same time a difficulty in this philosophy of history as in no other before. It implied a total comprehension and thus that every action was in some way justified. Was there, then, no moral choice? Was the development of human mind necessarily determined, as some historians and the behavioural scientists who have succeeded to this philosophy of history have believed? In that case the world of history is without morality, without choice and not open to judgment, solely a set of changing manifestations of thought. Thus Gentz, for example, argued both that the partition of Poland in the late eighteenth century was inhumane and callous and yet that, once it was a *fait accompli*, it became part of the necessary *status quo* in Europe, forming the basis of a new balance of power.[13] Gentz was left in a position which justified any situation as it developed from the interplay of states which were obeying an historical logic. It was this historical imperialism against which Nietzsche inveighed in his essay *The Use and Abuse of History*. He claimed that all capacity for judgment and choice was destroyed by this cloying and fatalistic philosophy of history.

II

Yet such a philosophy of history does not lead in a single direction. The way divides. One path no doubt leads to determinist behaviouralism. But equally it is possible to argue for what A. C. Danto, in his *Analytical Philosophy of History*, has called 'methodological individualism', the path of 'those who regard social processes as the complicated outcome of the behaviour of human beings'.[14] The task of the historian, on this view, is to reveal the tensions and contradictory perceptions which go to make history and to deduce the historical reality from the human thought and action, not the other way about. This was, above all, Tolstoy's position. In his terms, the task is to reveal the interplay between 'free will' and 'inevitability'.

We should not be deterred from this task by the apparent remoteness of events, whether in time or space, as the events of international relations often are. We know about the politics of our parish in some ways differently from the politics of other states, and yet all events are in the parish of such a philosophy as Tolstoy's in *War and Peace*.

The world that is there described is one in which morality and judgment can arise because the individual is responsible for his choices. He must face the consequences of his decisions and actions. The individual is compelled to act, to choose his action, and the appropriateness of his choices will be revealed and judged by their history. There is no escaping the judgment of events and, thus, of history.

It is this that forms the basis of the moral novel. The decisions and weaknesses of the characters bring their inevitable reward as the plot unfolds, although at the moment of decision a real choice was open to the individual. Thus, George Eliot heads a chapter of *Middlemarch* (Book 1, Chapter 4) with this quotation, displaying the relationship between decisions and the constraints of the actual situation in which the decision must be made:

First gent: Our deeds are fetters that we forge ourselves.
Second gent: Ay, truly: but I think it is the world that brings the iron.

The ability to explain and understand the past no doubt appears at first to remove all necessity and possibility of judgment: if the context of the time can be understood, then the basis for judgment, for approval or disapproval, is undermined. Yet judgments are possible; but afterwards, in the light of history when we can perceive the relationship of events and the appropriateness of action. The place of human action in history can only be assessed, and must be assessed, by the historian as he writes his history. He necessarily judges in writing. The problem is not simply one of understanding the facts but, as Collingwood puts it, of 'getting inside other people's heads, looking at their situation through their eyes, and thinking for yourself whether the way in which they tackled it was the right way'.[15]

To write this sort of history is not to narrate the past but to face, in Croce's words, an 'ethical problem of changing' the facts, 'that is, of creating new facts'.[16] An 'event' is created by the historian. It is not simply the sentences linking events, the selection of events and their interpretation that are the creation of each historian, but the events themselves. A. C. Danto writes: 'The whole truth concerning an event can only be known after, and sometimes only long after, the event itself has taken place.'[17] Events themselves have a history; they can be recaptured only through their history and judged only through their history. The assassination of the Archduke Franz Ferdinand in 1914 was at first just a 'shocking assassination'. Later it 'began the First World War'. In the same way, Collingwood uncovers the significance of Caesar's crossing of the Rubicon by referring to subsequent history. The history of an event is an integral part of the event itself, not simply an interpretation. Actions and the passage of time are linked by the historian.

To sum up so far: political action is to be judged on its own terms, by criteria created by the historian and not imported from outside. Belief in an anterior morality does not affect this process by which political action is judged on the basis of values deriving from the realm of politics and its institutions. Indeed a tension will be set up between the belief in an anterior morality and what amounts to a political morality, and a choice must be made between them. The action of the state must be understood as part of the history of mind, of how a given action was possible in its historical circumstances. In this way, history must be constantly rewritten in order to give expression to judgments which themselves have a history. The implications of this philosophy of history are that the actions of mankind have to be judged, for judgments are inseparable from history, presented as the history of mind. At least in this sense, history is the study of psychology and not its rival – *pace* Philip Windsor in the previous chapter of this book, and even Collingwood who claimed that mind regarded as psychology 'ceases to be a mind at all'.[18]

III

The purpose of the theory of international relations is the judgment of the behaviour of states, not simply the explanation of their behaviour. Judgment is to be made on the basis of values established by international relations and not on the basis of an anterior moral order. The philosophy of history here outlined has the potential of specifying historical criteria by which those relations can be judged.

That philosophy of history came together with the theory of the state in the early nineteenth century in the work of Hegel and in the work of such historians as Guizot. The events of the past were to be understood and assessed from the point of view of the development of the state. The state established a special context in which human action and thought was to be understood historically; the politics and the history of the state had now to be brought into the making of judgment, as had not been the case before. Men must now judge conduct by studying political history, by understanding the different political situations in which mind had worked. Actions were justifiable from the point of view of the state which might otherwise be condemned.

Yet, once the political theory of the state had joined with this philosophy of history, the question arose, did, then, history end with the state? For us, the answer is that this philosophy of history presents the study of international relations with the opportunity of showing that history does not end with the state; rather that it ends in, or at least can be seen to proceed towards, international relations, a new context within which human action and thought can be judged.

The state was once the sole concrete reality and international relations were at best simply 'becoming'. But the study of history need not end with the state, nor yet be replaced by other disciplines, but may develop as international history. The philosophical purpose would be to find in international relations what Vico called 'a demonstration of the historical fact of Providence',[19] a demonstration that Providence was evident in international relations as well as in the history of the state.

Such a demonstration was achieved for the state and its institutions in the nineteenth century but not as yet for international relations. It was not achieved by the exhortations of the time to create international organisation. This introduced an unhistorical element into the discussion, something which was a prescription and not consistent with the history of the world and the fact of the state and its separateness. Neither, however, did stress on the need of states to compromise, as forming the essential element in their relations, give the study of international relations a clear, distinctive basis. Such ideas could still be expressed and corresponding judgments made in terms of the state and its development.

On the one hand, then, there were prescriptions for improving relations between states: the building of international organisation, international law, contacts (especially commerce) among the citizens of various states. On the other hand, and equally inadequate as a theory of international relations, there was the idea of *Realpolitik*, the assumption that whatever the historical differences between states, common ground existed which could be attained (or perhaps created) through diplomacy, founded upon the presupposition of the equality of states or an acceptable hierarchy among states. Here the basis remained the primacy of the state, not a new primacy of international relations. *Realpolitik* was not international relations because it was only a further expression of the world of states. The historian analysed the international relations of the state as part of the development of the state. International relations as a field of study was subject to the history of the state. Judgments in international relations were on the same basis as those in the domestic politics of the state.

The assumption of a world of independent, though inter-related, states restrained the development of theory in the study of international relations. Moral issues remained in the realm of the state, the conventions of the interstate world notwithstanding. The world of international relations did not enter the philosophy of history. Moral judgments stopped with the state.

Thus, Heinrich von Treitschke rested his arguments on the moral quality of the state even when saying that war and the rules and conventions and treaties that accompany this apparent collapse of civil society are the moments of mankind's greatest moral and rational achievement. He seems momentarily to be admitting a truly autonomous sphere of international relations, and yet the necessity for this sphere is in the end assessed in terms of the state. All the moral and rational devices which Treitschke saw as brought into being by the conflict between states were to be judged by the criteria of the state and not by criteria drawn from that international world. Perhaps this is why he has been dismissed as unconvincing in his arguments, if not abhorrent.

International relations are still not yet completely within the domain of history; the distinctive basis for judgment there is still not discernible. The tension between individual and state is clear; and between state and state; but not as yet between the state and a new context of international relations.

To say no more than this, however, would be to neglect the contribution of those in the past who have begun to point in this direction. Some of the great political theorists have tried to comprehend this tension. Machiavelli achieved insight by political intuition, pondering the clash of virtue and necessity in the political arena in which the Prince and Republic operated. Kant proceeded on the basis of a philosophical theory of Peace and the logical extension of this to international relations, but without history and separate from the history of the human mind.

From the early nineteenth century, with the development of the new philosophy of history, at the very moment when the philosophy of history could absorb the state, the possibility arose that theorists of international relations could begin to write history with the international world as its end beyond the state. Events could, from this time on, be judged from the point of view of international relations. These relations were, thus, more than the reassertion of the individual states, and constituted a separate realm with its own history.

The crux of judgment was the relationship of Good and Evil, the accommodation of Evil in the description of the past, its condemnation or comprehension. The tradition called Machiavellian (if not actually initiated by him) had accommodated Evil by the deeper analysis of politics: wickedness was justified to prevent greater wickedness. The state had thus been made relevant to the judgment of Good and Evil. This was at least consistent with history as the story of the development of the state. The new philosophy of history opened up the possibility of judgments and the comprehension of Evil in the latent world of international relations.

So Ranke in *The Great Powers* judged the actions of states and individuals from the standpoint of international order, uniting the philosophy of history and international relations. International relations began to emerge as 'a framework for choice' in the sense in which Philip Windsor discussed this in the previous chapter in terms of the state.[20] Ranke (whom I cite again here because he is an early and clear example of an historian who is also a theorist of international relations, that is, one who makes judgments about the history of those relations), analyses, for example, the attitude of Frederick II in refraining from crushing the Austrian armies in these terms: he 'wished to feel free and to assume an independent position, based upon his own strength between the two powers', France and the Austrian Empire.[21] Ranke comprehends and does not judge action on the basis of external moral criteria; he relates all parts to the whole and does not need to pick and choose, approve or condemn, but only to say, in terms of historical context, whether action is appropriate or inconsistent. And action is here approved by reference to the international context.

Yet despite such nineteenth-century foreshadowings, the history of international relations has still to be written. The Hegel of international relations has not yet appeared because the world has not yet escaped from the historical limits of the state. It is possible that the state may never be transcended by international relations. We cannot know, for history is neither about the future nor to be written in the light of a desired future. But it seems, at least, that the history of international relations is beginning to be written.

It seems so from the spirit of a great body of contemporary historical writings; not the writings of those who still interpret the world in terms of *Realpolitik*; nor yet of those who impose on events concepts, 'transnational relations', 'integration', and the like, in line with their desires; but the writings of the many scholars who set out to do no more than present the policies of states as faithfully as they are able, and who in doing so, who in their manner of doing so, who in their selection, their interpretation, their judgments, reveal to us the movement of contemporary mind towards a context of judgment wider than the state.

The movement of history continues to be revealed through the writing of historians. The significance of events continues to depend upon the unfolding of the modifications of the human mind. Philosophy of history provides the study of international relations also with the capacity to make judgments of the Good and Evil quality of action. Without judgment there can be neither responsibility nor a study of international relations which is not simply another way of studying the politics of the state. Philosophy of history makes theory of international relations possible because it enables it to make judgments in its own right.

NOTES FOR CHAPTER 11

1   Richmal Crompton, *Just William's Luck* (London, George Newnes, 1952), p. 59.
2   *War and Peace* (London, Macmillan, 1942), Second Epilogue, p. 1332.
3   *The Idea of History* (Oxford, The Clarendon Press, 1946), pp. 333–4.
4   *The New Science*, trans., T. G. Bergen and M. H. Fisch (Ithaca, Cornell UP, 1948), bk 1, s. 3, p. 85.
5   ibid.
6   ibid., bk 2, ch. 2, p. 100.
7   ibid., bk 1, s. 4, p. 92.
8   ibid., Conclusion, p. 353.
9   Vico insists always that it is a hard task to follow the changes of human mind 'which we cannot at all imagine and can apprehend only with great effort' (ibid., bk 1, s. 4, p. 89).
10 ibid., bk 2, ch. 4, p. 113; bk 1, s. 3, p. 85.
11 *Leopold von Ranke: the Formative Years*, trans. Th. von Laue (Princeton, The University Press, 1950), p. 217.
12 ibid., p. 189.
13 *Fragments upon the Present State of the Political Balance of Europe* in M. G.

Forsyth *et al.*, *The Theory of International Relations* (London, George Allen & Unwin, 1970), pp. 288–97.

14 *Analytical Philosophy of History* (Cambridge, The University Press, 1965), p. 313.

15 *Autobiography* (London, OUP, 1939), p. 58.

16 *Politics and Morals*, trans., S. J. Castiglione (London, George Allen & Unwin, 1946), p. 128.

17 *Analytical Philosophy of History*, op. cit., p. 151.

18 *Autobiography*, op. cit., p. 93.

19 *The New Science*, op. cit., bk I, s. 4, p. 91.

20 See pp. 171–2.

21 Th. von Laue, op. cit., p. 199.

12
Schools of Thought in International Relations

STEPHEN GEORGE

My conclusion is not startling: it is simply that now is the right time for doing some new fundamental thinking about the nature of international relations and the ways in which we study them. On the content of the rethinking, I have little to say, and would prefer to refer the reader to the preceding chapters of this book. What I am prepared to say is this: when, from some future vantage point, we come to look back, we may well realise that all our thinking was more determined by our circumstances than we supposed.

But let me start elsewhere. Thomas Kuhn's *Structure of Scientific Revolutions*[1] deals with the activity of doing science. It identifies science as a communal activity, carried on by a community of scholars who share a common set of basic assumptions about the nature of their subject matter. These assumptions constitute a paradigm within which normal scientific activity is conducted. Normal science consists of solving problems which are suggested by the paradigm and are considered to be important and relevant by the community of scientists. Only occasionally a problem is attempted to which no solution can be found within the framework of expectations constituted by the paradigm. In these instances, the response is either to drop the problem altogether and turn to other problems which are more amenable to solution; or to produce a solution to the problem by producing a new set of rules for problem solving, which consequently involves a complete restructuring of the paradigm. The latter response constitutes what Kuhn calls a scientific revolution. What Kuhn does not explain is why there is sometimes a scientific revolution in response to an awkward question and sometimes not. Nor, indeed, does he consider why the awkward problem should be raised in the first place.

I believe that the reason why Kuhn does not have answers to these questions is that he treats the community of scholars as a self-sufficient social system, and disregards the fact that all scholars are also part of a wider community, sharing many of the values, beliefs and concerns of their nation, class and generation. Certainly this social influence could be held to be less of a determining factor for the thinking of the scientist (at least on matters scientific) than it is for those who may be less scholarly and self-conscious. But that does not mean that the influence is negligible. And it could well be admitted that the influence of social constructions of reality would be stronger for the scholar who is studying society than for the natural scientist. Which brings us back to the study of international relations.

International relations as a subject is in a situation which is exactly like that described by Kuhn as being the pre-scientific state of all existing sciences: there are 'a number of competing schools and sub-schools' all trying to dominate the field.[2] Each school is an independent community of scholars with its own language, commitments and criteria of relevance: in other words, each works within its own separate paradigm. And there is very little communication between schools. How little was shown by the exchange between Hedley Bull and Morton Kaplan in 1966, which Kaplan strangely chose to characterise as 'The New Great Debate'.[3] That exchange at least had the merit of showing how far from mutual understanding the 'classical' and 'scientific' schools were.

Both Bull and Kaplan stressed that the classification into two schools was a simplification and that there was a great deal of variety within each. But at least the categories were sufficiently real to allow each protagonist to identify himself with one side against the other. From the point of view of this chapter, it is also extremely interesting that the stronghold of the 'classical' approach was 'the British academic community' and that it was in the United States that the 'scientific' approach had 'progressed from being a fringe activity in the academic study of international relations to such a position that it is at least possible to argue that it has become the orthodox methodology of the subject'.[4] I would like to suggest that this difference of approach represented the effects of cultural differences between the two countries and the different positions of the academic communities in the two societies.

Perhaps because I am an outsider to the 'scientific' school, I consider the influence of cultural and situational factors on that approach to be more obvious than in the case of the 'classical' school. The need for a science of international relations was felt strongly by United States policy makers, faced with a situation in which the United States for the first time had to fulfil a world role.

In a quest for guidance, the policy makers turned to the academic world, and ample funds were made available for research into the fundamental guiding principles of international relations. This attracted scholars into the field, and they brought with them ideas about the most suitable methodology for the study of the subject, which were derived from other fields of investigation.

The three analogies which were most likely to impress members of a technological–managerial society were analogies with the three branches of human knowledge which had played the biggest part in creating that society. First, there was the analogy with the methodology of the natural sciences, the aspiration being to control international relations in the same manner that knowledge of the natural sciences had allowed the United States to control nature. Second, there was in the nature of American power a powerful stimulus to worship of the mechanical system, the computer and the guided missile: thus, cybernetics found a place in the study of international systems. And third, there was the temptation to adapt the techniques of business studies to the problems of international politics in the light of their success in promoting the economic strength of the United States.

All these analogies were called upon in the attempt to establish a new science of international relations, as well as in other areas of the social sciences. This produced a diversity of competing approaches within the 'scientific' school, but all had one thing in common: they aimed at the achievement of a form of knowledge about social and human affairs which would be exact knowledge within the context of a cumulative enterprise. This aim embodied the most fundamental value commitment of those who adhered to the 'scientific' approach, which was a belief in the idea of man's ability to progress in his understanding and control of his environment.

The idea of progress had been linked in nineteenth-century Britain with the study of history. By the mid-twentieth century that link had been eroded by the changes which had occurred in the position of Britain and Europe as much as by the experience of two particularly nasty European wars, which had not borne the signs of progress over previous wars except in their destructiveness. After 1945, although it took Britain a long time to adjust to the idea that her power was distinctly in decline, British culture was no longer vigorous. Indeed, it was distinctly on the defensive against the powerful, materialist and expansionist ideologies of the Soviet Union and the United States. Although in no doubt as to which side in the Cold War they were on, the British political and academic worlds continued to cling to a sense of separate identity from the Americans. History remained the vehicle of this sense of identity because the one respect in which the British definitely felt superior to the United States was in tradition and experience.

In terms of international relations, the fact that there were established British procedures for dealing with foreign policy matters meant that there was no pressure on British academics from policy makers to undertake research to discover the secrets of the process. Academics did study international relations because there were in existence several Departments of International Relations (or International Politics), which had been set up mainly between the wars as a part of the idealism of the League of Nations era. But most of the work done in those departments would not have been out of place in a Department of History.

Typically, English historical scholarship has been based on a rather crude philosophical empiricism. With a few exceptions, of whom the most distinguished is E. H. Carr, this has been as true of history written under the label of 'International Relations' as of history called 'History'. This view of history as a search for hard facts which exist independently of the historian, whose task it is to discover and report them, is perhaps a remnant of a more confident period of English history, when there was no question about what constituted a correct perspective (it was an English middle-class perspective); or perhaps it is a bunker response to the attacks which have been launched against English culture in the post-war period. In either case, the effect has been to make the historical approach essentially unselfconscious and somewhat anti-theoretical. Hedley Bull wrote in defence of a 'classical' approach to international theory,[5] but in respect of most of its empirical work, the classical approach has had no theory.

What theory there has been connected with the 'classical' approach to international relations has been separated from the empirical study of the subject. It has taken the form of philosophical speculation about international relations, and particularly about problems of ethics in this area of human activity. But such philosophising has been separate from the writing of the history of international relations because the empiricist division of the subjective from the objective has meant that judgment has been seen as a secondary activity which might or might not be engaged in once the facts had been established.

Although the 'scientific' school did not display a great awareness of the roots of its basic assumptions, it did at least attempt to make those assumptions explicit. One of the least valid criticisms made of the 'scientists' was that they were liable to mistake their models for reality, because, as Kaplan pointed out, the traditional historians were even more likely to mistake their models for reality, and even thought that they were not using models.[6] By not making explicit his assumptions and organising principles, the empiricist historian does not abolish the need for such principles, but simply imports implicit ones which are just as firmly derived from his own values and beliefs as are those of the 'scientific' school.

The values and attitudes which have informed the writing of history in England have been those of the English academic community. And the English academic community has taken as its typical values those of the élite of the community, the scholars of Oxbridge. For a long time the highest ideal of English academic life has been to achieve a position at Oxford or Cambridge. And to reach that goal has been to join an élite of cultured individualists. Lower places in the academic hierarchy have attempted to be as like Oxbridge as possible, either to prepare those who still have hope of one day getting to Oxbridge, or to offer some consolation to those who have evidently failed. Consequently the values appropriate to Oxbridge life have been adopted in provincial facsimiles throughout Britain. And the values appropriate to a community consisting of an élite of cultured individualists are, clearly, élitism, individualism and traditionalism. These have been translated into the implicit organising principles of an historical approach to international relations which has seen individuals as the motive forces of world affairs, concentrated on Great Men, and focused on the foreign policies of particular states rather than on the wider international system.

Such an approach remained satisfactory for those using it so long as it appeared to them to raise important questions and to provide a framework for answering those questions. The same applied to the 'scientific' approach. But in recent years there have been signs of discontent with each approach on the part of members of the academic community which had in the past been associated with that approach. What I believe is happening is that each school is going through the equivalent of a scientific revolution, that each is in the process of fundamentally revising its paradigm. The old paradigms are being called into question because they no longer provide a satisfying framework for the investigation of what appear to be important problems. The criteria of what is an important problem and what a satisfying framework are established by reference to the dominant values of the respective academic communities, which in turn are closely related to the values of the wider communities within which the academic communities exist, and to the position of the academic communities within those wider communities.

Again it seems to me that the social bases of the reorientations of thought which are occurring within the 'scientific' school are the easier to identify. As one part of a wide-ranging re-examination of the bases of behavioural and social science, the developments within the 'scientific' school of international relations are clearly traceable to a crisis of consciousness of the technological–managerial society of the United States. The process began in the late 1960s with the failure of the Kennedy–Johnson social reform programme. The 'scientific' solutions to social unrest resulted in the ghetto riots, not the promised harmony. In international relations, the same approach contributed to the Vietnam entanglement, which became increasingly unpopular, increasingly desperate, and ended in ultimate failure by anybody's standards. And the Watergate trials drove home hard the message that a technological–managerial society may not be the fulfilment of the American dream nor the route of inevitable progress. Staggering under these blows, there is little wonder that the scholars who had placed their faith in the values of such a society should begin to do some serious rethinking.

At this point it might be expected of one who was nurtured in the classical tradition that he would exult at the rout of the old enemy. But all is not quite well in the 'classical' school either. There is a sense of unease here too, though it is less easy to point to than in the 'scientific' school. Perhaps that is because we English are a bit more reticent than those brash Americans about saying that we may not have been right all this time. Perhaps the changes in social conditions which are prompting us to question our commitments have been less spectacular. But the doubts are there, and I interpret every chapter of this book as an expression of those doubts.

The book is the product of a group of scholars who are all working within the academic field of international relations, who are all clearly sympathetic with the 'classical' approach, and who have felt a certain dissatisfaction with the state of their subject. It seems to me vitally important that those of us who have felt this sense of dissatisfaction should attempt to face up to the social origins of the feeling if we are to move at all towards a more satisfactory position. This is bound to be a more difficult task than that of tracing the roots of someone else's discontents, and one which it will be very much more difficult to agree about. That is why I would like to stress at this point what is taken for granted throughout – that what follows is a purely personal understanding of the situation and in no way a group perspective.

The undermining of the values which underpinned the 'classical' approach, I see as being partly a consequence of internal changes in the nature of British society and of the place of the academic within it, and partly a consequence of the changing position of Britain in a changing world, which presents new perspectives to students of international relations.

The decline in Britain's relative prosperity, following a period of unprecedented expansion in higher education, has led to the rather sudden change in the status of the academic from being a quite highly paid professional working under remarkably good conditions, to being a rather poorly paid, increasingly pressurised and somewhat lowly regarded member of society. The economic preconditions of the good life are being fast eroded. And this has been part of a general reorientation of British social values, in which old status distinctions have begun to disappear, and the old systems of expectations have had to be revised. It was the attempt to arrive at a political arrangement consonant with the changed social realities which produced the idea of the Social Contract in the context of the British political debate of the mid-1970s.

These changes in the structure of British society have been paralleled by changes in world relations. The easing of the Cold War in an era of *détente* has led to a movement of the centre of attention away from East–West relations to North–South, rich nation–poor nation relations. At the same time as the stimulus to cling to fixed ideas has been reduced with the reduction of East–West ideological tensions, the values themselves, and the structures which those values have supported, have come under increasing attack from the Third World. And the questioning has been listened to the more readily when backed up by an effective display of power, as it was by the oil-producers of the South. The oil price rises revealed to the West, and particularly to Western Europe, that it was not necessarily able to count on winning any confrontation in international affairs, that it had a firm interest in seeing the conduct of international relations regulated by rules, not power, and that the old rules were no longer acceptable to a large number of those who were being asked to abide by them. Clearly what was required were new rules, which would be acceptable to all the parties concerned – a new social contract in the international sphere.

At the same time, Britain has been having to rethink its international position in another context, coming to accept the realities of institutionalised interdependence as a member of the European Community. Since she became a full member of the Community, Britain has been made starkly aware of the fact that she is one of the weaker members. In a Community context, Britain has had to defend the position of the least advantaged and has thus had to consider the same type of questions as have been raised in the North–South dialogue, but from a different side of the table.

These questions are questions concerning the constitution of a new and more just international order which will be acceptable to all the participants, and will thereby form a consensual framework for co-operation. Their consideration has, therefore, demanded a total retreat from entrenched values and a questioning of all that once was held as true. The question of justice has been placed firmly in the centre of the concerns of students of international relations, thus undermining the artificial separation of theory from the empirical. The problem of relativity of values has to be faced up to: where can we stand in order to pass judgments? The whole problem of what we can learn from history has to be reposed. For what we need from history in order to understand where we are now is not what we have hitherto been concerned with in our writing of history.

Developments such as these could not fail to influence the nature of academic thinking about international relations. A whole new set of questions are raised by them which cannot be satisfactorily answered within the context of the existing paradigms of either the 'classical' or the 'scientific' school. What is demanded is not so much a new start as a further development of the dominant schools. Perhaps those who start from behaviourism and are now attempting to go beyond behaviourism will arrive at one set of answers, or, rather, one framework for posing what seem to them to be the relevant questions of the day. In the meantime, it is my personal view of the nature of the successive chapters of this book that, starting from the 'classical' side of the theoretical divide of the 1960s, they attempt to move one stage further towards providing a framework which meets more nearly our contemporary experience of the world. The effort is opportune.

NOTES FOR CHAPTER 12

1   Thomas S. Kuhn, *The Structure of Scientific Revolutions*, 2nd ed. (Chicago and London, The University of Chicago Press, 1970).
2   ibid., p. 12.
3   Hedley Bull, 'International Theory: the Case for a Classical Approach', *World Politics*, vol. xviii (1966), pp. 361–77; Morton A. Kaplan, 'The New Great Debate: Traditionalism vs. Science in International Relations', *World Politics*, vol. xix (1966), pp. 1–20.
4   Bull, 'International Theory', op. cit., p. 363.
5   ibid.
6   Kaplan, 'The New Great Debate', op. cit., p. 17.

Index

Compiled by Moorhead Wright

Adair, E. R. 42
Addison, Joseph 35
Adkins, A. W. H. 152
Africa 22, 42, 128, 129, 131, 134, 141, 191
Aix-la-Chapelle, Congress of (1668) 42
alliances 13, 27, 32, 95, 147
Allison, Graham 154–5, 158–9
Althusser, Louis 186
Amin, Idi 191
ancien régime 30, 36
Anderson, Perry 193
Aquinas, Thomas 66, 103
Arab-Israeli conflict 142, 147
arenas, public 94–5, 113–14; *see also* public domain
Arendt, Hannah 94, 101, 113
Aristotle 75, 78–9, 93, 101
art 180–1, 187
association, political 12, 28–40 *passim*, 52, 61, 79
Athens, Laws of 160
Augsburg, Peace of (1686) 16, 191, 193
Augustine, Saint 75, 78, 80, 82
Augustus III of Saxony 45
Austria 31, 34, 58, 203
Avenal, M. 62

Babeuf, Gracchus 177
Bacon, Francis 65, 83, 87
balance of power 27–9, 32, 40–3, 57, 60, 64, 75, 110, 198
barbarians, relations with 65–6, 127, 130, 139
Barbary coasts 42
Bateson, Gregory 193
Baxter, Stephen B. 41
Bedouin 70
behaviouralism 125, 164, 182–3, 187, 199, 210–11
Bentham, Jeremy 66, 156
Berkeley, George 86
Berlin, Congress of (1878) 128
Berlin, Sir Isaiah 193
Biafra 141

Birch, A. H. 62
Bismarck, Otto von 70
Blackmur, R. P. 93
Blackstone, Sir William 160
Bobbio, Norberto 98, 101
Bolsheviks 73
Bossuet, Jacques B. 196
boundaries 11, 94–5, 109–10, 119, 124, 131, 136, 169; *see also* frontiers
Bozeman, Adda B. 130, 134, 141
Brest-Litovsk, Treaty of (1918) 73
Britain, *see* Great Britain
British Committee on the Theory of International Politics 74
Buganda 129
Bull, Hedley 74, 207, 209, 213
Burke, Edmund 43, 66
Burke, Kenneth 95, 101

Caesar, Julius 200
Callières, François de 36, 41, 43
Cambridge University 35, 210
Carlowitz, Congress of (1699) 30
Carr, E. H. 64–5, 209
Castle, Barbara 175
Chamberlain, Neville 72
China, communist 73
China, imperial 131
Christendom 26–8, 32–3, 40, 42, 127, 129, 132
Christianity 58, 66, 68, 137, 173–4, 176; *see also* Judaeo-Christianity
Civil War, American 98, 101, 134
civitas maxima 62
claims 68; imperial and papal 26; of justice 151; moral 58, 81–2, 145–6, 160, 175–6, 186, 188; political 73, 95; of state 112
Clark, G. N. 42
Cohen, Morris R. 92, 101
Cold War 208, 212
Collingwood, R. G. 91, 196, 200
compact, *see* contract theory
conduct, human 31, 37–8, 40

congresses, diplomatic 32–3, 36; *see also* under individual congresses
conscientious objection 148–9
consciousness 108, 114, 179, 184, 187
Constance, Council of (1416) 26, 68
Constantinople 26–7, 34
Constitution, American 107, 176
'constitutions' in international relations 32–3, 94, 124, 137
contract theory 39, 46, 51, 104–21 *passim*, 140, 144, 146–52, 160–2, 169, 212
Convention on Human Rights 138
Counter-Reformation 31, 67
Crane, Stephen 96–8, 100–1
Crimean War 73
Croce, Benedetto 196, 200
Crompton, Richmal 204
Cuban missile crisis 154–5
cuius regio, eius religio 119, 176, 193
cultural diversity 129, 132, 136–43, 151
Curtin, P. D. 141
cybernetics 16, 182, 208

Dante Alighieri 66, 171–5 *passim*, 184, 187
Danto, A. C. 199, 200
dar al-harb 67
dar al-Islam 67
decolonisation 128–30
Descartes, René 83
deterrence 120–1
Devil, the 116
De Witt, John 42
diplomacy 12, 29–44 *passim*, 58, 132, 134, 202
Dostoievsky, Fyodor 172–5 *passim*, 178, 187
Dresden 73
Dumont, Jean 43
Durkheim, Émile 108, 178

economics 16, 17, 91, 133–41 *passim*, 147–8
Eichmann, Adolf 144
Einstein, Albert 23, 164, 182, 196
Eliot, George 199
Engels, Friedrich 178
England, *see* Great Britain
equality of states and nations 33, 52–4, 61, 128, 132–3, 148, 151, 157, 202
ethics, *see* morality
Europe 21, 22, 25–44 *passim*, 45, 56–60, 61, 70, 72, 109, 126–41 *passim*, 143, 171, 176, 178, 187–8, 195, 198, 208

Europe, Concert of 32, 41
Europe, Eastern 191, 193
Europe, Western 212
European Community 146, 149, 212
European Economic Community 141
European states-system, *see* states-system, European
everyday life, world of, *see* Lebenswelt
expansion 125–30
explanation 115–18, 125, 182, 193

Fenwick, Charles G. 56, 62
Ferdinand, Archduke Franz 200
Findlay, J. N. 96, 101
Fleming, Sir Alexander 156
Florence 171, 175
Foreign and Commonwealth Office 166
Fox, Charles James 177–8
France 12, 21, 27–8, 30–1, 34–5, 43, 72, 108, 196, 198, 203
Frankfort, Congress of (1681), 42
Frederick II 203
Freud, Sigmund 65, 84, 117, 164
frontiers 29–30, 125–6, 136, 170

Galileo Galilei 181, 190
Gandhi, M. K. 68
Gellner, Ernest 115, 118, 141
General Agreement on Tariffs and Trade 140
General Assembly (UN) 38
General Will 84, 107, 113
Gentz, Friedrich von 198
George II 59
Germany 12, 27, 32, 71, 73, 138, 149, 161, 196
Gladstone, William Ewart 72
Glaucon 155–6
God 105, 115–17, 120, 138, 157, 161–2, 172, 178
Goethe, Johann Wolfgang von 177
Goffman, Erving 108
Goldsmith, M. M. 62
good, the 76, 79–80, 109, 113, 121, 144–5, 195; and evil 203–4
Gramsci, Antonio 186
Gray, J. Glenn 153
Great Britain 12, 21, 27–8, 30–1, 58–9, 64, 72, 80, 83, 131, 142, 144, 174–5, 207–12
great powers 31, 41
Greece 33, 79, 143, 151–2
Grotian tradition 65, 74
Grotius, Hugo 35, 41, 54, 56, 66, 77, 130
Guizot, François 198, 201

Hanover 59
Hapsburgs 32
Hegel, Georg Wilhelm Friedrich 18, 75,
  164, 186, 203; on concrete institutions
  158; on epistemology 86–7, 107, 114;
  on history 96, 179, 183–4, 198, 201;
  renewed importance of 153–4; and
  realism 65, 81; on the state 84, 169–70,
  187–8, 191–2
Henry IV of France 58
Hinsley, F. H. 120
historical materialism 185–6
history 96; of international society
  126–30; and morality 125, 195–204
  passim; nature of 171, 179–80, 184;
  philosophy of 195–204; and political
  theory 82; and study of international
  relations 12–14, 209; Wight's
  traditions on 65
Hitler, Adolf 65, 72, 161–2
Hobbes, Thomas 18, 57, 65, 75, 77, 80,
  82, 104–6, 109–13, 164
Holland 30
Holmes, Roger 194
Holy Alliance 67
Holy League 28
Holy Roman Empire 32
honour 70
Howard, Michael 98–101
Hulme, T. E. 96, 101
human nature 46, 65–8, 79, 167
Hume, David 86, 182
Hungary 27
Huss, John 68

India 88, 131, 134
institutions of international relations 32,
  35, 39–41, 43–4, 110–11, 146
interest 29, 31; of individuals and
  groups 57–62 *passim*; and justice of
  social order 146; national 65–6, 81,
  144–5, 150, 162; of princes 42; 'real'
  42, 120; of state 36
international law 18, 29, 32–4, 36, 39,
  41, 43, 45–63
international organisation 13, 41, 201–2
international relations, science of 12,
  16–17, 20–1, 109, 124–5, 163–4,
  182–3, 189–90, 206–13 *passim*; study
  of 163–9, 206–13
international society 33, 50, 55, 65–9,
  122–41, 151; *see also* states-systems
international system 12–13, 15, 17, 167;
  see also states-systems
international theory: difficulties of

110–12; and history 202–4;
  importance of international society in
  122–4; nature of 11–24 *passim*, 69–71,
  200–1, 206–13 *passim*
international trade 51, 140, 150
intervention and non-intervention 18,
  119, 125–41 *passim*
inverted revolutionism 65–73 *passim*
Iran 133
Ireland 71; Northern 191
Islam 67, 127–8, 132, 137
Israel 190
Italy 27, 34, 42, 196

Jan Sangh 134
Jerusalem 116
jihad 67, 138
Johnson, Lyndon B. 211
Judaeo-Christianity 68, 79, 84; *see also*
  Christianity
judgment 191, 195–204 *passim*, 209
Jung, Carl 192
jus gentium 33
jus inter gentes 33
justice 23, 80, 142–52, 193, 212–13: of
  belligerent's cause 54–5; definition of
  155 6; ethic of redistributive 135;
  existence of 114; and obligation 161;
  universalisation of 169

Kahler, Erich 92, 101
Kant, Immanuel 65, 75–7, 84, 86; and
  contract theory 151; on peace and war
  96, 99–101, 203; and revolutionism
  67, 74; and structures of mind 115
Kantian tradition 65, 74; *see also*
  revolutionism
Kaplan, Morton A. 194, 207, 209, 213
Kedourie, Elie 141
Keens-Soper, Maurice 42–3, 62, 124
Kennedy, John F. 211
Khrushchev, Nikita 73
Kierkegaard, Søren 153–4, 170, 186
Kissinger, Henry 142–4
Kojève, Alexandre 184, 188, 193
Kuhn, Thomas 206, 213

language 19–20, 92–100, 132, 134, 187–8
Laue, Theodore von 204–5
law of nations, *see* international law
law of nature, *see* natural law
League of Nations 67, 209
Lebenswelt 93–4, 96–8
legitimacy 45–63, 108, 120–1, 130–3,
  162
Leibniz, Gottfried Wilhelm 43, 77

Leviathan 77, 105–6, 112–13
Locke, John 17–18, 57, 66, 75, 77, 80–2, 86, 90–1, 110, 176, 193
Lomé Convention 141, 149
London School of Economics and Political Science 64–5
Lonergan, Bernard 91
Louis XIV 27–8

Mabillon, Jean 43
Machiavelli, Niccolò 34, 65, 70–1, 74–5, 80, 82, 106, 164, 186, 195, 202–3
Machiavellian tradition 65, 74, 203; see also realism
Macquarrie, John 96, 101
mankind, community of 18, 66, 76–91 passim, 122, 141, 163
Manning, C. A. W. 43
Marlborough, Duke of 28
Marx, Karl 75, 84, 87, 106, 164, 178–9, 185–6, 191, 193
Marxism 117, 153, 185–6
Marxism-Leninism 68
Mattingly, Garrett 41, 43
Mauretania 131–2
Mazzini, Giuseppe 67
meaning 92–100, 102–21 passim, 138, 170, 180
mechanisms, role of 110–11, 115–18
Mediterranean 42
Mexico 98
Middle Ages 16, 26, 33, 42, 68, 108
Middle East 129, 191
Mill, John Stuart 107, 178–9
Millett, Kate 179
modernisation 133–41, 143
Mohammed II 27
Mohammedans 26
Mohl, Robert von 56
Montaigne, Michel de 37
Montesquieu, Baron de 66, 75, 83–4
morality 121; of consequences 139–40; and history 195–204; and international law 56–60; and international society 122–41; and politics 153–70; and the state 171–93; Wight's traditions on 65–8
Morgenthau, Hans J. 65, 70
Morocco 131–2, 138
Moynihan, Daniel 188
Münster, Treaty of (1648) 12, 42; see also Westphalia, Peace of
Murdoch, Iris 95, 101
Muscovy 30; see also Russia
Mussolini, Benito 20
myth 108–21 passim, 181, 190–1

Nadel, S. F. 44
Nagy, Imre 68
Napoleonic Wars 98
Nash, Walter 73
Nasser, Gamal Abdel 65
Natanson, Maurice 101
National Health Service 175
nationalism 18, 117, 133–4
nations, nature of 46–7
natural law 33, 45–9, 52, 54, 60, 85, 122–4, 179–80
nature 23, 102–21 passim
Navari, Cornelia 193
Nazis 161, 165
Nehru, Jawaharlal 134
New Left 106
New Zealand 73
Newton, Isaac 196
Nietzsche, Friedrich 153–4, 170, 198
Nigeria 129, 134, 141
Nijmegen, Congress of (1676–9) 42
Nine Years War (1689–97) 27
non-intervention, see intervention
norms 16–17, 22, 88, 93
Nussbaum, Arthur 42, 62
Nyerere, Julius 141, 188–9

Oakeshott, Michael 44, 91, 108
obligation(s) 23, 90, 153–70; general and special 159–62, 169; international 144; to international society 136; to mankind 82; moral 62; political 18, 122, 190; voluntary and involuntary 159–62, 169; see also responsibility
Old Testament 33, 172
Oliva, Congress of (1660) 42
opinion, and world affairs 11
Organisation of African Unity 134–5, 141
Osnabrück, Treaty of (1648) 12, 42; see also Westphalia, Peace of
Ottoman conquest 27; see also Turk, the
Oxenstierna, Count 12
Oxford, University of 35, 210

Pacey, Arnold 193
pacifism 68
Palestine Liberation Organisation 121
Palestinians 61
Papacy 42
Paris, Treaty of (1856) 30
Parliament, Acts of 144
Parry, Clive 41
Pascal, Blaise 123, 137, 141
patriotism 161–2, 169

peace 15, 27, 55, 58, 67, 96, 99, 119; *see also* war
Pecquet, Antoine 43
Pelagius 80
perspectives 21–3, 93, 167–8
Peter the Great 30
phenomenology 93–4
Philonenko, Alexis 99, 101
Pius II, Pope 27
Plato 96, 155
Poland 27, 34, 198
political theorists, and international relations 14–16, 75–91
politics, definition of 37–8
Popper, Karl 189
power 15, 41, 118; concert of 41; configurations of 25; and international politics 11, 31, 90, 212; and international trade 150; Leviathan's 106–7, 112–13; and modernisation 133; and moral problems 127; 'real' 120; of the state 131; and Wight's traditions 65–8
Providence 201
Prussia 31, 198
psychology 192–3
public domain 61, 77, 94–5, 98–9; *see also* arenas, public
Pufendorf, Samuel 32, 42
Pyrenees, Congress of the (1659) 42

raison d'état 31, 36, 57, 85, 139
Raj, British 72
Ranke, Leopold von 198, 203
rationalism 17, 39, 65–74 *passim*
rationality 13, 120, 144, 151, 158, 184
Rawls, John 109, 114, 146, 148–9, 151–2, 160
realism 17, 25, 65–74 *passim*
reason 76–91 *passim*, 100, 113, 196–7; moral 17, 78, 80, 196–7
reciprocity 93, 136
Red Cross 77
Reformation 31, 67–8
relativism 83, 137
Religion, Wars of 98
Renaissance 26, 33, 71
responsibility 34, 48, 60, 62, 157, 160, 166, 173, 188, 199, 204; *see also* obligation(s)
res publica Christiana 27
Revolution, French 43, 188, 198
revolutionism 17, 65–74 *passim*
Reynolds, Charles 44
Richelieu, Cardinal 42
Ridley, F. F. 44

Riezler, Kurt 94
right 15, 29, 31, 45, 71, 80, 121, 136, 138, 142, 144–7, 179
rights 45, 47, 53–4, 56, 61, 90, 107, 122, 124, 132, 150
Rijswijk, Congress of (1697) 42
Roberts, Michael 41
Rohan, Duc de 42
Rome 33, 58, 66, 72, 80, 152
Rome, Treaties of (1957) 149
Rousseau, Jean-Jacques 57–8, 66, 75–6, 81–4, 87, 107, 113–14, 151
Royal Institute of International Affairs 64
Ruddy, F. S. 63
rules 12, 16, 29, 33, 37, 40, 52, 127, 146, 202, 212
Russia 31, 73; *see also* Muscovy, Soviet Union
Rutherford, Lord 175

Sartre, Jean-Paul 186
Saudi Arabia 190
Scheler, Max 95, 101
sciences: human 11–24 *passim*; natural 14, 16, 20–1, 23, 124–6, 163, 189–90, 193, 208; social 181–3, 187
Scottish Nationalists 61
sea, law of 33, 150
Sermon on the Mount 68
Shafarevich, Igor 193
Singer, Peter 156–7
Skinner, B. F. 192, 194
Smith, Adam 17, 75
Sobieski, John 28
social contract; *see* contract theory
societas christiana 30
Society for the Abolition of the Slave Trade 177
Socrates 143, 155–6, 160, 165
South Africa 190
sovereignty 13–14, 18, 23, 32, 57, 61, 127, 130–1, 150, 191, 193
Soviet Union 73, 185, 191, 208; *see also* Russia
Spain 27–8, 31
Spanish Succession, War of (1702–13) 27–8, 98; *see also* Utrecht, Treaty of
Spectator, The 35
Spengler, Oswald 65
Spinoza, Benedict de 186
Stalin, Josef 191
state 102–21, 171–94; central to problems of international relations 23; as framework of moral choice 171–4; justification of 58, 171–94; and

knowledge 102–21; as mediator 158; modern industrial 141; as organic unity 95; one and many 76, 78; paramountcy of idea of 61; as perspective 167; and philosophy of history 201–4; a product of agreement 12; as self-regarding entity 187–8; separate 75–91; theory of 21

state of nature 66, 85, 104–6, 118–21, 146

states-systems: Chinese 37, 102; European 25–44 passim, 127; identity of 25–44, 189; institutions of 39–40, 43–4; legitimacy in 45–63; Mughal 37; as perspective 167; as political association 28–40 passim; practices of 37–9; v. world community 168–9

Staude, J. R. 101

Steiner, George 92, 100

Stoicism 66

Sully, Duc de 58, 63

Sussex, University of 64

suzerainty 131–2

Sweden 30–1

systems theory 16, 110, 118

Tanzania 141, 190

theory and practice 14–17, 25, 40, 90

Third Reich 138

Third World 133–5, 188, 212

Thirty Years War (1618–48) 12, 32, 141; see also Westphalia, Congress and Peace of

Thucydides 69

Tibet 131

toleration 176–8, 193

Tolstoy, Leo 68, 195, 199

Torcy, Marquis de 35

traditions of thought and practice 65–74

treaties 49–50, 144, 202; see also under individual treaties

Treitschke, Heinrich von 65, 202

truth 13–14, 103, 107–8, 112–15, 125, 180, 187

Turk, the, 26–34 passim, 42

ultimate realm 95–6, 99–100

United Arab Republic 138

United Kingdom, see Great Britain

United Nations 38, 131, 188

United States 73, 98, 150, 155, 175, 178, 207–9, 211

universalism 39, 122–3, 130

utilitarianism 144–5, 156–9

Utrecht, Treaty of (1714) 27, 41; see also Spanish Succession, War of the

values: absolute moral 173; and Cuban missile crisis 155; and Lebenswelt 93; political 200–1; and scientific approach 16–17, 122, 164–5; ultimate 130, 139–41; Western 130, 134; and Wight's traditions, 73

Van Velzen, H. U. E. Thoden 95

Van Vollenhoven, C. 62

Vattel, Emmerich de 15–16, 18, 45–63, 77, 128, 141

Vico, Gianbattista 196–7, 201, 204

Vienna, Congress of (1814–15) 32

Vietnam War 155, 175, 211

Virgil 66, 171–2, 189

Voltaire 30, 196

Waltz, Kenneth 167

Waltzer, Michael 160

war 11, 19, 27, 35, 38, 62, 126, 143, 148, 167, 202; concept of 120; and conscientious objection 148–9; holy 138; just and unjust 48, 54–6, 66, 120, 147; law of 33, 47–8, 54–6, 139; meaning of 93, 96–100; and nature of state 77–8; as state of nature 119; Wight's traditions on 65–8; see also peace, and under individual wars

Watergate 211

Weber, Max 106

Webster, Sir Charles 74

Western expansion 127–8

Western and non-Western civilisation 122–41 passim, 212

Westphalia, Congress of (1648) 31–2

Westphalia, Peace of (1648) 12, 16, 35–6, 39, 41–2, 127–8, 132, 139–41, 176, 191, 193; see also Thirty Years War

Wicquefort, Abraham de 36, 39, 42, 44

Wight, Martin 40–2, 64–74, 141, 152

Wilberforce, William 178

Wilson, Woodrow 67, 72

Windsor, Philip 200, 203

Wittgenstein, Ludwig 194

Wolf, John B. 41

Wolff, Christian 46, 62

Wollstonecraft, Mary 177–8

Woolf, Virginia 197

Wordsworth, William 70

world community 168–9

Wórld War I 67, 98, 200

World War II 68, 98

Wright, Quincy 163–4

Zimbabwe 61

Zimmern, Sir Alfred 66